REFLECTION'S

OF

a

STRANGER

D1254741

1

ACKNOWLEDGEMENTS

To my sister Michael Ann Davidson we never   judged one another and for that our bond is everlasting I promised you that I would finishing this book, In your memory I will always weep, In our legacy I will forever succeed I love you!

Landia my beautiful daughter to whom I have single handedly raised into a strong gifted and fine young woman your smile shine's so bright, Success is what you make of it never dare to dream and never stop believing in yourself and trusting in your heart I love you Infinity!

Lance my handsome son through miracles and blessings I have accomplished the impossible a single mother can raise a well rounded and respectable, intelligent man continue to be a leader never follow the sky will never be your limit stay in an honoring roll as you did in school I love you Infinity!

To my Ghost Reader
Winston without your feedback I would not have gotten
my groove back to restore and complete my first novel listen to #5 then
Hollulude it equals
Black Roses in reverse I'm sending them to you forever!

To my parents Mary and Wayne

Thank you for loving each other enough to marry because it started my foundation also for bringing my sister and me into the world it is big and bright, thank you for introducing me to God. The two of you were on one accord caring for your first born my sister you are amazing in my eyes through your love I am going to let my little light shine I love the both of you. To my little brother who has not been little in quite sometime you are talented, and your blessings are yours they will never come from anyone else nothing can validate you but you I love you truly since the day that I named you by your nickname with out any repercussion.

Finally, to all my motivators near and far I appreciate all your kindness believing in me keeps me believing in myself sometimes, you have to encourage yourself. Life is much simpler when people have your back you know who you are if you do not then this message is not for you to my motivators I love you all.

Special thanks to Tyler Abner for my amazing book cover on such short notice!

This book is   Fictional any   characters and places or likeness to anyone or anything is merely coincidental

Email me at patriciardavidson@ymail.com

This book reads about a young girl named India Hype she learns at a very young age whom and what not to trust. After the tragic death of her older brother Ronald, India reluctantly leaves her abusive childhood home to expand her adult journey to become an independent woman she moves back to her hometown in Indiana were she seeks to find peace within herself and the world that stands behind her the journey becomes long and hard. India is quickly forced to learn more of life's disappointments living with her father Steve and all of his new found secrets to help her escape she looks to her cousin Dena who knows all the ways of the world. While finding relief through teaching young children India meets, her new friends Leah and Jill they take India under their wings and together they become the best of friends. Through trails and tribulations, many broken promises together they fight to make it through, even though Peter Leah's brother wants to accomplish the inevitable breaking the women's true bonds it became his main agenda. Peter was convinced that with or without India's consent his desire to become her one and only consumed him. With many failed attempts to have her love, his only thought was if he could not have India for himself then no one would.

It would take India 30 years to breath, to stop looking at her shadow and see her silver

lining who knew India would be capable of love finding that someone especially for her,

India had so many things locked up inside of her heart things far from love far from a

man any man that was never in her truth. All India ever saw as a child in adult

relationships was resentment along with despair and resentment from women that she

knew.   The men that where around would beat and disrespect the women they claimed to

love India promised herself when she grew up that she would never be submissive to any

man the cost would be to great.

Once India turned eight, she was always the one elected to baby-sit for family or family

friends. she was very good with children India loved to read to them, comb their hair and

since she still played with Barbie's that made things even better. Even though she was,

only a few years older than the kids she would be watching India was much more mature

then your average eight year old.   India was a natural born protector, without fail,

whether it was the middle of the day or night. Whomever India was baby-sitting, the men

that their mothers were with would either be waiting or already be in a altercation with

them by the time India would be done babysitting. It did not matter the time or the day

the   men would take out whatever trauma or frustration they had that day on their women and India would be right in the middle. Ms. Kia would ask India to baby-sit some Saturdays India liked Ms. Kia she always had plenty of snacks to eat and was the only one that would always pay India up front. Ms Kia was very pretty she had long hair and always wore pretty dresses and high heels India loved her style in dresses. They were always pretty some of them were somewhat short that is what India liked about them too but that's what her man Frank always said made him angry even though Ms. Kia said it was probably all the other women he would mess around with around town. India had not noticed Frank around in a couple of weeks India wanted to ask about him made sure he was never coming back to hurt such a sweet lady and terrify her two kids none of which were Frank's. Ms. Kia was dressed sharp India hoped she had found her a nice man someone to protect her from Frank but not long after Ms. Kia left India and Rita and Wanda were playing Barbie's. When Ms. Kia's phone started ringing off the hook India normally didn't answer because she knew who it would usually be after a half hour India answered and the strong voice started yelling into the phone and before India could respond he warned her not to run her smart mouth to only answer his questions.

"How long has she been gone?" Frank yelled

"I don't know ask her?" India said

"Little girl, you need to stay in a child's place." Frank replied

India hung the phone up loud right in his ear two hours later India was glad to hear Ms. Kia's keys in the door she was getting sleepy and both the girls had already gone to sleep India lifted her head off the couch to greet Ms. Kia before putting on her high top gym shoes. Ms. Kia greeted India back with a silly smile she turned to lock the door behind her and there Frank was he busted right through the chained door .

India jumped up she shook both the girls awoke grabbing them by the hands and ran into the kitchen then up under the table. It was a long wooden table with six chairs India pulled them back under the table as if he hadn't seen them go under there she covered both the girls faces with her little hands as she always did when Frank got physical. He was ranting and raving all India could see was Ms. Kia face going side to side from Franks hard slaps across her thin brown face her hair the parts he wasn't pulling with his other hand was flying all around. She was yelling for frank to stop all he would scream out was "Make me" India never covered her face or closed her eyes she didn't ever want them to get to close to her are maybe one of the girls getting caught in the cross fire. Frank broke both pictured mirrors on the living room wall he put Ms. Kia head threw one of them   India could see the blood on the flood she told the girls to stay put India jumped up ran a few feet to the freezer she got four ice cubes out the ice tray and wrap them with clear wrap.   Without thought, India walked into the living room Frank was at the door telling the downstairs neighbor to mind her own damn business them slammed the door back shut. Then locked it he turned to see India trying to hand Ms. Kia the ice while she was helping her off the floor Frank yelled to the top of his lungs slapped the ice from India's hand then grabbed her by the arm.

"Get your trouble making ass out my house." Frank said

"This isn't your house." India said

Frank raised his hand to India while she was still standing between the doorway and outside in the hallway India gave Frank the coldest look he had ever seen from any child and it was not fear as he usually saw. Frank was from the streets and had seen many faces but India's eight-year-old face made him have a second thought about swinging at her the way he was beating his woman he held back. He put his hand down then he pointed and told India to go home India heard Ms. Kia gasped for air,

"India, I'm ok go ahead India I'm fine I promise."

India stared at Frank for a few more seconds she rolled her eyes she looked at Ms. Kia then India walked out.

India did not run home she knew where she was headed would not be any better the apartment complex were mainly mother's raising their children everyone's kids got along and most had the some story but the stories effected people in different ways. India was always told she had an old soul was always told she was to pretty not to smile she could never figure out what they thought she should smile about. Seeing her mother get hit was a lot different at home then seeing Ms. Kia India wouldn't just stare her stepfather down. She would go even farther to protect her mother grabbing whatever weapon that was closes the one she thought at such a young age would do the most damage mainly knives. India had gotten in the habit of hearing her stepfather say,

"Go ahead, India be the little protector run get the knife."

India would already be coming with knife in hand, India's mother Sharon and her stepfather Bobby Bradley were married when India turned four years old and her older brother was six years old. Just a few months after they met India took on the responsibility of being her mother's protector she did not feel she had a choice unaware that living such a battle would slowly but surely stir a hole into India's soul. That could not be mended by nothing or no one there was one time Bobby started beating Sharon he didn't need a reason although he always had one. India got angry and mumbled under her breath and Bobby heard her he came flying toward her and tried to grab her by her shirt India came to her own defense in the struggle and while he was reaching for her shirt he ended up busting India in her lip. It immediately swelled she was not allowed to visit her father Steve that week Sharon told Steve that India had gotten into trouble at school and that was   the reason why India couldn't visit.   That is also what was told to anyone that wanted   her to   come outside to play no one thought anything of it since India stayed missing in her room reading and drawing a lot of the time India loved Danny and the Dinosaur   books. India never told her father what happen not because she was scared for herself but what he might do to her mother Bobby definitely had no rule over his own spirit. India had to spend the next fourteen years with this man she would learn that bible quote like the one to put God first your spouse second this verse has been misapplied for centuries. Because when you   don't have God in the house at all its should be called hell on earth India was confused she would learn late in life the only time that you are to put your husband first is when   he is totally allowing God to be the head of his life and household.   Bobby and Sharon fought the day before their wedding It was Saturday night May 15th they were to be married Sunday afternoon they were arguing Sharon said that she no longer wanted to   get married Bobby continued to yell.

"Oh you're going to marry me Sharon, you can be sure of that." Bobby said

 After an hour of slamming doors Sharon said she would not marry him again after that India and her brother heard the loudest slap, he had slapped her so hard she ended up inside their bedroom closet on the floor. When   India didn't hear her mother cry out she opened their bedroom door then saw Bobby naked on his knee's reaching inside the closet he was choking Sharon with both hands. India started screaming for him to let her mother go Bobby stopped and turned to look at India he lounged up and rushed out at her with his hands still cuffed as though they were still around her mother's neck.

"Get the fuck out of here." Bobby yelled

He was coming straight toward India with this big black wrinkled thing hanging from between his legs it startled the hell out of India she immediately turned and ran out the door hearing it slam loudly behind her. Even though Ronald India's brother was the oldest, he just could not deal with the fighting he did not have the fearlessness that India embraced early on. Wherever Ronald would be when they started fighting that is where he would stay Ronald never knew his father their mother told them Ronald's father died he was killed in a car crash when their mother was 7 months pregnant they were to be married but that never happened.

India's father was happy to have a son and that is how he treated Ronald as his own if anyone asks he would introduce Ronald as his son Sharon always felt every child needed both a mother and a father. Close to two years into Steve and Sharon's marriage, India arrived she was a bundle of joy head full of hair with the prettiest brown eyes Sharon worked part time at a cleaners so that she could be home when the kids got out of school. Steve worked in a factory he was going on his fifth year thing were pretty good they seemed like the perfect couple all the women in the apartment complex envied them but Sharon wasn't happy. Steve really didn't know why other then the fact that they married pretty young they would argue he would try never to have disputes in front of the kids they had even had a few shoving matches. Steve felt like all they needed was each other they would party but at the end of the day, he wanted to be home with his family,

"Steve I want a divorce." Sharon said

This was not the first time Steve had heard this so he was going to ignore Sharon once again until Sharon shouted it aloud.

"Sharon you're not taking my children anywhere we've been through this you don't know what you want." Steve said

"Steve all we do is argue and Ronald is not your son." Sharon said

"No Sharon all you do is argue and like I said you're not taking my children anywhere."

"I'm leaving." Sharon said

"Sharon all couples have problems nobody is perfect so now that you've found someone with a bigger wallet your ready to run out on our family? "

"This has nothing to do with money Steve."

"Oh sure it does." Steve said

 "You think I don't know that you and that Cherokee looking friend of yours the one that can't keep a man you think I don't know. You and her have been sneaking around acting like sluts over there at the Soul Lounge you think people haven't seen you and some want a be solider painting up the town feeling you up is that what you think Sharon well think again ?"

Sharon smacked Steve across the face as though he was telling a lie he held his face and then he raised his hand up and smacked her back Steve's anger was about to get the best of him. When Ronald walked into the living room carrying India Steve pulled back when he saw them Steve took India out of Ronald arms and patted Ronald on the top of his head.

"What's wrong dad why are you guys fighting.'

Tears were coming from Ronald eyes,

"Me and your mother were just talking it got a little out hand hey I think I hear Mr. Softy outside."

Steve reached into his pocket and handed Ronald a dollar,

"Go out and get you and your sister an ice cream cone." Steve said

Ronald got a big smile on his face he didn't want to deal with any fighting anyway he had always been fidgety since a baby crying all the time for no reason everyone said Steve always tried to find ways to toughen Ronald up. Putting him in little league most sports Ronald did really well in he always made friends six months after that argument Sharon filed for a divorce from Steve. He moved out and into an efficiency apartment her new love Bobby had two daughters only one living in the city and their mothers did not deal with Bobby. Sharon never asked him why Bobby moved in and did not waste anytime getting on Ronald case calling him sissy then told Sharon she needed to stop babying him he also did not waste any time. Stating that India even at her young age was as mean as a rattlesnake Sharon tried to convince Bobby that the kids did not like to see them argue. And that he needed to be more patient with them that she did not like the name's he was calling them Bobby immediately let Sharon know that he did not give a damn. if she wanted to get married and that he would continue paying all the bills. That she had better get control of things even though Sharon had no problems out of her kids Sharon wanted this relationship to work as she did all of them. She was going to put her all into this one she wanted to give her children all the things she didn't have growing up and the very first agenda on his list. Of things Bobby did when he moved in was make Sharon quit her time job he told her she didn't need to work especially for pennies.

Ronald had an art project and had left flour and water everywhere on the kitchen table one afternoon he was so proud of what he had made even though he didn't know himself what it was he had created.

"Boy get in here and clean up this mess and take out the trash." Bobby yelled

He never talked only yelled sometimes he acted like he didn't even know Ronald's name he would just yell out boy whenever Ronald didn't respond fast enough he would pop him in the back of his head or pop him in the chest said it would make him a man. Ronald would come in the room India tried everything to consoled him Ronald tried to hold back his tears because Bobby told him only punks cried are shed tears real men never cried. Ronald came into the room with anger building he told his sister India if Bobby pops him in the head or chest one more time that he was running away. Ronald would go into the closet and cry India would always try to convince her older brother he had a right to feel the way that   he was feeling. She would tell him in her little voice that everything would be ok and that she would try to do more to protect him. Ronald looked at India and his response was always to tell India   that he was suppose to protect   her that's what dad always told him to and it devastated Ronald that he wasn't brave enough to do that.

"Daddy will come and get us if he hurts you again Ronald." India would say

Times did not get better even though Steve would see them on weekends both India and Ronald would not say what they were going through out   of fear for their mothers safety once Bobby moved them out of the apartment complex and into a nice house. Things really got worst Bobby would get upset and put them out in the middle of the night, Sharon would plead with him not to put them out one night became too much for India to bear. Sharon had come into her room Bobby had followed behind her ranting and raving about who's house they were in she told India to pack a bag

India looked pass Bobby and her mother and saw Ronald standing in his room doorway. He was looking at everyone wondering what he should be doing then Bobby pulled Sharon back out of India's room by her arm yelling India knew that he was drunk. They started to go back downstairs where their bedroom was Sharon still pleading   for Bobby to stop beating her both still yelling at the top of their lungs.   Bobby would always tell us to come back in the house once we hit the bottom step India picked up her bag after noticing how nervous her brother was. He had his jacket on and his book bag on his back India grabbed her brother's hand at 2 am in the morning they left while glass was breaking and the yelling continued. No idea where they were going India and Ronald started walking for blocks until someone driving pass finally noticed they were children a woman stopped. She told them to get in her car she had just come from work she stopped at a 24 hour convenient store and had the store clerk to call the police.   India and Ronald telling the police where they had walked from they told the police where their dad Steve lived Steve awoke from a deep sleep with officer knock at his door. He spoke with them for a few minutes and told the police he would work things out in the morning not knowing what was going on but they convinced Steve that was the right thing to do they didn't say much but they were tired of Bobby and their mother fighting all the time. Steve assured them he would talk to their mom and things would be all right. They went along with that plan the next morning before Steve went to work he took the kids home when he arrived he asked to speak with both Bobby and Sharon but Sharon told Steve that Bobby wasn't at home. Which made Steve upset he wanted to know how he could be gone and not out looking for the kids truth was Sharon didn't know they had left and she was more concern with Steve not noticing any bruises on her so she turned it on him. Telling him how irresponsible it was to not call and tell them where the children were and that Bobby was very concern and would never let anything happen to her children.

"They are our children Sharon." Steve said

"Look Steve, Bobby won't be back off the road until tomorrow so it has nothing to do with him so we can end this discussion Steve."

Steve slammed his hand on the kitchen counter Sharon jumped and started fidgeting around the kitchen like she was cleaning the children refused to get out of the car until Steve told them that everything was ok India and Ronald hoped that Steve was whipping Bobby's ass not knowing that he wasn't home. Steve had never seen Sharon so nervous this was the first time that Steve had even been into the house he always dropped the kids off and continued on his way. That the way Bobby demanded it Steve did not care about the big house or anything else as long as he could see his kids. Steve walked outside toward the car with a confused look on his face until he remembered what he promised the kids knowing he had to get to work he put a big smile on his face and reminded himself that he knew that Sharon wouldn't allow any harm to come to the children. India got out of the car and held on to her father's hand for dear live Steve had to carry Ronald out of the car.   Sharon came outside gathering the children and assuring Steve that if the children needed anything Bobby would make sure that they had it and the little child support he sent didn't amount to anything Steve kissed the kids and then left.

 Two weeks had passed this time before Bobby returned home he had not even called this time it was around 9:30 at night and some woman called to tell Sharon that she was the

15

only big wig that Bobby was driving in his truck. Bobby drove big rigs hauling metal parts in and out of town when Sharon went to see about his check, which she always picked up the office manager, came out and said.

"Mrs. Bradley, I'm sorry but your husbands already picked up his check yesterday." Sharon was getting worried because they had pretty much ran out of food things were getting like that more often than not   one thing she never had to worry about was her children going hungry before. The phone was constantly ringing for days Sharon kept answering the phone and when she answered, they would wait until she said hello then hang up.

"Mommy please stop crying." India pleaded

Then tried to console her mother India and Ronald did not care if they had to eat beans everyday when Bobby was gone there was no fighting. Bobby finally came home Sharon had already washed four loads of clothes she cooked what seemed to be a full breakfast and had started dinner. She knew how to make ends meet Bobby made more than enough so that they did not have to struggle in anyway but thank God that she was putting the little checks from Steve into a saving for the kid's college. Dinner was pork chops homemade mashed potatoes with gravy homemade biscuits pinto beans she had soaked all night with oxtails. Sharon did not want to go too far out in case Bobby came home and wondered where the money come from Ronald and India were ready for school, India watched her mother as she drove off. They usually took the school bus but Sharon needed a reason to leave the house for an hour she went to an old friend's shop where she use to work. They both knew each other's family since childhood they were like family Sharon

16

walked to the back of the cleaners to see her friend and her friend's husband they were happy to see her she asked her friend if she could speak to her alone.

Sharon was concerned that Bobby would stop her from getting his check again and she didn't want to keep tapping into the kids savings and she certainly didn't want to not be able to feed and cloth her children. She and Bobby had a mortgage car payments furniture bills and child support from his two other kids she didn't have anything to fall back on so she asked her friend Monica if she had filled a position for a presser that she was hiring for,

" Your kidding Sharon , girl how long have you been gone you know you gave me one days notice last time what's going on Sharon you know Bobby don't want you working is this some kind of joke?" Monica said

"Monica I need to feed my kids no this isn't no joke we go way back you know that and I apologized a thousand times for running out on you like that."

Sharon's longtime friend could see the despair in her eyes,

"Follow me to the back Sharon we can talk." Monica said

Monica's husband was in the back of the dry cleaners running the machines

"Hello Ed sorry to be so abrupt at first I'm just a little on edge." Sharon explain

"Hey sugar long time no see how have you been don't worry I know how my wife love's to gossip you look a little tired you don't even get your clothes clean here no more you moon lighting on us or something?" Ed asked

Ed and Monica were at least 10 years older than Sharon she just gave a friendly smile hoping that Monica wouldn't give him to much information about what was going on,

"Well you know Bobby brought us a brand new washer and dryer they clean your clothes better than a cleaners, (laugher) nothing against you two they cost so much I'm such they wont be putting you guy's out of business no time soon." Sharon replied

"It's that right? " Ed said

Sharon tried to keep her composure but was not doing a good job of it Monica noticed her sadness.

"Sit down Sharon we haven't seen you at church in I don't know how long and that really isn't like you, we are here for you girl you know me and your older sister use to get down back in the day we were the two baldest chicks around I was the finest though I know she told   you that ." Monica said

"Yeah I think I heard you were, yeah." Sharon laughed

It felt good to laugh she has not been laughing let alone smiling lately Sharon couldn't figure out what was going on are how to fix things,

I told your sister I'd look after you, but you make it hard I don't mean to say I told you so but I told you not to marry that boy." Monica said

"Monica, honey bite your tongue Sharon came here for our help just listen." Ed replied

"Everyone has hard times Monica every couples argues right." Sharon said

She was not even convincing herself of this,

"Now I have to say this one thing your right about ups and downs but that man don't have no right going upside your head no right it isn't your daddy but he act like he is." Monica said

Ed tried not to but shook his head in agreement and repeated,

"No right Sharon you're a beautiful girl you should be treated like a queen just as a man should treat his wife as I do."

Sharon jumped to her feet,

 "Who has told you'll this mess that's not why I came here I just need to make some extra money to make ends meet." Sharon said

"Makeup can't hide everything Sharon as Ed stated you're a beautiful girl we don't mean to hurt your feelings we are here for you; we have an empty apartment available in one of our two family houses."

"We will not charge you much hell we won't charge anything until you are ready it is your's if you want it he makes damn good money at that trucking company has he stopped taking care of you and the kids." Monica pleaded

Ed decided this conversation was for women only at this point he went back up front to wait on the customer coming in the door.

"Monica do not be ridiculous of course not those kids can eat you out of house and home you know." Sharon gave a fake laugh

"All I need is a couple hours a week as long as I'm home when the kids get out of school. Sharon replied

 Bobby never came home from the road until evenings so he'd never know Sharon thought to herself.

Well when can you start Ed and I can use a break I usually take the money to the bank myself but it isn't to safe anymore you might be a little rusty and we can't pay much for part time but the job is yours.

"The kids don't get home until 3:30 pm I can work till around 2:00pm ."

"Good I'll let Ed know we'll be back in a couple of hours nothings changed so you should be fine." Monica said

Then she stopped walking and looked back at Sharon

"Remember no family discounts." Monica said then smiled

Sharon had been happily working for about four weeks she did not realize how much she had stayed cooped up in the house. Bobby came home on a Wednesday, Monica had giving Sharon a weeks pay in advance she bought food and did all the laundry and cooked Ronald and India favorite liver and rice gravy and homemade biscuits. Sharon was home by the time India and Ronald came from school Sharon was happy and waiting for her husband she felt good about her decision to get the job it felt good having her own money getting out the house. Sharon had just finished four loads of clothes Bobby walked in the door and walked swiftly over to Sharon dropping his clothes bag at the door as he always did he walked past India and Ronald without speaking Sharon started to smile and lifted her arms thinking a hug was in store. Having her arms open made the grip to her neck easier for Bobby he took hold and started dragging Sharon across the kitchen floor through the living room and into their bedroom then slammed their door. "God damn it bitch why in the hell didn't you pick up my check I just talked to George they done mailed the shit which take's an extra week what the hell you been doing." Sharon was trying to hold herself up before he pulled her hair right out of her head, Sharon had been busy working and enjoying the out doors besides she figured Bobby no longer wanted her to pick up his checks but this week he had had a little too much fun. Sharon could not believe this was the man that swept her off her feet the one that told her she was the most beautiful woman in the world, and one week after getting together told her that neither she nor her kids would ever want for anything again. The second week of their committed relationship he took Sharon to Canada moved her into a big house he wined and dined her gave her a blue fox coat treated her like nothing but a lady. Now he was beating her on the regular basis he gripped her hair more firmly and lifted her head so that she could do anything but look up at him he was pulling her hair so tight her eyes could not cry just filled with tears.

   Bobby smashed the back of Sharon's head into the dresser drawer then yanked her up to her feet and smashed her head and his hands through the glass dresser mirror the shattering of the glass was so loud and Bobby was yelling to the top of his lungs. Ronald ran outside India was getting ready to go to the kitchen and get a knife she could hear her mother choking gasping for air calling for Bobby to stop. India was trying to decide between the knife or the round sharp pizza cutter she choose the knife on the way to the bedroom India stops in her tracks when she heard the knock on the door it was forceful India had a strange feeling.   Even though she was told never to open the door that Bobby owned she decided that she was going to beg who ever it was for help the knocks became harder then the bedroom door opened.

"India you better not touch that damn door." Bobby yelled

Bobby was holding Sharon by her neck from the look on her face India decided opening the door would be more useful then the knife that she was holding India looked toward the door and ran to open it. Standing in front of India was an officer Bobby quickly pushed Sharon in to the bathroom he quickly told her to wipe the blood from   her face he was boiling hot when he saw the look on India face.

"Hello pretty girl you look kind of young to be answering the door is your mom home?"

India wasn't a   fan of crying but sometimes the tears had control over her she looked at the officers this wasn't the first time she'd seen them and the fact that she was still holding the knife didn't make matter any better India reluctantly whispered.

 "My mother needs help." India said

India slowly moved the knife behind her back the officer smiled at India leery about the knife they noticed she possessed they didn't want to scare her with questions so they decided that hopefully she would put it away when she went to go get her parents.

"Ok can you go and get her for us please I'm Officer Dole and this officer Sheen."

 They walked into the house both with caution   on their face gave India hope. Before India could make it to the kitchen to get rid of the knife, she heard Bobby's dreadful voice,

"Yes sir officer's how can I help us guys?' Bobby said

He had the biggest smile on his face India knew how charming Bobby could be even at her young age she took notice of this it caused her to become tense most people loved Bobby he always invited everyone over for parties.   Nevertheless, for India's young age, she understood that at the end of the day they would all leave once the party was over and the nightmares would become realities. Bobby put his arm around India, which made her shake uncontrollably.

"Officers did my daughter mistakenly call you, I've told her about playing on the phone it's the new faze the kids are doing since the 911 stage came along it's a great idea but it give's kids the notion that it's the new toy of the century. Bobby said

Still smiling and holding India by the shoulder, he directed the officers into the house when he noticed his smile needed much more convincing.

""Sir we got a call about a domestic disturbance from a neighbor and it's our duty to check and clear every call if we could just talk to your wife we can let you get back to your day." Officer Dole firmly stated

"Well officer I'm on the rode a lot and when I get home my wife and I spend a lot of time in our bedroom if you know what I mean, we get a little excited sometimes that may have been what our neighbors heard."

"After all this is a big house as you can see I'm surprised they heard anything at all." Bobby said

"I understand sir, really I do unfortunately we have to speak to your wife to make our report official if that's ok with you. Could you please get her for us we can make this quick" The officer firmly stated

Bobby pushed India back and told her to go and get her mother India didn't want to go in the bathroom to see her mom she didn't want to see anymore black eyes or bruised face's she loved her mother to much and was losing sight of how to protect her. Bobby looked at her and firmly directed India to get her mother giving him more time to charm the officer's India looked at the officers they were now in the middle of the living room Bobby offering them a drink and laughing at the fact that they had to be bothered with nonsense. India opened the bathroom door then closed it behind her Sharon was sitting on the toilet crying holding her head in her hands. Sharon looked up at India's innocent face, "India where is your brother, go get him I'll be alright I'll be out in minute." Sharon said softly

Trying desperately to hide her wounds holding her head to the side and trying to stand, "But mom, you need to get us help if you tell the officers they will help you know like on

'Good Times' the episode were they helped penny mom they will help us moved to a better place." India pleaded

Bobby came bursting through the bathroom door pushing India out of the way and grabbing Sharon by the arm.

Get up you know those damn cops are out there get your ass up and get yourself together bitch. "

He grabbed a scarf out of the bathroom closet where Sharon kept all of her night things he   grabbed a shirt off the back of the bathroom door where Sharon kept her nightgowns.

"Put this shit on you see all that blood on you I don't have time for this shit Sharon." Bobby said

Before Sharon could react, he grabbed her up by her bloody shirt and whispered.

"You trying to be funny aren't you, you and your kids are going to find yourself on the streets if you don't get yourself together you hear me." Bobby spoke

He took notice of India and smiled as he walked out the bathroom to continue his usual con game with the officers.

The officers stood when Sharon entered the living room putting their cups of whatever Bobby had given them on the end tables.

"Officer Dole, Officer Keen here is the best thing that has ever happened to me my wife Sharon sorry it took her so long we were looking for our son he's always into something you know how kid's are Sharon where is that boy?"

Sharon was looking down to the ground as she knew she should she looked up at the officers with only a glance.

"He's probably playing with friends you know Ronald." Sharon said

"Hello ma am as we explained to your husband we have to make a report on all calls we needed to talk to you I know that there has been a few calls to your home and officer Keen and I felt it was important this time if we spoke with you directly. Not just your husband you know the laws are changing no big deal I can tell your husband is a hard working family man and sometimes neighbors can confuse an argument with violence we just need you to confirm this for our report and we'll be on our way Sharon alright." Officer Dole extended his hand,

 "Officer umm Bobby's is a hard working good man sometimes our arguments get loud but everything's fine."

Officer Keen notice Sharon's face when she glanced up he stepped closer to Sharon, "Ma am you look to me like you might be hurt is that a bruise on your face if it is you can tell us we are here to help and we can get you the necessary help that you'd need." Officer Keen firmly stressed

Sharon all of a sudden had no control of her speech she lifted her head and looked officer Keen in his face and boldly told the officer that the dispute was over her having a part time job and that her husband didn't agree nor did he like her working .

Bobby looked like Sharon had finally assaulted him back and like the knife was still in his chest he thought to himself working he tried to speak.

"Sir is this true do you have a problem with your wife working has this caused you to be violent toward your wife." Officer Dole quoted

With a confused look on the officers face Sharon knew that this was as good a time as any to confess to her husband about sometime that he was sure to find out and maybe just maybe the repercussions would end the abusive.

Bobby's answer didn't follow his mouth he held himself for losing all control he was in disbelief he had no idea what Sharon was speaking about he quickly caught up with his destructive thoughts,

"Well officers my wife of course knows that a wife's place is of course in the home cooking my dinner and having it hot when I return home from the road that's how I pay for this nice house we live in and that nice car that my wife drive's don't I take good care of you woman.?"

 Again, Bobby is almost losing control of his temper but not to the point where he would acknowledge his abuse to anyone but Sharon's children

"Well I mean a wife's place is in the home right we have our children to take care of?"

Bobby said with confidence

 Bobby watched as the officers wrote things down in their report,

 "Do you have any other children in the home?" Officer Sheen said

Bobby quickly answered,

"Yes we also have a son Ronald. Bobby said

"Well can we talk to Ronald and how old is he?' Officer Dole asked

Bobby yelled out for India to get Ronald not knowing that he fled   he knew he could not take his mother being beating again. Bobby looked around in confusion not knowing if Ronald had hidden under the bed again he motioned for India to look for Ronald thinking he was surely close by. The officers were getting a little frustrated and asked Bobby if he could fine his son to end the matter without incident.

Despite Bobby's command for India to find Ronald India ran to her mother side and would not leave India listened intensely she watched the officer reaction thinking this is it everyone has had enough of Bobby's abuse. Bobby walked away calling through the big house for Ronald's response that he usually got because he was too scared to hide from Bobby's wicked voice that controlled every corner of his house.

"Ma'am your neighbors say it sounded as if you were being beaten and that they have intervened several times your husband can't hurt you if you need for us to help you we can and will protect you." Officer Keen replied

"Officer like I said it was just an argument I'm ok." Sharon replied

India looked up at her mother and put her hand on her mother's arm, Sharon continued talking,

"I mean my husband can get a little out of control and my neighbor's can be confused by his sudden anger but he would never hurt me or my children."

"And the matter of you working how will you handle this." Officer Sheer inquired

India again gripped her mother's arm tighter she was thinking mommy please get us out of here I will take care of you Sharon pulled her arm away from India. Feeling after this session Bobby would surely know that he could no longer get away with beating her she gestured India to go sit on the living room couch while she once again handled the matter that was destroying her and her children's life.

Bobby was back in the living room with a troubled look on his face,

"Officers I assure you the last thing I would do would be to harm my family."

He had finally found Ronald hiding in the garage out back after threatening to do bodily harm to him if he did not show his face immediately. Ronald looked like he could shit his pants but India knew the officers would help them so she ran downstairs to the basement to get the suitcases that were still packed from the last time they were getting put out it was heavy. But India struggled with each an every step that lead to the top of the basement doorway she didn't care she felt it was time for her and her brother and mother to get to safety she did not care any longer   what was said   to who she was ready to go. The officers were facing her mother handing her a clipboard to sign.

 "Well ma'am it's very apparent that you have bruises on your face and neck but if you don't want to press any charges there is really nothing further that we can do if we have to come back to this residence someone will be going to jail here's a card for a domestic abuse and violence counselor." Officer Dole said

"No disrespect ma'am but you have your children to think of too." The officers both tipped their hats

Sharon took the card despite Bobby's objection and still had an act of confusion about the whole matter.

"Officer my wife would be needing this I promise you. "

Bobby once again tried to stop the transfer of the card,

"Sir this is my job to make you wife aware of her options she has the right to protect her and the children."

Then officer Keen gave Bobby a look that only an officer could give to assure that his wrong doing   was duly noticed.

"Oh sure officer I understand it's a nasty thing when a man harm's the one that God has honored him with as the most important thing in his life. And believe me I know what I have and again I assure you I would never hurt my wife but I thank you'll for your concern and let me escort you all out Bobby gladly directed the officer's to the door

knowing Ronald would never say a word and hoping India would know what her words

would later bring for the family.

 The officer gave Ronald a firm handshake advising him to take care of his mother and

sister Ronald was sad feeling the task would be impossible for him but nodded in

agreement. As Bobby showed the officers to the front door, Ronald quickly ran to his

room India was out of breath she hadn't notice that she and her family were not going to

be saved. She was finally at the top of the stairs with the suitcases when she saw the

officer shaking Bobby's hand it felt like her heart stopped then she watched as the front

door closed she heard the loud voice that had always determined if her family's life

would be destroyed.

"Put those God damn suitcases back downstairs what in the hell do you think your doing

this is your home and I run this house and no one I mean no one is going any where until

I say so you hear me girl now get your ass in your room." Bobby's voice sounded like

chalk to a chalk board,

India's desperate look focused toward her mother Sharon she was looking at India. Tears

were feeling both Sharon's eyes India couldn't speak or move she had at this point been

defeated all she could think was the officer's were gone and that they were not going to

safe her family in her little mind all she could think was how could she save her mother

now. Sharon walked over to India and took the suitcases from her tightly gripped hands

Sharon gave India a smile then walked down the basement stairs with the suitcases.

Bobby continued the beatings once Sharon found her way back up the basement stairs braking Sharon's left arm in two places the officers never returned and Sharon never went back to work at the cleaners.

Four years later things at one point thing were a little better for a while they moved about four hours away to a little town in a nice neighborhood and an even bigger house. Bobby transferred his job to the town and to another company he promised things would be better with a new town no problems and no one to remember the old ones. India was 15 years old, Ronald was disappointed everyday at 17 years old Sharon had, had her third child this one from the man she had adored, and thought would take away all her heart ache and pain away.

Bobby was excited and viewed his disappointment when the baby came out a girl Shay was now four years old and Ronald was now twice as scared three women he knew he should be protecting India was still his biggest fan. These days when it came to convincing Ronald that it was up to their parents to protect them India's protective skills had not lessened she knew what was right and who was wrong. Ronald had become really good in baseball he would stay gone all day in practice almost everyday he had made many friends and had become very close with his coach. The coach and his family embraced Ronald they would help him with his homework to keep his academics up for sports he was smart but he struggled a little with math. The coaches son and Ronald were the same age both excellent at their game Ronald would work all day practicing the game then Ronald would eat dinner at the coach's house with his son Harry and his mom. India would hear Bobby complain about Ronald's absence from the house fearing

Ronald would divulge the evil that haunted their family but Ronald was nothing like India every chance he got he blocked out the horror he felt from Bobby. He kept any memory separate and tried to maintain a normal life but at the same time always feeling guilty about not being able to protect his two sisters India and now little Shay. He had spent the Thanksgiving holiday at the coaches house and had only come home to get more clothes

India tried to convince Ronald to spend Christmas at home and that the tree that was full of toys of course had his name on them too their phone conversation was short though. "India I'm not going to spend one more day in this house." Ronald proclaimed

"India I talked to Harry about you and Shay and he said he'd talk to his dad and he was sure they could help us I won't leave without you and Shay but I need you to know that I can't help us alone." Ronald said

Tears filled Ronald's eyes and India's too she didn't know how to make her brother feel secure he reminded India about the social worker that let him talk at school but Ronald stopped seeing her when she said she had to visit his home.

It was just too much now that they were not spending summers with Steve India would not leave Shay and Ronald would not leave India.

Ronald was torn between his image of Steve one day saving them and the thought of him escaping he even mentioned to India that she and Shay could stay at her friends Toshiba he was sure that she and her family would protect his sister. Toshiba was someone that India had met once that arrived in the new town they had become very close Ronald was not sure if India had confided in Toshiba as he did in Harry and his family Ronald was comfortable with India's friend. Mainly because their family was from the same town that they had moved from they were just as welcoming as his friend Harry's family. India urged her brother on their last phone conversation that he shouldn't tell Harry's family their personal problems what goes on in their home he knew Bobby wouldn't like that and it could lead to them fighting but Ronald was way past tired of the madness.

"India it's time to start thinking about ourselves we're almost adults I can't take this any more." Ronald said

Their conversation went without notice he had not come back home in two days he was coming into his own. Ronald felt normal when he was at the coaches home their family spats felt like a cool summer breeze compared to what went on at his house,

Sharon felt bad she knew why things were happening the way they were she had contemplated leaving Bobby yet again. Ronald had discussed with her what his coach had said about having children in a safe environment but Sharon convinced herself that no one knew what she was going and that she was to providing a good life for her children.

Bobby come in the door upset what a surprise he noticed that the trash had not been taking out although India had tried to sneak it out once she'd heard him come in Bobby said leave it for your brother that it is a man's job.

"Where in the hell is he anyway?" Bobby said

Ronald was easily unnoticed because Bobby was always gone on the road but Ronald swore the next time that he saw Bobby that he was going to man up and let him know to kiss his ass and take his own damn dirty ass bags to the laundry room.

"Where the hell is that boy, boy you better get your ass in here and get this trash?" Bobby

said

Sharon   hesitated before answering saying Ronald was studying over his friends house

and that he'll be home soon Bobby slammed the trash can down scaring Shay making her

causing her to cry.

"You call that boy right now and tell him to get his ass in this house and do his chores

and never go anywhere again with out them being done or getting his permission." Bobby

said

Then told Sharon him she knew he was hungry he walked right pass his bags and down

the stairs to their bedroom   India knew the number but knew the conversation should

could from their mom because she had   been trying to get Ronald home for days.

Ronald was very respectful to his mom but told her he was not ready to come home,

asked if he could stay another   couple of days he quickly said goodbye then hung.

Sharon took Bobby's plate downstairs before he could come up Bobby had just gotten out

of the shower. Sharon stressed she knew how tired he'd probably was so she brought his

plate hot to him Bobby smell the good smell and couldn't resist he flopped on the bed

while Sharon pulled the tray on wheels close to him he looked up at her,

"That boy here yet   there had better not be no trash out their on that ground Sharon he

starting to get real lazy I am not having it." Bobby said

"Oh he wanted to spend another night so I told India to take out the trash there is no trash

anywhere." Sharon said

Bobby pushed the tray back away from him tied his robe in a knot   slipped on his house

shoes grabbed his keys and told Sharon to get in the car and tell him were Ronald was

he'd be damn if this boy is going to disrespect him or his mother. He refused to let India

ride when they pulled up to Harry's house Bobby pulled into the driveway it was 9pm at

night Bobby started blowing his horn non stop then yelled out Ronald's name. Coach

wasn't their but Harry's mother walked out the door she wanted to let Sharon know it

was ok they have talked a few times Sharon cutting her conversation short every time

Ronald stopped Harry's mother her in her track he didn't know what would happen

Bobby rolled down his window and blurted out .

"Boy you better hurry up and get in this car disrespecting your mother didn't she tell you

to come home."

Ronald gathered his things then told them goodbye and walked to the car with his head

down Sharon stuck her arm out the window and waved as if everything was all right

Bobby yelled all the way home Ronald never said a word.   Sharon talked to Bobby

discussing the fact that her only son was thinking of staying with the coach and his family

so that he can better his game. She stressed that Harry and Ronald had become

inseparable. She made that up off the top of her head Bobby was not hearing it he asked

Ronald what was going on but he did not answer.

"Boy you hear me."

Jumping slightly from the roaring sound of Bobby's voice but still no response from

Ronald   Sharon once again tried to distracted him saying if they did not get home he was

going to miss the rest of the game. He knew it had already started he hated missing the

game or being interrupted during sports Bobby thought for a moment about   the game and for a minute and a half there was silence in the car. Bobby did not have a load to deliver for two days and those two days he took Ronald to practice trying to show Ronald's friends that he was the best dad a kid could ever want and need. Even told the coach they could have a man to man anytime, he yelled out to Ronald when he missed the ball something that never happen when he was at practice alone. Bobby told Ronald to come over to him so that he could give him some pointers Ronald looked at him as if he was crazy Bobby repeated himself something he did not like to do. Coach spoke up saying to Ronald he would get it on the next round gesturing to Bobby he was all right and the ball was a little curved. Bobby didn't want to hear that and told Ronald not to be acting like a punk Ronald threw down his bat and walked off the field walking past Bobby who turned and reached for Ronald then smacked him in the back of the head. He took off running the coach tried to reason with Bobby telling him that his behavior was unacceptable and asked if they could talk in his office.

"That's my son not yours , we don't need to talk all that nonsense your filling my son's head with better stop or I'm taking him off the team." Bobby walked away

Calling out to Ronald he was gone walking through the trail making it home before Bobby to pack the rest of his things when he got home Bobby told him he was being disrespectful and that he could no longer be on the team.

In fact, that he could not go around the coach or his family once again

Bobby made that clear Ronald started rebelling India had never seen him

act out this way. He was slamming his door and would not come out Ronald was barely eating or sleeping he was not allowed to use the phone and had extra chores but did not care Shay tried to get him to draw or read. She would listen to him read for hours but he'd just shut his door as soon as he got home from school in only a month he was failing out

of math   and heading for the same thing with chemistry which was his favorite subject .

Bobby told him that if another teacher called about his work that he would beat him into
a

man he better not be embarrassing him or his mother, Sharon tried to talk to Ronald

saying this summer he and India could go to Steve's and stay. If he would get things at

school in order she tried desperately to get her son to cheer up and to look at the bright

side she wanted Ronald to snap out of his spell after a month of misery her son

 had started sneaking into Bobby's weed stash even though he always hated the smell

he'd hide in the garage when everyone thought he was in school this day he'd smoked the

whole bag using school paper when he ran out of tops India was on the cheerleading

squad and drill team with Toshiba. One of their friends mentioned to India they had not

seen Ronald in class all week India laughed it off she knew Ronald would not get that

crazy but she was going to talk to him when she got home. She skipped cheerleading

practice and went straight home she walked up the few stairs that lead to the kitchen and

put her book bag down in the kitchen chair she looked through the kitchen sliding doors.

Their dog willow was softly howling he turned to look at India and jumped to his feet

waging his tail India laughed and thought {crazy dog} he was getting old she thought

Ronald probably had not fed him. India looked behind the kitchen door and got a big

scoop of dog food and a big cup of water for his water bowl she opened the sliding door.

Gave willow his food and came back inside she called out to Ronald shaking her head

because she knew he would be cooped up his room he didn't answer of course she grabbed some cookies from the cookie jar. Eating them as she walked to his room, she did not see him or his book bag so she closed his door back after picking his pajamas off the floor and putting them in his closet.

"Ronald where are you we need to talk you better not be smoking that stuff are I'm going to kick your butt myself." India said

India stopped in her tracks and wonder if he'd missed his bus she stepped down the first kitchen stairs headed for the basement when the phone rang she rushed to answer it,

"Hello."

"Yes my I speak to Mrs. Bradley please?" The woman said

"She's not here whose calling." India asked

"Mrs. Smiley, Ronald's math teacher." The woman responded

"Oh ok, well my mother's not here right now but I'll tell her that you called." India replied

"Great, I need for you to give her a message please can you write it down please. " The woman said

India pretended as if she was writing what the women stated she said that Ronald could not return to class without a parent conference as soon as possible. India agreed she had taken the message and hung up the phone frantic to talk to Ronald and get to the bottom of everything she was going to straighten things out get him back on the team and back into class long before the parent conference India called out even louder for her brother.

India got a weird feeling that maybe Ronald had ran away he had to know that his teacher would call and her friend telling her she'd hadn't seen him in class India went out the patio doors to check the garage she knew Ronald was sneaking out there smoking

hopefully he was just fixing on his bike. When she didn't see him inside India thought

maybe   Ronald was mad at her she'd threaten to tell on him if she caught him smoking

again he was pretty mad India thought his action was do to the effects of getting high.

Ronald wasn't there willow started back howling India told him to stop then rushed back

inside to check in his room leaving the patio door opened for his things they were still

there his baseball card collection that Steve had started with him he'd never leave that his

baseball caps, and drawing equipment. India closed his door back and headed down to the

basement if Ronald was in the house he be sure to have heard India in all this time the

phone rang again run back up the stairs to answer it,

"Hello." India voice was shaky

"India what's wrong with you sounds like your crying." Sharon asked

"No mom, did you pick up Shay from daycare." India asked

"India I don't need to be reminded to pick up my own child, now I'm at the car repair

shop they are trying to say the brakes are bad when I have a warranty they can't get over

on me.

" Now go downstairs and look in my box where I keep my warranties the box in the

middle on the shelf in my walk in closet hurry up I need to know the date and the ID # on

the top." Sharon said a mouth full

"Ok I'll go look."

India put the phone on the kitchen table and put a rush on it when India reached the

tripped once she got to the bottom of the stairs she tried to caught herself with the banister but her hand went straight to the wall. She had forgotten that Bobby ripped it out

the wall falling down the stairs drunk last week. India hurt her hand she shook it off

then noticed the light in the family room directly across from her mothers room was on

India reached in to turn it off she and her brother got into trouble all the time for leaving

lights on she didn't need anything extra causing friction. India stopped in her tracks when

she notice the light in the laundry room adjacent to the family room was also on,

"Ronald you asking for trouble aren't you."

India called out again to him forgetting all about her mother waiting on the phone India

was fighting back the spider web she hated spiders and their web she turned the light off

when the light from the large storage room across from the laundry room shined through.

Ronald had to be playing tricks on her because the storage room was spooky and always

full of spider web she and Ronald always by passed that room when playing hide and

seek they also knew that's where Bobby kept his weed stash it always smelled like

burned grass.

She called out to Ronald yet again India's voice a little more faint fighting the spider

webs were grossing her out the light didn't do much there were no windows in the room

the door was slightly closed and there were lots of large wooden boards against the walls.

It made it harder to get around and India was about to give up when she spotted a

kitchen chair. Directly under the light India eyes followed the cord that was dangling

above the chair within seconds it felt like her brain had exploded the vision attached to

the cord was her brother Ronald hanging from a wooden beam in the ceiling. It felt like

India was screaming but she couldn't tell her body shook uncontrollably she was trying to

call out his name but still not hearing anything her vision became clouded with tears she felt her legs about to buckle when she tried to reach up to wrap her arms around Ronald's limp legs she could not reach them that made her even more frantic his face looked swollen she could imagine him not alive. India was short and tiny she kneeled on the chair and reached up feeling Ronald's feet in an instance India fainted what seem like eternity had passed India come too her head was throbbing she felt her hand rubbing her forehead which felt wet there was a smell then she notice it was willow licking her conscience. She could feel the hard cold basement floor under her head she did not know where she was until her vision became clearer and there he was still hanging body without any life. It looked as though he was looking right at India she started breathing hard holding her chest trying to get up leaning on willow still licking her face. India got up from   the floor she felt dizzy then she yelled out hysterically,

"Ronald, why what happen." India waited for a response

She went to him this time using all of her strength and her might, she pulled the chair from under his body and stepped up toward him trying to lift her brother's lifeless body. Hoping that maybe she could help him India almost fell out the chair she released him jumping out of the chair then tripping over some on the borders that were on the floor. Trying to get out the room to the phone, she knew how to get help everything was going to be all right she yelled back to Ronald lifeless body now laying on the floor to hold on. India reaching her hands out in front of her to feel her way through the basement after turning out all the lights she made it to the family room she picked   the phone off the end table and started dialing 911. There was no response coming from the receiver India started pushing down on the buttons harder and harder pushing the hang up button repeatedly. Then she heard a loud dial tone she ran upstairs to the kitchen hung up the phone then picked it right back up checking for a dial tones she finally heard one hands shaking   India dialed 911.

"911 what's your emergency? '

"Please help me my brother's needs your help he's hanging downstairs in the storage closet help him please." India pleaded

"Ma'am your brother need an ambulance how old is he, did you say he's hanging I need you to slow down please."

"Lady we need help I think he's dieing we need help I can't get him down I've tried please."

"What's your address?" The operator asked

It took India a minute to think then she blurted the address the operator wanted India to make sure the brother was alive India didn't want to hear that she told the women to send help then she hung up.

India opened the side door then rushed back downstairs to her brother she slowed down when she got to the storage door she felt her emotion running high again so she took a deep breath then entered the room telling Ronald help was on the way she wanted him to hold on. She wanted him to know that she was sorry for not protecting him and convincing him to stay in the house she knew how it was killing him she pleaded with him to forgive her. Not looking at him, she was walking around in circles kicking anything she could move that was in her way then she started screaming again asking Ronald why

India jumped when she heard the horrible sound of Bobby's voice yelling out.

"What in the hell is going on this is my Got damn house who in the hell call you what's going on."

"Sir we were called on a possible suicide can you direct us to your basement." The EMT ordered

Bobby was in shocked he directed the E.M.T's to the basement he was sure they'd made a mistake he mumbled under his breath as he was fighting back the spider webs he was calling out his wife Sharon's and India's name. Waiting on someone to answer him and explain what was happening Bobby was looking around he could hear crying but didn't understand why he knew the kid's didn't go pass the laundry room   Sharon, India what the hell is going on who back here.

India screamed out no repeating it over and over she didn't want him around she wanted help for her brother not the man that killed him India turned and slammed the door shut get the hell away get out of here there coming to help him.

Bobby was shocked that it was India in the room the police were now taking charge they both put directed Bobby and the EMT's to the side they no longer knew what they were walking into.

"Ma'am were here to help are you the young lady that called for help."

India yelled out through her crying,

"Yes we need your help telling that son of a bitch to get away."

"Bobby you better watch your damn mouth and open this got damn door."

"Sir let us handle we need to found out who's in here and what is going." The officer said

Bobby stepped back he did not know how to take control this time,

"Young lady tell us what's going on we're here to help nothings going to happen to you."

"It's already happened he wanted to leave I talked him out of it, it's all my fault." India said

"Can we come in you told the 911 operator that your brother needed help now we have some EMT's standing next to me and my partner now I'm going to open the door slowly so that we can get help in there ok?" The officer slowly opens the squeaking door

India had backed up she was still walking slowly backward she stop when she bumped into the chair she turned around looked up and started screaming uncontrollably again telling them to help her brother. The officer open the door all the way he and his partner slowly entered the room once they slowly got around the border there eyes hadn't imagine the sight they were forced to see officer Langer ordered the EMT's inside after cutting Ronald's limp body down. There was nothing they could do but pronoun Ronald dead no more then five minutes after they'd entered the room India could take no more a female officer had arrived and was consoling India.

Sharon pulled up and rushed into the house leaving Shay seat belted in the car she didn't know what was going on she knew Shay would be safe one of the officer outside waiting on the coroner tried to stop Sharon she stated this was her house and that her kids were inside. The officer face changed he was about to give his condolences after telling her what happen   but Sharon ran passed him almost knocking him into the side door. Sharon called out for her kids she ran up the kitchen stairs she ran around toward the kid's room when she saw an officer trying to calm India Sharon blacked out when the officer forced her to sit down in the living room and told her what had happened to her son.

The neighbors were starting to gather and one of India friends had called Toshiba she had her mother bring her over they were shocked and saddened   they convinced India that she and Shay should leave and go to their house. Once the officers and everyone left they even offered for Sharon to go they knew it would be too hard on all of them Sharon refused but insisted on the kids going. India packed a bag for Shay then herself as if she was never coming back and she did not until the day of the funeral that night Sharon tear apart the house   looking for a suicide note. Looking for something some sign that Ronald wanted to tell her why.   She did not find anything she cried for days she did not care what Bobby said Toshiba's mom helped Sharon with arrangements Bobby did not want the coach and his family at the services. He had to have someone other then himself to blame they did not listen they along with other teachers and baseball parents and friends rallied together giving Sharon a large donation Bobby refused the generosity. Everyone agreed to put it toward the teen suicide organization India reached out to the coach and his family introducing everyone to her father Steve he let them know he had heard a lot about them and was glad he had gotten the opportunity to thank them. Steve felt confused he was consumed with guilt Bobby wanted to have the funeral as soon as possible he said no need to prolong things.

Quite a few family members were not able to make it the funeral   India mind was racing it right then she decided she was not going to stay in that house any longer she did not care what anyone thought. Her mind was made up she would have to figure out at a later time how she was going to keep the same thing from happening to Shay she had to go as soon as she saw her father she told him. But India was told she couldn't leave she had another year she had to finish in school Steve told India it would be best to finish out her last year while he got things ready for her to come stay   if she wanted   it was time for

the casket to be closed

India went to the podium to read her poem Ronald loved her poem's and she knew he

would be listening this poems was one of the first she'd written around the age of 12   she

would read it to Ronald   all the time he said it made him feel better.   Steve took India by

the hand than lead her to the podium   India stood with grace she couldn't feel any pain

she had been hurting all her life not being able to protect Ronald killed her inside all she

felt was numb she was ready to run right out of the funeral home. Then get into her

fathers car she wanted him to drive until the gas ran out but she knew she needed to be

there for her friends her mother and family.   India held on tightly to the podium looking

at no one she straightened her paper and began to read.

"When the morning time comes no more pain."

"When the sun shines no more pain."

"When the rain hit's the window pane no more pain."

"The moon gets brighter then the shooting stars all are at large no more pain."

"Don't open your eyes keep these things in you mind and you will have no more pain."

India wrote those words to put Ronald to sleep at night she never thought she would read

those words that would put him to sleep forever she rushed   down from the podium gave

her mother a hug. Then she carried Shay over to where she and her dad were sitting they closed the casket India whispered goodbye   Steve was inside the church speaking to

Sharon's brother after the burial he and Bobby had words. When he arrived, he wanted to

know why Sharon had not called to let him know that Ronald had been depressed Bobby

told him that it was not their job to do his job. That almost lead to a fight but out of

respect for his son and Sharon, Steve stayed settled he felt that in a way Bobby was right

he ignored many signs trying to keep the piece.

Everyone had gone Sharon grieved everyday crying sometimes for hours in the dark after

almost a year had past went by Bobby started to tell her to get over it all the crying was

not going to bring him back. India's heart stopped every time he mention Ronald's name

she wanted to tell him to shut the hell up and never mention her brother's name again.

But instead she did her usual thing rolling her eyes and stomping around what more could

he do to her   Sharon was talking back a lot and Bobby told her he wasn't going to take

much more of it. There was one of the usual come home take a shower get cleaned up put

plenty of cologne on then pack a bag and out the door Bobby would go.

Sharon was yelling telling him the whore's in the street did not give a damn about him

and that she was not going to take much more of his disrespect he had not been there for

her since Ronald left. Bobby reminded her that Ronald didn't leave that he was dead

Sharon ran into the bathroom slamming the door   he picked up his bag walked pass Shay

as he always did   told India to check on her mother   and left out   the side door. India

was on the phone talking to her best friend Toshiba and putting a movie in for Shay to

watch. She did not hear a word Bobby and her mother said she had learned to ignore

them grabbing knives made Shay crazy so India learned to just turned up her music and

keep Shay calm.

She and Toshiba were talking about the new Prince movie purple rain India was a Prince fan and Toshiba was a Michael Jackson fan Shay started jumping up and down on the couch she was so happy when Bobby wasn't home that was the only time India would invite friends over. India got up to turn up the television she hadn't notice the side door closing Shay pointed and jumped into India's lap India turned around to see Bobby walking through the kitchen.   She was praying he'd left something behind she was even tempted to offer to help him but said nothing he then headed for the bathroom door the door was locked India hadn't noticed if her mother had come out. Bobby banged on it a few times he had left his favorite cologne and could not find it.

"Sharon open the door you hear me woman." Bobby said

India sat up on the edge of the couch standing Shay to her feet Bobby knocked on the door harder turning the knob back and forth India's heart started beating fast usually they started their fights in their room   but they were upstairs Sharon was   using the upstairs bathroom. India was thinking mom he is trying to leave open the door and let him go please.

"Damn it Sharon I don't have time for this shit I told you not to do this shit."

Bobby got so angry that he started to   try and knock the door down first with his shoulders then he kicked the door in India called out to her mother Shay began to cry. Bobby rushed in Sharon was laying on the bathroom floor she had taken a whole bottle of valium still holding the bottle in her hand. Bobby was smacking Sharon on the face then looked up at India and told her to call 911 India froze she couldn't move Bobby jumped up and got on the phone to call 911 they rushed her to hospital. The emergency room doctor pumped Sharon stomach and decided to keep Sharon for a few days for observation once they checked her in to a room Bobby told India to call her friends mother to see if she could come get them. Which they immediately did and as soon as they left Bobby kissed Sharon on the forehead telling her she needed to get herself together then he headed for his car. Sharon was to drained   two days later she had to call a cab when the doctors released her Bobby was no where to be found and she couldn't remember her neighbors or Toshiba's number. Bobby came home two days later Sharon was trying to cook and clean neither he or Sharon ever discussed what happened that day after a while it seemed as though it had been a bad dream but the hurt in Sharon's heart was present and heavy.

It was now two more days until India's graduation India counted the seconds the days and the hours India's mother didn't want her to go but her soul was now at state she told her mother she wanted Shay to visit every summer. India was going back home to Tennessee   there were people she hadn't seen since she was a little girl she wasn't real excited she had not been away from her mother   for more then a week or two she hadn't been away from Shay at all and her friendship with Toshiba was priceless. But Toshiba was selfless she was glad India was getting away she deserved happiness even if it meant she'd be miles away they knew each others address and was going to write and keep in touch everyday. They had some good times in cheerleading going from game to game competition to competition they laughed at the memories saying they were going to have many more they were eating at the local pizza restaurant with some other seniors giving India's their   goodbye's and reminiscing. Especially about prom night, India was still mad that everyone had left her but Toshiba promised India that, that was not what happened   she was the one that got herself lost she and Harmon had claimed to be boyfriend and girlfriend for the last seven months. Toshiba was dating Rick the two guys weren't close but friends Harmon was also a boxer and on prom night came to pick India up all decked out with a black tuxedo he was sharp he was a real nice guy but out of all of India's friends she thinks she was the only deer in headlights that night.

She was the only naive person who didn't know that on prom night that the girl was suppose to give it up, rather It was her first time or 100th she was suppose to turn her prom date out. India didn't have time to get caught up with the fast girl life nor time to please a boy the most she had ever done was let a football player put a hickey on her neck. She thought since Harmon was always hanging around with fast girls that he knew she did not have to do anything with him but India had no idea what the night had in store. Sharon and Toshibas mother helped the girls get all dolled up then sent everyone on their way looking like princesses India and Harmon had a ball at the prom all the guys who were convinced that India was the meanness but the cutest cheerleader including Eric the captain of the football team approached Harmon and asked him would it be ok to give India a hug India didn't understand why but she fit in his arms like a hand in a glove perfectly until she opened her eyes and remember she was there with the guy staring them down India never gave him the time of day before she knew he had every girl for miles and he never pressed his flirted because India thoughts were right. Everyone looked amazing   the ballroom   in the hotel was decorated with pink and white balloons with matching table clothes and vases with pretty pink flower there were champagne glasses on all the tables with the same words of the song that   played "If only for one night" by Luther Van dross. India and Harmon got along great she thought because he respected her and was ok with the fact that she was a virgin but he was just so busy with his fights and working out in the gym. He knew when he and India would go all the way from the day he met India she motivated Harmon's mind in ways he had never been motivated she was his main squeeze. Prom night all the fellows were talking and then he quickly realized she had him whipped without doing the do they had plans with about five couples which followed each other to the local   pizza restaurant. Then after leaving there, Harmon pretended he could not keep up with the other cars that were driving to a house party he said he wanted to stop at his house to call one of his friends. He said to see where everyone had went India told him she would stay in the car Harmon purposely stayed inside long enough to make India get out the car and knock on his side door. When he said come in Harmon was standing in his kitchen butt naked India head snapped back as she reached for the kitchen chair to hold her amazement.   He struck a pose, which made things even worst India did not know rather to curse him out or throw something like her high heel shoe. He was about to get on her last nerve,

"Look Harmon I've had a great time tonight but I'm ready to go meet my friends let go."

"India don't play stupid this is exactly what your friends or doing don't play stupid."
Harmon said

"Look brother I'm not playing and don't call me name's." India said

Harmon laughed saying he was sorry and started walking toward her telling her she did not have to be shy or scared he reached for India telling her how beautiful she was tonight.

"Look Harmon, I'm not scared or shy I just don't want to do this now please lets go."

Harmon ignored India's demands and started kissing her and putting his hands all over her India pleaded with Harmon asking where his mother was he laughed at her and lifted

her up onto the table trying to pin her down. India didn't want to hurt him but it was

obvious he wanted to be since he had already hiked her dress up it was easy for India to

reach and take off her high heel shoe she took to beating Harmon upside his head with it

until he was off of her he yelled out,

"Girl you hit me in my eye or you crazy?"

"Your trying to take something that isn't yours now are you going to take me home are

do I have to walk besides you've been hit in the eye before aren't you a boxer."

Harmon mumbled under his breath,

"Little Bitch."

India was already outside, Harmon it took all his might not to hit her they opened the car

door together but by the time India got in Harman was backing out of his driveway he put

the car in drive then haul off. Toward India's house going at least 50 mph in a residential

area, India lived at least 15 minutes away but they got there in just 7 minutes he never

said a word nor did she.   Harmon put on his brakes so hard in front of her house that

India's entire body jerked forward she could barely get her seat belt off before Harmon

was switching gears to pull off. India was getting ready to say goodbye with no hard

feelings until Harmon yelled at her to close his door he pulled off before it could close

then he turned the corner while the door was swinging back and forth. He was burning

lots of rubber India stood on the sidewalk for a minute then slowly walked inside the

house not knowing what to think or feel. She laid her pink satin dress neatly on the extra

twin bed then put her matching pink satin shoes next to it she put her shiny bobbie pins

on top of her dress showered then said her prayer's. Mellow moods was on the radio wishing all the graduates a happy and safe prom night India shook her head she went to sleep. The next day when her mother asked how the prom went she told her she had a great time and continued to make her sandwich no need to cry over spilled milk that she was not aware she was suppose to pour on prom night India was still clueless. Harmon came by a day later to apologized he said he talked to his mother about what had happened and she told him virgins have the right to remain a virgin. Harmon assured India that he had never had a virgin for a girlfriend and that he did not realize that she was he told her that he was sorry and that he should have told her of his plans he just though she knew the deal. Then he started to laugh as he remembered how his mother smacked the shit out of him for treating India that way. Harmon talked with a whisper which made getting smacked by his mother funny India forgave him mainly because she could tell he was sorry this wasn't a usual feeling for India to acknowledge. But Harmon was actually a good guy to her he gave her anything she wanted and most things she didn't ask for like jewelry. He wanted her at all of his fights and his family loved her being around that didn't really mean anything to India she didn't know how to really channel their relationship it was her first serious relationship and she didn't really care if it was her last. Harmon had their prom pictures he had picked them up after paying for them they were beautiful they looked great together they talked for a while sitting in the living room. When India finally decided to tell him she was leaving going back to live with her father she figured they both kept their intentions a secret. Harmon begged her not to go but India she felt a little sorry for him but at the end of the day he disrespected her trust and feelings, India told sent him on his way looking like a sad puppy. Her girls were on their way and after they arrived India reminded Toshiba once again in between her big bites of pizza. That she would never be forgiven for leaving her that night she wished she could be seriously mad but their friendship was solid. Toshiba was the sensible one she was good for India who was always hot headed they finished eating pizza then her friends all signed a card and gave India a goodbye gift. It was an enlarged picture of her with the entire cheerleader team and band in Florida while they were on their senior trip for a parade and then Disney World, it was in a frame and each one of them had signed the picture. It made India emotional but she rarely cried only when she looked at her picture albums that were filled with Ronald's pictures and artwork India kept it dear, and near to her, some of the pictures were in frames she'd packed them carefully. Toshiba dropped India off she had already gotten her license India kept putting it off all she had to do was take the written test she'd passed Driver's Ed . India hated taken test she figured she'd take care of it once she got in town with her father Sharon was sitting at the kitchen table watching Shay eat her lunch India asked what they were eaten Sharon snapped at India which was unusual India blow a kiss to Shay she blow one back then India went to her room to finish packing.

India was about to close her door and do her favorite thing listen to music when Sharon stopped the door with her hand,

"Your father called from the hotel room he said he'd be here around 5pm I don't know why you'll are leaving so early I haven't finished cooking dinner."

India could tell her mother was upset but this time there was nothing that India could do she had to for once think of herself as hard as it was to do she could no longer live in this house. India walked over to her mom and thanked her for giving her the message she reached to give her mother a kiss on the cheek then told her that Toshiba would be stopping by to keep her company from time to time. Then she gave her mother a hug

India did not want to let go but Sharon turned releasing India's tight grip,

"I guess I'll go speed dinner up Bobby said to say bye and if you need anything to call

home."

Sharon walked away still talking India knew Bobby was happy that she was leaving but

yet instill he'd called India ungraceful a few times once he found out she was leaving

India wanted to cry but didn't know how her heart couldn't take any more pain. it had

been a year since her brother passed and a week since her mother was last beaten   for

asking Bobby who was the strange woman that kept bringing him beer at his company

picnic once he reminded her that it was none of her business and never to question him

again. Steve had arrived Sharon tried to convince Steve to stay until after dinner that was

the most she'd said to him in years Steve didn't feel comfortable entering Bobby house

and India didn't want to be rude rushing to bring her bags to the front door. She had over

heard Bobby telling her mother that Steve wasn't welcome in his home she was very

surprised her mother was almost pleading to defy her devoted husband demands.

India slow down she knew this would take a lot out of her she even requested that

Toshiba not see her off once out on the front porch with her things India did not go back

inside. She walked around to the back yard to give willow who was getting so old   a

goodbye kiss she was convinced that even he was sad she was the only one left to walk

and talk to him he was a good dog India waved goodbye telling him she'd see him soon.

Even though she had no intentions of returning not as long as Bobby lived there, India

walked back around to the front of the house where her mother, Shay and her father where talking. It made India feel weird to see Sharon and Steve talking she was little the last time this had happen they said little to nothing at the funeral and the graduation hell since the divorce. India walked toward them slowly Steve had his hand on Sharon's shoulder looking at her in a serious manner India stopped in the tracks when she notice they didn't notice her Shay ran over to her and jumped into her arms.

Steve was apologizing for whatever responsibility he had in the ending of their marriage and that if Sharon needed anything that she could call on him. He also apologized for putting his hands on her twice during their marriage.

He was sorry for letting Ronald down and that he was not going to do the same to India not any more   it was no longer on her India had a responsibility to protect herself Steve asked Sharon if she wanted to go she could. Sharon declined she snatched away from his touch and denied any wrong doing on Bobbies behalf   It was then that India continued on her way. She whispered in her little sister Shays ear that she would always be there for her and their mother no matter the time day or night. She just would not be living at home any more once India got in the car and started to put her seat belt on Shay reached for her it was then India started to cry. She asked her father to leave he backed out the driveway waving at Sharon Steve never had a relationship with Shay and he never got use to that it was weird for him. India was   quiet   for the most part after about an hour into the ride she looked over at her father to confirm what she heard.

"So is it true you hit my mother before." India said

Steve thought about his words before speaking,

"Yes India it was stupid you where just a baby I realized early on that it wasn't the right thing to do I apologize to you also baby a man should never put his hands on a women especially a woman that he loves."

"Did Ronald see you hit our mother daddy?'

Steve knew there was no thought out answer that could make this question go away and he knew India was a smart girl and that the last thing he should do, was lie so he answered his little girl.

"I an not sure India,"

The look on her face hit Steve deep he knew a long time ago that he was wrong."

"Did your father hit my grandmother?"

"I mean India they had thier arguments but I don't remember him ever hitting her not once." Steve said

"So you don't even have that excuse." India said

Steve tried to keep his cool composure as he always did,

"What do you mean India?'

"Most men and women try to use the excuse that the reason they hit on their mates is because their fathers beat their mothers women see their father's beating their mother's but they don't use it as an excuse they just think they deserve to be beat what's your excuse then dad."

India didn't really want a reason there wasn't anything reasonable that he could ever say she was just venting she knew why she was leaving but didn't know why everything had come to this.

"India I didn't control myself when I should have I'll regret it for the rest of my life."

India rolled her eyes and turned to look out the window that was the longest ride of both their lives.

Steve had moved from his two bedroom apartment into a two family house with a nice back yard he was so excited that India thought he was going to say he had put a swing set out back the house was nice. It was very cozy India and her father had always been nice clean people Steve had India and Ronald's picture positioned the exact same way as he had in the old apartments. On the walls above the big screen television, they had just come out and India was not surprise he had gotten one he no longer had child support and was still at the factory he had a nice black mercury cougar and had changed his hair from braids to a nice short afro. India tossed and turned the first few weeks without much sleep she never went to bed without praying to God that her mother and sister would be safe.

The silence in the morning and although the night was unsettling for India the guilt of it was getting to her she was ready to pack up and go back to home. Steve worked third shift which made it worse when they talked about it India thought it was a good idea they would have the day to get to know each other better since India hadn't spent much time with him in the last few years. The last thing India thought she would be doing is freaking out from to much piece and quite she had started back having   bad dreams about Ronald, things weren't suppose to be working this way Steve introduced India to at least four women in the first few weeks they were all nice. And of course thought they were all numero uno knowing that was the only thing India had to laugh about lately. Steve would tell India she needed to get out meet some friends maybe even a boyfriend that was the last thing on India's mind Steve taught India how to make the best cheese

Coney's and club sandwiches along with homemade hamburgers. Her stomach was normally use to homemade full course meals three times a day but the footlong Coney's were to die for India made it through the first year. She and Toshiba sometimes talking through the night Shay came down that next summer it was hard for India when she saw her she was getting so big Sharon had driven her over while Bobby was off with his family. India looked her mother up and down Sharon didn't say much wouldn't get out of the car only asking India why she hadn't sign up for college yet. It surprised India because that was the first time her mother had ever mention college to her but one of Steve's lady friend worked at the University . She told India with her father's benefits at his job she could get India right when Steve came out to say his hello's to Sharon she told Steve that Bobby would pay for India's education. Steve didn't take the news well ignoring her in fact he said his goodbyes to Sharon and said going to college would be India's decision Sharon yelled out the car window reminding Steve that he was still a wimp. And that he needed to make India aware that he was the parent and that if India were still at home that she would have India at the college as soon as summer was over. Steve put his hands in his pockets walked up the steps and into his house   India had already thought about using her two years Early Childhood Education certificate she had received in vocational class from her junior and senior year to teach head start all she needed to do was take an early childhood test through the board of education to get in to one the elementary schools. This test India wasn't nerviuos about she'd taken a practice test before getting her certificate and aced it she just hadn't made any moves yet she was ready to enjoy her visit so she quick got off the subject not before Sharon mumbled that India could have stayed home to do nothing. Sharon said she needed to leave to pick up

Bobby his was giving a barbeque India told her mom she wanted to take Shay shopping she would be staying for a few weeks and India wanted her to look hip. India had started driving a few weeks after getting out of high school and Steve wanted her to take him driving on the street that was a lot different then driving around in drivers ed vehicle. India's first time out Steve was so busy dictating that India ended up going right through a red light at an intersection wrecking Steve's brand new Cougar he had it fixed without malice there was no yelling no fighting something wasn't right India wasn't at ease. The next day India and Shay went to a local outdoor mall where they had their pictures taken in matching outfits she had Shay's hair fixed so cute. India slept every night that Shay was in town she loved having Shay with her Shay talked her head off Shay cried when India told her she wouldn't be going back home with them Shay told her that she hated when her mother and father fought. India told Shay that as soon as she could she would convince her mom to let her come to stay with her she knew it probably would never happen but it was the only why to calm Shay down. India thought about packing and leaving when her mother and Bobby returned to pick her up at the end of the month but her dad's friend Pricilla had called her for a position India had been waiting on. She put in for the board of education to teach head start just what India was waiting on she could not wait to tell her mom the good news.

Steve was excited that India would be getting out of the house and meeting people working in head start with four and five year olds they will definitely be keeping India busy. Sharon and Bobby arrived India thought they would be staying the weekend they blow the horn Bobby called out for them to come on, India and Shay were carry plenty of bags India had braided Shays hair and put plenty of beads in it. Bobby fussed he said he better not find one bead on the floor Sharon had on dark glasses and did not get out the car it was cloudy and slightly raining. India always cried like a baby every time they left she didn't really get a chance to see her mother when they came because she had to follow Bobby around she only saw her when she had visited her side of the family. India reached inside the car and held on tight to her mother she held back her tears for the sake of Shay she told Shay her mother said she would have to think about letting her come back soon and maybe stay. She hated lying but she had to she blew Shay a kiss as Bobby put the car in reverse letting India know he was ready to go. She waved bye as the car backed out the driveway she went up to her room and cried for hours she knew why her mom was wearing shades

On a raining day she didn't have much time to be excited about her new job she would be starting in a few days. Sharon just smiled a little when India told of her good news her mother told here there were baby sitting jobs in Michigan India's head hung low she was putting she and Shays pictures in nice frames she only had one picture of Ronald up she kept the rest in a jewelry box that she kept on her bed. India talked to Toshiba that night until she fell asleep the next day India thought about how she was going to decorate her classroom she couldn't believe it her own classroom. India was glad to be getting out of the house since Steve had started having many parties some of them lasted until early morning Steve had many friends male and female it seemed as though he knew everyone in town. She would be making her own money Steve had already opened her up her first bank account and showed her how to keep up with her finances, She didn't need to do much shopping India was a nerd and dressed like an old lady India could not believe she would be turning 21 years old in a few weeks Steve would throw India a nice birthday party mostly his friends India invited a few cousins.

India was learning herself slowly but surely, the first year was great India had a great group of kids the school was nice and clean. Since she started working she has not really talked to Toshiba the last time she called, she was not at home she was dating heavily India felt guilty about not talking to Toshiba as often as she should be. India always felt better after they talked but she didn't like Toshiba asking about her nightmares all the time sometimes they were visions of Ronald in a dark room sometimes she wake up in a sweat from dreams of her mother screaming out her name for help. India fibbed the last time she asked she said the dream had stopped so that Toshiba would not ask any more. Maybe she would stop suggesting counseling since she has found her prince charming no the less she still tried to convince India she should do the same, India told her she had better things to do then chase after sex hungry boys. It was the weekend, India was upstairs working on her lesson plans she started to hear her father, and his friends downstairs she was glad he choose this house because her room was on the top floor. It was huge with two walk in closets just like having her own little apartment since India didn't have a life she turned her music up Shirley Murdock 'As we Lay' was on the radio. India loved all of her songs she watch television and listened to music until she fell asleep.

The next morning India went downstairs, she has been cleaning up after her father friends a lot lately India was not sure if Steve had changed his hours she did not really know what he was doing lately. He was in and out acting a little strange the last time India tried to make breakfast for him he did not eat much and did not seem like himself she could not believe he was already gone since it seemed like his friends had just left.

The phone rang India knew it wasn't for her she let the answering machine get it, it was a message from her father's job they wanted to know why he had missed work again and that he needed to call them as soon as possible. India stopped cleaning in her tracks.

"Missing work?" India said aloud

She knew Steve took pride in his work and he liked nice things she needs to find out if everything was ok when he got home. India waited and waited he finally came home around 4 pm India had falling asleep on the couch she heard his keys hit the glass tray he always put them in India did not wasted any time.

"Dad your job called there message is still on the machine you've been missing work are you alright can I do anything for you?"

Steve looked up at India he was sitting on his bed he looked like a train had hit him, India didn't know what else to say she didn't know what was going on   she had never really seen him drunk maybe once or twice when she and   Ronald would be with him in the summer time. This look was different   she didn't know if this look was from the smell that sometimes comes from   underneath the closed kitchen door India didn't like wondering or assuming so she ask Steve which had laid down as if she wasn't there India sat down on the edge of his bed she put her hand on his arm

"Daddy what's that smell that comes from the kitchen when your friends are over it smells funny not like a joint or cigarette." India asked

Steve mustard up some energy and gave India a smile,

"What stuff honey there aint nothing going on for you to worry about Ms. Teacher."
Steve said

"Are you going to work to night or at least call they sounded serious?" India asked
reluctantly

He didn't answer her she left out and closed the room door behind her Steve had always
tried to make India aware of her surrounding keep her informed about the news and
current events sex and so on. But he was now shutting her out India has mentioned once
or twice to Steve that he was too old, to be partying with so many different people he
promised her he would never let anything happen to her and that she should let him be
the parent.

Monday morning India was heading out for school she was greeted when she opened the
front door by one of her father's friends Jerry he was carrying a T.V.

"Excuse me Miss Lady uh."

Steve was at the top of the stairs trying to signal Jerry to take the T.V back out but he was
already squeezing his way through. Jerry looked up the steps when he heard   Steve's
firm voice India still stuck in place on the front porch she was counting the televisions
already in every room. Not missing the one in the big bathroom Steve keeps threatening
to take it out because India keep falling asleep in the bath tub it's one of the old tubs that
stands on legs India fills it with hot water and bubble bath from Avon one of Steve's lady
friends kept India stocked. Between the hot water then the over sized deep tub his kept
telling India it was dangerous but that pretty much was the only time India slept the
television Jerry was carrying was not   in a box. India shook her head then left she could
not be late for her class   her kid's were to important   to her she would count how many

television there were when she returned home. Steve yelled out for India to have a good day as he always did but normally he they would be passing each other him coming in from work and India leaving out for work.

India was always glad when the weekend came it gave her a chance to think of ways to change   her classroom around   time to unwind she was able to hide her sleeping habits because as soon as India would hear one of her students call out her name she was at attention. India rested well Friday night she did not see the televisions and her father was not at home when she came home.   Saturday morning India woke up excited she had a new friend she met a teacher from school they were meeting for lunch, Leah welcomed India the first week of school it took India a while to open up luckily Leah is very patience. She reminds India a little of Toshiba in that manner God must really know the type of friends she needs because India knew that she could be a hand full.

But Leah had a lot of differences for one she had Blonde hair that she kept in a nice bob and blue eyes thinly built 5ft 7inches in height   she was 24 and India had made it   to the big 20 India didn't realize what she had going on physically she never did and she never really cared. She had very nice hair not to thick full a little past her shoulders the prettiest brown skin cocoa she'd say c cup and 36 , 24 , 36 she had just enough ass to give a man a nice warm grip   for sure 5ft 5 inches tall she and Leah   hit it off right away. She has been asking India out for happy hours brunch whatever India was tired of partying with her dads friends from her room. From   time to time she would hang with her wild cousin Dena so she's getting out   India was kind of excited about having an adult friend who didn't know anything about her past her pain her nightmares to everyone at school India seemed just as normal as them. Never someone that could never recognize her own shadow Leah and India eat and talked as though they have known each other for years just as they did on their lunch at school. When India got home, there was a new red Celica in the driveway she was admiring it when her father and Jerry came outside they were discussing something.

"Nice car who's is it dad?' India said

"Why, baby girl you like it?" Steve stated with a smile

"It's nice my favorite color."

Steve walked to the bottom step and threw India the keys, she caught them without malice there was one key dangling from a key chain that had a red letter I dangling from it India noticed.

"Daddy are you serious." India said

"I told you as soon as you got out of your rut, I had a surprise for you, you're a professional now baby girl." Steve said

India embraced the car then opened the car door it was so clean inside India was smiling so hard that her cheeks were starting to hurt she sat inside then looked over at her dad then Jerry. He looked happy and healthy so India turned the ignition and took off she passed by a park where all the neighborhood guys liked to play ball she gave a quick glance as she always did she hated when they yelled out are made noises at her. She stopped at a little store around the corner to get an air freshener for the car. When she got out of the car

The guys standing around always stared at her India never spoke back they thought she was a major stuck up girl India wasn't she just didn't care what they thought are who they were. The guy that worked behind the store counter stared at her for a minute or so before he rang her honey bun and grape pop along with her yellow leaf air freshener.

"Your Steve's baby girl right?" The man said

India started to get smart with him addresses her with baby girl wasn't an option she rolled her eyes handed him her money then looked him straight in the eyes.

"My name is India sir.'

"Sir, do I look old to you." The man said

"Don't really care can I just have my change.' India griped

"You have such a beautiful name with such a ugly attitude just know if you ever have any problems with any of these knuckle heads around let me know Steve's my main man you know."

"No actually I don't, I have no idea who you are." India said

"I'm sorry my name is Mel I've said hello to you when ever you come through." The man said

He extended his hand to India she just looked at him she couldn't help but notice that he was tall he didn't look old at all he was nice looking very well built muscular even. Without shaking his hand, India took her change and left out the store.

"Wow nice car India I can assure you my salary doesn't compare to yours and I have been teaching for years." Leah said

India pulled in to her same spot at the same time Leah did they have been parking next to each other since their newfound friendship.

"Funny Leah it's a gift from my dad." India responded

"Nice gift does he want another daughter?" Leah stated

"You would off set the family portrait just a little Leah."

"You can always say that I was adopted you know."

"I always wanted a big sister." India responded

Leah was gulping down coffee and India a grape pop they had 2 minutes before their day

was to start.

"India you never did tell me how the visit with you little sister went." Leah asked

"They came down for Labor Day Leah it   seems lie the older Shay gets the more she

resents me and my mother has the same attitude we don't hug are talk like we use to my

dad and I had to ride around trying to catch up with them to see them. I don't know what

to say enough of my junk time for class." India said

Before Leah leave out her classroom she notice India face turn sad,

"India trust me we've all got family problems and don't forget to call and tell me how

your date goes this weekend." Leah said

"That's if I go.'

India thought Leah would not hear her but she stuck her head back inside the classroom

door,

"India don't start you said he was a hunk he's got a job and he knows your dad go have

fun for a change for me." Leah perked her lips upside down

India shook her head yes she did not care what he was she wanted to chicken out besides

she never told Leah that her father was adamant about her not dating anyone in the

neighborhood would not say way. He specifically pointed a couple fellows out that he knew wanted to holler at India but Mel from the store was fine as wine so India did not tell Steve besides it was just a date she drove her own car to the movies. Mel had on a nice black plain button up shirt and some Levi jeans he was a little bow legged India was a little flushed it was something about this guy his confidence made him interesting. No matter how facetious India was, Mel always had a come back for her with a smile on his handsome face. Besides she had not been out on a date since she has been back she talked on the phone to a couple of guys they never held her interest for long as Mel did the two of them went to a small Italian restaurant after the movies. Half the time he was talking or asking questions about her dad Mel made Steve sound like he was some type of super hero India looked at him confused he was Steve her dad the one that needed to stop partying and keep up with his schedule at the factory.

"Look Mel do you want to be on this date with my dad or me." India asked

"What a silly question India, I'm just saying your dad is the man around this parts." Mel said

He has always talked about you but he left out the fact that you are fine and sexy as hell where are you from."

"I was born here in Indiana and I'm just trying to fit in I left as a little girl I'm not into any mess." India said

Mel continues to talk about stuff India had no clue about they never even talked about the movie he was nice and polite so India went with the flow.

A few weeks later India noticed about three more TV's , four or five VCR's and some boom boxes in one of her walk in closet upstairs usually her dads never comes upstairs India hadn't seen her dad all weekend. A few days later, he came in before India left for work she was thinking that at least he is still going to work.

"Hello dad." India said

"Hey baby." Steve said

"Dag, you could have called to let me know you were all right and wouldn't be coming home I've been worried.'

Steve just smiled a handsome smile at his very mature little girl,

"I'll be home tonight did you need something I thought you were a big girl now I promise I'll call next time ok.' Steve said

Then gave India a kiss on the forehead

"Real funny daddy, there's no one to cook and what's with all the stuff upstairs the phone been ringing off the hook are you sure everything is fine?' India asked

" I'm going to church on Sunday do you want to come?"

"Maybe next Sunday honey you going to be late for work you better get on out of here.' Steve said

India left but when she returned home from a long days work without fail the kitchen door was closed and full of people with the weird smoke smell. The music was loud India went straight upstairs she was very grateful to be away from all the destruction at her mothers but this was starting to drive her crazy in a different way its like her father had changed over night India didn't even know who he had become. She was glad she had brought Kentucky fried chicken home she took the whole bucket up to her room and ate she fell to sleep and didn't wake up until she had one of her nightmares it was 3am and she noticed it was quite downstairs. India needed something to drink she went downstairs Steve's door was shut India started straightening up the kitchen she cleaned all the white powdery stuff and the small glass mirrors off the kitchen table got her a grape pop then went back to bed.

The next morning Steve told her he had quite his job India was shocked he'd been working at this factory for over 18 years he said that he and his friend Jerry would be opening up two clubs.

He was calling them Main Stream 1&2 he said the clubs had already been opened for about two weeks. He was talking a mile a minute he said he did not want to tell India until things were finalized he banded her from the clubs of course. India was speechless she didn't know what to say Steve seemed very excited as though he had things in order so India went with the flow but banding her from the clubs was ludicrous after all she was 21 years old now. So India decided a few weekends later to get dressed and check out one of the clubs she called her cousin Dena and her girl Leah, Dena was always asking India out and Dena said the clubs are always jumping she knew since she hadn't been banded especially on Friday nights. Steve had warned India that they probably were not her type of crowd but still courage her to get out and mingle. Mel was hired as head bouncer for the club his eyes lit up when he saw India especially since she had refused to go out with him again.

"India my, my, my no one has entered this club as fine as you I welcome your presence please save me a dance." Mel said

India pulled her money out her purse when she saw the cover charge sign $10.00,

"Don't be silly my lady you know I can't charge the first lady around this here parts."
Mel told her

Dena was all smiles she extended her hand although she had been to the club a few times

70

she never knew the treatment that awaited her with India's presence.

"I'm India's cousin and I can safe you a dance too?" Dena said

"India's all the dance I need Ms. Lady but it's nice to meet you." Mel said as he directed

the women into the club

Mel whipered into Dena ear,

"Have her save my dance Ms. Lady and all your drinks are free."

Dena get anode that India's virgin ass is getting all the attention she rolls her eyes at Mel

but does not take it   lightly with what he has said. Once in the club safely India turns to

Dena to ask what she wanted from the bar as if she was an expert she than wandered

where Jerry and her father where,

"India I know that wasn't the lame you told me about."

"Yes that was him Dena it's cool we are in now chill out." India said

Dena rolled her eyes at Mel as to say she was not India's babysitter India assured Dena

that there had to be plenty of men other than Mel in the club tonight Dena was extra

anoid at the fact that India did not even want Mel but India insisted on Dena getting her

groove on with someone else. Steve was standing in the corner talking to two Hispanic

looking guys their conversation looked serious so he hadn't seen India with Dena yet she

saw him but she didn't disturb him.

Dena spotted him too she mentioned that he looked as if he was talking to some tuff

looking guys India told her not to say anyting negative about her father. Dena told India

that she had better wake up and smell the strong coffee that had been brewing for quite

some time. India started to comment but Mel was right in face.

"Mel you ready for that dance yet?" Mel extended his hand

But Dena's comment has pissed India off but she ignored it and went to dance before Mel did the same thing. There was so many people on the dance floor little did Mel know this was India thing to dance and she definitely loved all types of music the song 'Renegades' came on India had never really been to a club like this before it was crazy when the people started gathering to the dance floor like flys. Leah was to wrapped up in her new relationship to come out India was not jealous she did not think the club and music was diversed Leah wouldn't probably like it they mostly went to sports bars when they hung out. Dena had made her presence known by the time India made it off the dance floor to wipe her sweating forehead Steve was holding his drink looking like he had lost his mind or something to that affect.

 "Baby girl, I told you this is really not your type of scene I don't want any of this guys getting hurt." Steve said

"Daddy I'm almost 21 years old I like the club and I love the music I will be alright I can take of myself you taught me that ." India smiled

"I know how old you, and what are you doing with Mel?"

India looked back to see if Mel wanted to answer the question he was clear across the room she was on her own. India turns back and smiled at her father again then pointed to Dena and walked away quickly.

Steve motioned for Mel, India followed them with her eyes they walked over to the same corner Steve had been talking to the other fellows. Steve was swinging his hands and arms pointing back and forth at India she kept trying to turn her head when his finger was pointing at her but she could not keep up. India was thinking he needed to chill he knew that she was responsible and this is what he wanted her to do get out and mingle India rolled her eyes and drank her cooler she could sip for hours. This one didn't take long she finished her last sip then got off the stool at the bar to walk over to Mel and her father when Jerry grabbed her by the arm with a surprised look on his face.

"Hey baby girl your father knows you're here good to see you."

India pulled her arm from him then started to confirm that it was not ok for anyone but her father to call her baby girl and question why everyone keeps asking her that question. However, the cooler made her hesitate then answer slowly India was not use to that and she did not like it but it didn't stop her .

"Jerry I'm a grown woman I'm 21 years old."

Jerry looked at her as if she could have been 32 years old and if Steve has told him to make India leave; he would have to kick her out himself.

"Be careful I'm going over here to speak to your father." Jerry said

Then eyeballed India as he walked away,

Dena presence was heavy on the dance floor Mel never looked India's way the rest of the night guy's continued to asked her to dance India declined thinking over why this wasn't her type of club she drank another cooler she had never made it to two coolers. India watched her father watching her while all types of people were walking up to him Dena was finally off the dance floor and walking over to the bar where India was sitting.

"I'm ready, I hope you are?' India said

"No, not yet go ahead I see someone that I want to take me to bed, I mean home." Dena said

"But you don't even know him and we came together." India said

"Correction I don't know him yet.'

Dena blew India a kiss then was off,

India yelled out to Dena she was mixed in the crowd India was so angry she jumped off the stool she waved bye to her father he acted as if he didn't see her Mel was talking to a couple of guys he yelled out to India. She was not able to hear, between the loud music, the coolers and her anger she kept walking as soon as she got around the corner within seconds she could hear someone running up behind her. She looked back and could see a person out the corner of her eye she quickly noticied he had a work uniform on which meant he probably was not someone she had brushed off in the club.

"Good" India said out loud

She continued to walk a few more steps and got to her car she started looking for her keys when she notcied the shadow of the guy in her car window he quickly put his hand over India mouth and stuck something in her back. He whispered in India's ear to stay quite and follow him with his body, he motioned which way to go India kept a small knife in her purse force of habit she guess the man was taking India futher up the street which sat on a hill.

India did not know what he had stuck in her back it felt as though it could be a gun she stumbled over her feet she was wearing heels.

"Walk faster." The man force the object deeper into India back

India thought to pray she instantly knew she could not let him take her any further she started to focus and a hissing sound that was coming from a car. She decided in her mind that whenever the sound got closer she would try and break free the car lights was about 15 feet from them they parked. India had managed to get her knife open and stabbed the man in the hand that around her neck. He yelled and India ran back toward her car she only had one shoe on now but didn't think about it she started screaming as loud as she could   hoping someone would hear her. She heard a shot behind her, she ran up on the sidewalk instead of in the middle of the street with the streetlight India could hear footsteps and heavy breathing behind her she ran right passed her car. She got to the corner, rushed around a tall brush, and ran right into Mel he as out of breath trying to figure out why India was ignoring him calling out her name India did not have a chance to look up she just started swinging and screaming. Mel was trying to grab her arms when he noticed the knife.

"Baby girl, India it's me Mel what is going on?'

Mel looked up at the footsteps behind India the man did not have a chance to stop Mel pushed India to the side almost into the brushes the man tried to do a quick u-turn   gun in hand Mel without fear took to India defense. He was tall and athletic the medium built man didn't make it but a few feet before Mel had   him in a choke hold dragging him down the street   he never took a shot at Mel India finally calmed down she was shaking from head to toe she extended the hand that was still holding the knife. Mel assured the man he had just made the biggest mistake of his life Mel reached India he told her not to worry there was two guys coming up the street to check on Mel's where about they saw the man dangling from Mel's big arm's gasping for air. They ran toward him Mel told them to walk India to her car then join him at the back of the club the men were as equally big as Mel. They took India by the arm   never asking a question nor saying one word   she was safely in her car they stood there as India sped off knocking someone side mirror off their car. It felt like it took forever for her to get home she was driving through stop signs running through yellow lights she rushed into the house and into then shower

the guys told India she didn't need to call the police that they would take care of things.

India washed her knife off with hot water and curled up with one of her father blankets

on the couch with every light on in the house at 1:30am in the morning she almost

jumped   out of her skin. When she heard a knock at the door she ran to the kitchen for a

much bigger knife then walked to the top of the steps with the phone in her other hand

then she   yelled out

"Who is it and what do you want.'

"It's   me India Evelyn your father called and asked me to come over."

"My father isn't here Evelyn.' India said

"I know baby girl he's at the club he told me what happen he didn't want you to be alone

until he could get here open up.' Evelyn said

Evelyn was nice she always hooked India up with Avon anything she wanted she walked

down the steps still holding her knife and still shaking. She looked through the

  window Evelyn looked like she'd just got out of bed India let her in they walked up the

steps into the bright house Evelyn gave India a hug she was holding India's arm probably

because of the knife India didn't give hugs often.

 'Are you alright baby girl?"

"Could you please call me India?"

"India sit down let me make you a drink you look like you need one."

'I don't drink.' India said

India hesitated,

"I don't drink liquor."

"Oh baby, you need this I'll make it light for you relax." Evelyn said

Then she went behind the bar that was in the large living room to make India a drink

India was scared to ask what the brown liquid was she did asked was it suppose to burn

going down   and Evelyn confirmed she told India to promise not to tell her father after

the second shot India promised .

"Evelyn were is Mel?" India asked

"I don't know I just do what ever your father asked of me India I love him.'

They were both sitting on the couch Evelyn's glass was a lot larger than India's

Evelyn reminded India not to say a word to her father about the drinks then proclaimed to

India that she'd never seen such love from a father to his daughter like the way she see's

in Steve to India. It brought tears to India's eyes but still it brought fear along with the

burning sensation from the drink India was a little confused she didn't understand how

Evelyn knew about her situation. She knew both her parents loved her but she did not

understand the need for any hard break that she was starting to feel. India the liquor was

starting to feel no pain from the incident that happened just hours ago she kept asking

was Mel ok and Evelyn assured her that her father was taking care of everything.   That

she needed to relax and not to worry India was feeling so good that she turned up the

music playing on the radio. She tuned off the television Rock the Bell by LL cool J was

playing the drinking forced India to start dancing and act silly. Evelyn join in she liked

India a lot most of the men she dated use her the other women never meeting their family

or children. But India was different even thought she'd has known her father for quite

some time India embraced the women in his life as long as they were drama free some of

them didn't pass the test but for the most part Evelyn did besides he wasn't married.

After all baby girl came first   he even told them about his son Ronald until this day that will never change.   India kept asking Evelyn for the number to the club until she did not even understand the situation at hand Evelyn was doing her job and even though Steve would not agree with the way she has gone about it she wanted to be Steve's wife even though marrying was the furthest thing on his mind.

India fell onto the couch after several failed attempts to get the clubs number from Evelyn exhausted from singing "It Takes Two" at the top of her lungs and dancing through the living room. Evelyn was rolling laughing   heavily she went into the kitchen to rinse out the shot glasses she had brought over she put her bottle of E&J back in her purse waited for India to fall asleep on on the love seat she stayed another hour she definitely could hold her liquior being a 45 year old woman with   five grown children.

India's head felt like a ton of bricks has fallen on it she peeked around the room trying to gather her where abouts   she pulled her cover back over her head then back down for another glance once her thoughts became familiar. India had to rethink her feeling for Evelyn and wondered if she was still around to whip her ass once her head stopped spinning her legs and arms were sore India didn't exercise she didn't have to then she remember dancing and the picture frame she'd broken the sun was shining through the tan curtains. Her mouth was dry she thought about getting up   to see what time it was get a drink and find out what day it was.   She made it to the kitchen the calendar stopped being a blur it read   that it was a Sunday the glass clock on the wall read 12 noon the glass of water went down slow she was about to go take a shower. When the toilet bowl became her best friend it felt like India's gust were trying to come through her throat she did not hear her father or Jerry caming up the stairs.

Steve rushed into the bathroom,

"India what's wrong."

He tried to pull her head up a litle but it would not budge Jerry asked if he needed help Steve snapped at him.

"Hell naw man this is my baby girl India what's wrong you pregnant or something." Steve could not think of any other conclusion especially not being drunk on E&J once India got herself together, she got her father out the bathroom she took her shower she confirmed that she was not pregnant. She wanted so bad to tell on Evelyn every time her head pounded she thought she was helping so India kept it quite she told Steve she was just shook up from last night.

Steve gave India a hug for the forth time all he would say is the guy would not be hurting anyone else he firmly told India not to question or worry about anything he did not think it was best he banded India again from the clubs. However, he let her know that not leaving with Dena the person she came with was irresponsible and better not happen again, no matter what club that she would be at. Steve wasn't firm with India maybe once in her life time today was different she heard him loud and clear he kissed her on the forehead she noticed he had on different clothes he looked fresh. He told her Evelyn would be back over in another hour she would bring India something to eat India did not declined she knew her father was not in that kind of mood. She was exhausted she went up to her room and within minute the aspirins worked she was knocked out she didn't even hear Evelyn at the door Steve made it back around 10pm that night he checked on India she didn't budge he went back downstairs.

He read   Evelyn's note he didn't go to the club that night or have any parties he stayed up as long as he could talking business on the phone in case India woke up and needed him he even called   his friend Linda. She was a counsler at a local community organization she mentioned that India might want to talk with someone that kept Steve still for the night when India came down for work the next morning she was a little nervious then she brightened up when she smelled breaskfast cooking in the kitchen. And her dad just finishing up to serve it they talked a bit he gave her Linda's card she had stopped by India said she was ok but if she needed it she would call. India got to school and gave Leah an ear full during lunch Leah couldn't belive what she was hearing she told India that she should probably called   the Linda. India ignored her she remembered she hadn't even talked to Dena she intended on calling her when she got home.

 When India got home from work the newspaper was still on the front porch Steve's car was in the driveway along with four others. India picked up the newspaper she nomally never read them but was instantly drawn to open this one she walked up the steps slowly the kitchen door was closed. She usually like going into the living room but the smell and loudness wasn't tolerable so she went upstairs threw everything off her bed closed her door turned her music on   Orange Juice Jones 'I saw you walking in the rain'.   India fell back on the bed with her arms stretched out singing to the words of the song she rolled over and notice the word Murder across the 3rd page of the newpaper. India sat up to read the article,

"Man found dead by near by club no witness the victims name has not been released black male around 25 to 30 years of age."

" There have been two rapes in the surrounding area in the last 3 months residents were requesting more police patrol especially since there was now a club in the middle of the neighborhood."

India did not know rather to cry or scream he could be the rapest he did attack her with a gun but he could be someone's father and what did all of this make her father. She wanted to know too many things, which were not adding up she knew she should do what her father instructed and forget about it, So she directed her attention on what was going on downstairs now she wanted to know what the smell was she started to knock on the kitchen door then she realized it was a kitchen door. She opened it then stopped quickly in her tracks from the smoke and the smell there had to be at least 10 people men and women. India couldn't tell who was who she then noticed Jerry who was trying to wave away the smoke a women patted Steve on the shoulder he was to busy doing what he was doing to notice India's presence.

"Honey what are you doing in here?" Steve said

 "You invited me to live here remember may I talk to you in the living room for a minute daddy.' India said

"Baby girl can you see I'm busy right now."

Steve was slurring his words his eyes were crossing India started to choke from the smell she was waving her hands back and forth in her face her eyes started burning. They all looked like robots scrambling around put things behind their back there was the white powder. That India always cleaned up all over the table glass mirrors and funny looking glass fixtures. Liquor bottles everywhere Jerry had managed to open the window India was wondering why they were acting this way they knew she lived here I guess as long as they never saw her they didn't think they were doing anything wrong.

"Daddy can I talk to you please."

"Baby girl you don't need none of this around you maybe you should talk to him later.' Jerry said

"Who the fuck is that talking to my duaghter none of you mother fucker beat not say shit.'

Steve was out of it, there was a glass mirror pulled up to him he reached and lift the mirror that had a razor blade on it an a small amount of white powder on it. He started chopping the powder then smoothing it out his body was moving around then he looked at India.

"Here you want to know what we doing." Steve said

India walked over to him and smacked the mirror right out of her fathers hand onto the floor Steve jumped up as though he was going to attack India Jerry and another man quickly restrain him.

"Man come on that's baby girl what you doing you know you don't want her to be a part of this shit.' Jerry said

He knew that Steve was over the top they have been there since 10 am it was 5 pm and if

Jerry didn't stop him after he realized what he was had done he would kill him. Steve did not resist them he did not have the strength. India ran out Steve was calling out to her while Jerry was trying to sit him down.

"Baby girl, where my baby go?'

India was upstairs stuffing her thing into an over night bag she could not fight back the tears she did not try she grabbed her things for school and rushed downstairs. She rushed passed the closed kitchen door she heard her father call out to her again but that did not stop her India had no idea were she was going but she was out of there. She stopped at a store near to use the phone booth Dena did not answer India drove and drove until she got nervous she realized she was in front of Leah's apartment. She couldn't believe she remembered how to get there she sat in the car wandering if she should tell her new friend of her dark secrets may she will leave out the part about her father and Mel being involved in a possible murder she does not want to scare her away.

Leah was now engaged to be married but was still living in her own apartment for a few months. Leah was coming down the steps to take out her trash when she and India almost bumped into each other. India quickly tried to wipe her tears away but her face showed all of her pain,

"India what a surprise how did you get in, what's wrong?' Leah asked

India hadn't gotten her stuff out of the car and she started to lie something she didn't

believe in doing maybe she just needed to talk maybe she should call the counsler and leave she and Leah's friendship was going so well everything was normal but her tears got heavier. Leah told her to sit down on the step while she ran out to take the trash.

"I'll be right back India it alright.'

If India had a dime for every time she heard it going to be all right she tried to gather herself before Leah got back this side of India was not like her especially in front of people.

"Come on India I'll make you some tea or coffee.'

India tried to gather her thoughts but Leah always told India your blues aren't like mine she meant that family life can be difficult for everyone. India felt comfortable around Leah she trusted her even though Leah might ran for the hills they had not been friends for long.

"Leah he offered me drugs, and then I was reading the newpaper and I think Mel killed the guy that attacked me."

"India you should take a deep breath calm down here drink this.'

"I thought you were getting me tea or coffee.'

"You don't drink that drink this." Leah said

She was handing India a small glass and some tissue India knew when it burned going down she did not want any more she quickly started to calm down. She handed Leah her glass back India leaned back and took a deep breath Leah changed her drink back to hot cup of tea.

"Leah I don't know how to explain this is horrible my father lost his mine I had to get out of the house I don't know if I can ever go back." India said

 Leah sat next to India she put her hand on her shoulder with compassion in her eyes.

"India you don't have to worry about anything you can stay here as long as you like."

India took a deep breath she sat up on the couch sip on her hot tea it was actually good she asked what Leah put in it besides honey a shot of Henessey she confessed.

"Why does everybody always try to get me drunk?" India asked

"Not drunk India you just feel that way because you're a beginniner."

"In a few seconds you will be saying,

" I feel a lot better now."

" So in laymen terms I'll be a drunk sooner or later.'

They both laughed India needed that her body started to calm down but her mind was still rambling on.   India tried again to gather her thoughts to think of how much she should say but she could not stop visualizing her father trying to give her drugs India has lived a somewhat sheltered life when it comes to the streets and the things she is learning she did not prepared for.

"My dad told me I'd be safe living with him he's a liar and a drunk and whatever else just like every adult that I have ever come across in my life no one has ever protected me. I've always been the protector I have no idea how to protect myself I have been around drugs and madness pretty much since I've been here this shit is crazy." India said

"It is official India you are upset I don't know if I've ever heard you curse it sounds devastating again your more then welcome to stay here I'll be getting married and moving into my new house ." Leah said

India got the newspaper article out of her purse and handed it to Leah,

"Look just read the article at the top." India said

Leah's eyes expanded as much as they can go.

"Leah's he's the guy that attacked me I know it, he's dead look what I caused Mel or whoever to do I'm shook up completely Leah my dad's house is in shambles I don't want to involve you are scare you away with what's going on." India said

"India if this is the guy it serve's him right I'm sorry and I'm not going anywhere we're good for each other and as far as being embarrass sweetie if you only knew in my family its smile then lots of tea and crumpets and lots of sweeping things and secrets up under the rug."

"Our rugs in my parent's house are so lumpy that it's not funny sweetie.' Leah said

"Leah I look in the mirror, and I have no idea who it is I see the bad daughter the bad sister, friend the only way I don't have nightmare's is not to sleep."

"Nightmare's what do you mean India.'

India stood and walked over to the window she moved back the curtain the sun was shining and in the back of Leah's building were tree's for days. Leah followed behind sitting down at a little table next to the window.

"India when I was little I had so many imaginary friends when I saw my real family I didn't even know who they were.'Leah said

In unison India and Leah looked at each other they could not do anything further but laugh they laughed at least 5 minutes tears were rolling down both of their eyes from joy and pain they stopped and started laughing again. By then Leah had filled India tea a second time India had found a little clock radio and turned it on to an R&B station. Before she turned up Joy and Pain by Maze she warned Leah to get rid of her secret, friends before she married her future husband Greg you do not want him to get jealous. Leah was on her third drink reminding India that laughing is good she told India to stop beating herself up that she is a good person. She stated that if no one else God and herself can vouch for that Leah promised that she was going to help India work things through she demanded that India stays at her place as long as needed India took her up on the offer they talked the rest of the night Leah took sleeping pills to settle her at night Leah mention them to India after she slip about her nightmares she would not think of taking any prescription drug to dangerous she always thought.

The next weekend after not talking to are telling her father where she was India decided to talk to him he'd been calling the school to no avail. India wanted to get some more things no smoke no Televisions, VCR, or stereo falling out of closets India was glad she stopped by the house after school Friday when she pulled up there were three cars in the driveway. There were more than usual amount parked on the street she parked behind the cars that were in the driveway then India sat in the car for a few minutes she was very nervous she didn't call she couldn't she didn't know rather Steve would be drunk or high all this drama in her life had to end.   No one answered the door India looked around at the apartment building next door nothing but silence things didn't seem right India must have lost are left her keys. For some reason India kept focusing on all the cars it was so quiet for so many cars India had been acting naïve since she had to start to smell that strong coffee Dena was talking about India decided to turn the knob sure enough the door was unattended and unlocked. She looked up then started up the third step the front door swung back open with force the next thing India heard were strong voices demanding her to get down on the ground.

"Get on the ground now." The masked officers said

Within seconds, the police had India down on her knee's then forcing her knees apart. Several officers rushed past her up the steps no one knew they were there India heard the ruckus upstairs door slamming yelling threatening of gun fire India was now standing and against the wall looking down at the floor she heard a deep voice demanding the her hands be uncuffed the deep voice was familiar but strange at the same time then the voice whispered in her ear.

"Don't worry you'll be ok just stand here and don't look back until I tell you too."
India was too scared to try to identify the voice she stood against the wall her hands to her side still looking down to the floor. She could feel people brushing past her while being escorted out of the house she heard Jerry call out her name then a bunch of scrambling around coming down the steps.

"Oh no not my baby girl motherfucker's let her go I'll give you whatever you motherfucker want, you dirty son of a bitches." Steve said

He was fighting down every step not listening to the officers commands when he got down the steps they slammed him against the wall his nose was bleeding he tried to reach out to India but was being forced outside India couldn't hold back she turned around.

"Please officer don't take my father what did he do leave him alone he'll straighten up I'll help him.'

The officers without masks where excorting people inside what were unmarked cars the masked officer grabbed India by her arm and escorted her through the already opened basement door. The steps were steep India had never even been down there before she was trying to resist not knowing what the officer wanted from her he told the other officer she may know where more drugs are located.

There was a little light shining from a small dirty window as soon as India focused the basement reminded her of the one in Michigan she started to hyperventilate with the masked officer in front of her she started to yell out then pull away. The officer

took off his mask he quickly put his hand around India mouth she bite down on it,

"Och India damn why did you do that I am trying to help you."

"What the, I didn't know it was you."

"Look you haven't been here in days and you're not driving your car." Mel said

India was driving Leah's car her car was in the shop she noticed the gun in his holster and

wandered if she could get it out   and shoot Mel before he could react if looks could kill

India would have killed a lot of people but she wanted Mel to die of slow death.

"Please India before you say anything this wasn't personal I was just doing my job I

never knew I was going to meet you or fall for you baby girl."

"Don't you fucking call me that you son of a bit,

"India please I had a job to do."

You had these people pin me to the floor like a dog you take me out come on to me you

call me all the time you were using me." India said

"India I couldn't hold them off any longer it was either we come in or the   Columbians

and you definitely didn't want that their orders were a lot different then the police."

'What in the hell are you talking about you betrayed me." India said

"I know I told you that your father talked about you that was a lie not on the street he

kept that part of his business very private when you arrived we didn't know who you

were." "From surveillance we finally figured you had to be a niece maybe daughter I

asked when I heard around time baby girl was off limits I figured you were her his baby

girl."

"Today you were just in the wrong place at the wrong time I'm sorry."

"He is my father Mel you must think I'm stupid you don't have to give me any explanation you were just doing you job right, like when you kissed me told me you wanted more that was just you doing your job right fucker." India said

Mel feeling for India were real but he knew the were not professional he could not say a word.

"I've never had any control over the bullshit that happens around me this is nothing what you want to do next frisk me find some more drugs go ahead."

India started toward Mel,

"Here I am this is what you wanted right?"

India started unbuttoning her blouse all the way down she was close enough to run her hands up and down his broad chest cover with a thick bulletproof vets. She put his hand on her breast he couldn't take it away he reached down to kiss her India pulled away then back and kissed him she leaned up and whispered in his ear.

"Is this what you like officer Mel if you'd told me you would not be taking my father to jail I would have been fucked you given this to you let's do this."

"India don't do this your not under arrest I really have feelings for you I promise you we've been investigating your father long before you ever came into the picture please lets talk later."

Mel was holding one of India arms he still had not taken the handcuffs all the way off he was looking at her with such compassion but not enough to make it matter. India stepped back from him she started laughing.

"Just tell me one thing did Officer Mel or did Mel kill that guy that attacked me?" India asked

He took the cuffs off of her   put his hand to India face she turned away waiting on his answer he looked her firmly in her eyes then kissed her lips softly. India didn't have time to react fighting back the tears and emotions were taking it's toll there was silence then he told her he wished things could have turned out differently. And that he would always be there for her day or night India didn't get her answer Mel warned her that if she wanted anything out of the house that she should hurry to get it   because everything would be seized   some of the officer were looking at them strange once they return upstairs.

India had no words she just shook her head she gathered as much as she could putting the things in Leah's car.   India came to reality that this too would soon become no more than just a memory, memories that were always painful and unforgivable India could hear Officer Mel's voice giving commands India looked around at the cars full of her father and his friend's officer Mel directed India to the dark blue car that held her father he wanted to speak with her. All her could mustard was that he was sorry India was numb she couldn't say a thing her face furious and confused only thoughts why was this happening. Her silver lining once again ended in a horrible ending that she had no control over. She looked at her fathers glassy eyes   he tried to reach for India with his cuffed hands he thought about all the things he should say but was to high to remember,

"India daddy loves you and I never ever meant to hurt you baby girl. "

India stood straight backing away from the blue car she could only think of one thing to say and she did in a whispered but toned voice,

'Fuck you daddy there is no one that I can trust and I have you to thank for that you had everything and me and that wasn't enough." India said

91

She walked away from the car she pulled the car keys from her pants pocket Mel tried to talk to her telling her what she could do to see her father she did not hear a word he said she got in her car despite the other officer's reluctance to allow her to leave without question. Mel was clearing the way stating he would take full responsibility for the report he stopped India at the end of the driveway

"Both India, sometimes when your under cover you get caught up I wish you the best you deserve it and I am sorry."

"You damn sure are right about that you are sorry."

The judge gave Steve nine to twelve years with possibility of parole   India could not bring herself to go to any of the court dates. She stood outside the courthouse the day he was bussed to federal prison there were many cars leaving out. That day several officers asked if India needed help, she continued to shake her head walking from corner to corner India left after lingering around for three hours. Over a few years had past India's aunt Veronica would touch base telling India that her father was alright and that he misses her and has once again sent money for her to visit him India hasn't seen   her father locked up she told her aunt to save his money for when he returned home.

Its been five years Mel stopped calling after the first year   India never answered   India still lived in the apartment she took over the lease when Leah got married to Greg they now live in a nice big home in the surburbs. They try to get India to move closer but the apartment is close to school India has two Godchildren Ezra and Le Ann. They are eleven months apart and a hand full but she loves them just the same India latest was Myron she sure knew how to pick them he is always saying India has bedroom eyes. He knew nothing about her that is why she liked him he was all about her looks he did not care about anything else. India was still built like a brick house nothing has gone out of place she let her hair grow past her shoulders even though she was devoted to fast food she still had one thing on her side a nice body and pretty face with smooth brown skin to match. India never went all out with her looks but she knew how she affected men. Myron was a ladies man he was about 6feet tall nice short curly dark brown hair you would almost think it was black he had caramel brown skin. He was India's mailman and for a while India did not know he was purposely leaving her mailbox door unlocked after about the fourth time India was convinced it was not her imagination. She tried catching him one day she hurried down the stairs four flights when she heard keys dangling and the sound of mailboxes slamming shut India looked a hot mess decked out with her white thick robe and rollers. India started cursing immediately when she turned the corner to face the mail person when she hit the bottom step she thought damn he sure is fine to be so dumb. Appartenly he has been noticing India but she's never paid any attention to him not even the fact that he was a mail carrier.

"My, my I didn't think you could get any more beautiful Ms. Lady.' The mail carrier said No he didn't India hadn't realized her wardrobe yet she looked him up and down fine or not fine he must be out his mind,

"Look my brother are you the one that keeps leaving my box unlock cause if so you'd better not make that mistake again are it's your .' India held her last word

He smiled just like a gigolo but a fine one nonetheless,

"I apologize if that has happened it will never happen again let me make it up by taking you out to dinner please."

His smile was mesmerizing but India would not let that faze her she looked him up and then down slowly he was bowlegged and his slim build showed them perfectly. India's head accidently tilted to the side when one of her rollers fell out. She calmly looked down but there was nowhere to hide so India decided she pick up the roller with grace then she replied smart again.

"Where are we going, Mc Donald's?" India asked

"Well maybe for our second date but no not for our first anywhere you want to go I'll take you."

India took her mail from his hand gave a smirk and turned and walked away to the top floor where her apartment was then closed and locked her door. After about a week of the mail carrier, leaving little notes and chocolate kisses in India's locked mailbox India finally gave in to the mail carrier. Myron took India to a nice restaurant in their downtown area called The Samuri they hit it off pretty good all things considering Myron had no kids which was surprising to India she could tell right away that he was a self confident ladies man   he drew lots of attention from all women young and old. But Myron was determined to get and have India to his surprise he was completely smitten with her, Head over hill and he didn't know what to do with all his energy and testosterone he was use to being the persude 6 months later he was hanging by a tread. His mother and sister could not stand India said she was stuck up and they did not like that Myron spending so much time with India. All the while getting on India's nerve she couldn't shake him no matter what she said are did the last two month's all they did was argue about one thing and one thing only he repeatedly told India that he has been waiting long enough and that he demanded that she have sex with him.

India once again told him that he wasn't waiting on a prize, that she was a virgin that he father's name was Steve and that he can deal with or leave she was hoping he do the second command. India had made this known to Myron on their first date he pleaded he wanted India to be his forever and he would do whatever it took, obviously, this has always been affective for him because he was becoming unbearable he came over as soon as India got off work. India could not get in the house good enough before Myron started in with his demands,

"India how in the hell are you going to be a 26 year old virgin that's for thirteen or fourteen year old girls why do you think God gave you all these hips and ass huh?"

'So you are saying God made all this just for you right?' India asked

Myron came closer and grabbed India by her waist his grip was tight he started kissing her on her neck then whispered in her ear,

"I know he didn't make it for you to waste."

India pushed him away and firmly reminded Myron once again that she was not running a marathon being a virgin was her choice when she decided to give herself away. It will still be her choice she told him that she was tired of always arguing about the same thing Myron walked up behind   India she turned around to face him,

"Girl you probably have cob webs down there let me help you once I give it to you, you won't never ever deny me again India."

India sat down on the sofa and started taking off her heels she look up at Myron,

"A real man wouldn't rush me."

"India a real man would take it then tear that shit up make that cherry explode and that's what I came here to do."

Myron ripped off all his clothes and was quickly on top of India they tossed around then India kneed him in the growing she jumped up trying to button her blouse back But Myron was not done he came toward her again full force.

"Look Myron its three days before New Years Eve don't make me put you out your trying to   start something that you know I'm not going to finish so get back." India said Pushing Myron back but he did not stop India backed up still pleading they were in the dining room that lead to the kitchen and when Myron would not stop forcing himself on her India went for the knife. Myron tripped over the kitchen chair injuring his foot after he stumbled he looked up and India was standing in front of him with the biggest kitchen knife that she could find. Myron immediately put his hands up and started backing away, "India what in the hell are you doing girl you crazy.'

"No, but I'd be crazy to let you take something that isn't yours now get out."

'I'm not going anywhere.'

India lunged at him,

"Is that right." India said

Myron ran from the dining room and before India could turn the corner, Myron was almost dressed he was tripping over his feet and cursing at the same time India did not give a damn.

"You cool your ass off and I'll be back.' Myron said

"Look, if your not planning on taking me out for New Years then keep your gambling self at your mother are were ever I don't care."

"I'll be back." Myron left

India showered and laid on the couch trying to unwind she had found out the hard way why she and Myron hardly ever went anywhere the last time they went to a popular spot almost every other person that approached them wanted to know the next time Myron would be at the house joint. They wanted to know if he was still on his losing streak India tried to discuss the situation with him but to no avail but India wasn't wearing blinders for no anyone again   if   she didn't get the answers she needed then she would ask friends or family.   Dena usually was a one-stop shop she knew everything and everyone,

"Girl he's a weed head gambling S.O.B leave him." Dena told her

India laughed to herself she asked Dena where she got the weed head part Dena said if he is not he will be India wandered why her Christmas gift was not wrapped. It was a gold bracelet it was pretty but there was no box or wrapping paper India was drifting off on the couch watching her favorite show Soul Train.

Myron came over the next day he was at it again like the day before or the time before that or before that had never happened. India was tired even though she was off school for the holiday break she was not sleeping and her nightmare last night was pretty bad. ""India who are you waiting to give it to, a girl I mean I've never had this problem with other women you know how many women want to have me, be with me." Myron said "Frankly my dear I don't give a damn can we talk about something else are we can brake up Myron it doesn't matter if I'm gay or not you aren't getting any."

"You know what I'm tired of begging you give it to me now or I'm out." Myron said

India got up from the couch and walked to the front door then opened it Myron walked toward her as if he wanted to choke the life out of her India assumed he would think about his decision after what happened yesterday Myron left peacefully. India shut herself back up in her apartment with her strawberry ice cream   her music and Soul Train with her favorite singers the phone rang India thought twice about answering it she didn't want to argue yet again listening to him say he can have anyone he wanted India wasn't trying to stop him.

"Hello hey girl."

'Hey Leah." India said

"India I'm going to make this short and sweet you know on New Years we are taking away the barricades from that house so what are you wearing and what time do you want Greg and I to pick you up." Leah said in one mouth full

'Girl I don't really have anything to wear and you know I don't really like the holidays." India said

"India I am not hearing you get up and lets go shopping I have to pick the kids up as a matter of fact I'll call Jill she's not doing anything I'm sure get ready I'll call you right back."

India continued to eat her ice cream shaking her head she does not know how Leah and Jill put up with her Jill was already Leah's friend. She introduced the two at her wedding and they've all been hitting it off every since Jill was fascinated with India especially how she handled men Jill never really had a friend out side of Leah India told her she didn't think knowing how to handle men took anything special. However, Jill was convinced she loved everything about India the way she did her hair the way she dressed the way she kept her apartment. Nothing fazed India and Dena was just crazy but she made her way in any now Jill was ringing the bell downstairs with in an hour.

Shopping was fun it took a load off India's mind her dress was red it was silk and it fit to her body like a glove she'd found some satin red high hills at Baker's in the mall with a black clutch satin purse since it was last minute everything was on sell. That really excited India Dena met up with them at the hair dresser they had a big sign inviting new comers at half off the last time India had been to a hair dresser once on for her prom she after that experience she liked to do everything herself and since she wasn't paying this time she agreed to get her hair pin curled whatever that means. She didn't like the way it made her hair hard but it looked pretty good Jill got her hair colored even though it looked the same she had pretty thick dark brown hair and she kept it straight and always an even cut on the ends $65 and it looked the same. Dena wanted everything under the sun perms tapers you name it hours later they were finished and India was so ready to go they got a quick bite and off they went when India got home she was glad to be tired she didn't wake until the next morning. Myron was ringing her doorbell India was making cheese eggs and bacon she went to the intercom to see who it was his voice was pleading. "Myron It's almost a new day and the last thing that I want to do is argue what you want.' "India I want to see you I don't want to argue either open the door." India buzzed him in but before he could make it up the three flights of stairs India, was dressed Myron looked like he knew what she had just done and the way she was dressed she had to have skills. Shirt tucked in socks and shoe's he immediately started watching Television he had a beer and a bag of grippos eating them as though he had not eaten in days. India ignored him and continued to eat her breakfast next to him on the couch after he eyeball her plate so hard she made he one too he was acting as though he had no clue that it was New Years Eve. He did not mention any plans which India knew it meant he did not have any plans or money.

Hours went by they both took a nap on the couch music playing softly and Good Times on the Television the phone rang India jumped out of her sleep she looked at Myron who's head was in her lap she reached over an answered the phone checking to make sure her hair net was still tightly on her head.

"Hello."

"India I can't wait until tonight I have a surprise for you Jill told me about the dress there was no doubt though I knew you were going to work it what are you doing girl?' Leah asked

"Nothing Leah I'm just laying around what's your surprise I'm not up to any surprises you know that." India said

"This surprise you will so you have a couple hours to lay on the couch before we'll be there so where is the stallion I know he's hasn't planed anything besides sex it's so time for you to leave that zero and bring you a hero you know.'

"Leah one day we're going to get you a slang book and were going to study it all day long."

"Am I wrong is he coming tonight.' Leah said

India looked down at Myron who had not moved a beat she knew he was awake and listening to every word, she said she did not want to elaborate on what Leah was saying she knew Leah and her lame game constantly trying to set her up after two months India never had any more interesting stories to them. Leah told India what time she and Greg would pick her up Dena and Jill were riding together India answered with uh huh then hung up.

Myron raised up and kissed India on the lips he didn't say a word he asked India to fix something to eat she didn't have any fight left in her so she went to the kitchen she started spaghetti with garlic bread and homemade green beans India loved homemade green beans. Myron stayed on the phone India could tell by the conversation that Gambling was a priority but she did not let it faze her the New Year would be just that a New Year and she knew it would not consist of Myron in anyway. That was just fine with her she told Myron to come get his plate India made her a small plate, she started to get excited about the dress she had brought. She knew eating a small amount would be the right amount the phone rang again this time it was Dena she was extra excited about tonight Leah promised the music and the men would be enjoyable for everyone.

"What does that mean?" India asked

Dena wouldn't divulge a thing which wasn't like her India became tense it was 8pm Myron was still pussy footing around making small talk India decided she'd had enough she showered and when she got out she put on her thick bed robe. Myron still was not mentioning a thing about the bring in the New Year she laid her dress on the bed she placed her shoes and clutch purse on the bed she turned the music a little louder. Myron was not stupid he could tell by India's phone calls that something was up but the only thing on his mind was making a come back from his losing streak. India was in the bathroom trying to fix a couple of curls that had fallen.

"Wow your hair looks nice when did you learn how to do that style.' Myron said

'"I went to the hair dresser they had a special going on and thank you I think.' India said

"Well I'm going to step out for a minute then we can maybe get a bite to eat or something.'

"Get a bite to eat or you serious.' India yelled

She put the curlers down in the windowsill then turned to look at Myron in disbelief even though she knew this was coming.

"What do you mean out for a bite we just ate its New Years Eve Myron Leah and Greg are throwing a party tonight and we are invited." India stated

"India you know your stuck up friends don't like me and they most certainly aren't trying to invite me to any party we'll go to the after hour spot tonight I'll be back."

He kissed India on the lips he was out of the bathroom before India could say another word she took a deep breath and walked outside the bathroom even though she knew Myron wasn't invited she knew this relationship needed to end Myron stopped by the bed and picked at India's dress.

"This dress will surely be to much for the after hours joint pick something else and I'll be back."

Myron quickly took his coat from the closet and left India could do one of two things call her friends and tell them they were right or get dressed and continue with her plans. But it would be so easy to just put on her p.js and curl up on the couch with some chocolate doughnuts and milk maybe some caramel popcorn but that might be over kill. India looked around her room then at the cozy couch in the living room India flopped down on the bed and without fell the phone rang she put her hands over her eyes and let out a big sound of frustration the phone rang and rang India finally picked it up,

'Hello," India dryly said

""Happy New Years Eve sweetie will be to pick you up at 9 pm sharp so be ready and be beautiful don't make me call Dena on you she's on standby you know." Leah said

Leah had a habit of starting right into a conversation she did not know if India was listening if maybe her voice was the machine instead of Memorex she just did not care.

"This   could be considered harassment you know."

"Yeah I'm sure it could and if I cared there might be a warrant out for my arrest but since I don't and I have proof that you're one of my best girlfriend in the whole wide world. I'll say this just one last time you have two hours use them wisely because I'm going to be looking fierce see you at 9 pm." India laid around another half hour then it was time for some music her dress was fierce as Leah would say she was already showered so she lotion herself up and danced around as she took her curlers out the front she would put in a few to keep her style.   An hour later she was done the mirror was doing a wonderful job capturing India beautiful essence India turned from side to side she didn't know what side looked better her hair and cherry jubilee lipstick was flawless. India rushed to the phone this time to answer it she was happy to tell Leah she would be ready,

"Hello.'

"Hey baby, what are you doing have you done what I said your under the covers waiting on me right." Myron said

"Myron I'm not even going to let you upset me right now I am looking to good for that this relationship has come to a wonderful end and I'm about to go have the time of my life."

"Look, India I told you I didn't want to be around your selfish friends."

"Good Myron because your not invited." India said

"Well you know what that means if I'm not invited then you won't be going either so I'll be there in a little while ok.'

India laughed so hard she dropped the phone she glanced at herself as she continued her conversation.

"Myron honey you never have and you never will be running me   I'm not waiting so you have a nice life ok."

"Well I won't be having a nice life unless you're in it and having my baby and you will be waiting by the way I took your keys out of your purse so I'll see you in about an hour." He said

Myron hung up and India thought she could see stars in front of her she hung the phone up and searched for her purse she had not switch to her clutch yet the doorbell rang at 9 pm sharp her keys were nowhere to be found.

"That son of a bitch, piece of shit, asshole."

India yelled out she stomped around the apartment then went to the intercom and told Greg she would be right down then stood in the middle living room looking up at the ceiling she turned the music off then the television.

"Think, think India." India said

Leah was always telling India and Dena that they should get extra sets of keys for years India only had one pair she got more heated when she thought about Myron getting copies of her keys India jumped when the doorbell rang again. She didn't answer she kicked off her heels and rushed to the front door with reluctance she headed to the second floor the hallway on the second floor was always dark the light bulbs were taking out. The entrance that lead to the apartment on this floor just didn't look right the one to the left has been empty since India moved in the door to the right was always cracked opened it smelled of smoke and cats and a weird lemons smell. India's heart started beating fast when she decided to knock but before she could the deep, smoky voice said,

"Come In Indian Hype.'

India was horrified and the fact that she missed pronounced her name meant nothing right then maybe she's a witch   India thought how did she know she was right here or that it was her India thought. She only dropped her rent in the slot outside her door India took a deep breath and slowly entered the apartment it was as dark as the hallway all the curtains shut. The woman sat in a dark green recliner it was dark green or dark dirty she rocked back and forth with a cigarette in her hand a drink in a small thick glass in the other. She had on an off yellow gown   with white socks and house shoes and a crazy looking wig India thought because it looked like it was on backwards. India could not figure out where the small glare of light was coming from there was a radio playing in the kitchen the television had a dark picture India looked around for the cats but all she saw and heard was a small black dog barking at her feet.

"Shut up Barney, what can I do for you young lady what did that dead beat of yours do now he is fine but a dead beat.' The woman said

 India did not have time to figure out how she knew her business she has never noticed the woman leave her apartment she would quickly take the rent money out of the slot and

India would quickly be on her way. India felt weird because she could not tell what race the woman was not that it matter she would like to know just in case it was one of the clues needed if she was never seen again.

"Yes I was wondering Mrs. Um. "

"Ms. Shiawassee." The woman said in a loud voice

"S.H.A.I.W.A.S.E.E you got that Indian."

"Yes ma'am I was wondering, well I was hoping you had an extra key to my apartment you see my dead beat boyfriend rather ex-boyfriend accidentally took mine instead of uh so."

"Oh sugar you don't lie to me I have been there done that look behind you on the wall look for your apartment number make sure you bring it back don't make me look for you do you hear me.' The woman said

"Yes ma'am I will thank you can I go now.' India said

"Yeah get the hell out you have someone waiting on you I hope he's not a dead beat.' India backed right into the door the dog was still barking at her she does not ever remember being so scared of someone she bolted once she felt her way out of the apartment. India raced back to her apartment put on her shoes grabbed her clutch purse locked her door then rushed down the stairs Greg was now blowing his horn which India knew was way out of his character. So she didn't care she opened and closed the hallway door Greg was standing outside in front of his BMW pacing around with worry convinced that India was trying to blow the night. But there she was as beautiful as ever the sweat on her brow hardly showed Greg gave her a relieved look because he knew going home without India was not an option.

"India what have you been doing you had me worried." Greg said

Greg motioned his friend to get out and open the door for India she gave a quick   smile she thought about what she should say but the moment was not the right one to come up with the jerk everyone hated had taking her night upon his evil hands so she just threw up her hands.

"You know me Greg perfection can never be rush but I will say Happy New Years oh and I'm sorry let's party." India said

Greg gave her a look who is this woman and where is India lets party Peter stepped out the car and escorted India inside Peter was Leah's brother they'd met at Leah wedding years ago India adrenaline was so high she didn't even realize that Peter must be her date. Peter didn't waste any time telling India how wonderful she look and how good it was to see her again she thanked him while trying to keep her composure Peter was a very attractive man he and Leah looked nothing alike he had dark wavy hair greenish eyes and a 6 ft 1 inch body and any woman would want him.   India had never been attracted to men outside of her race but she never denied a gorgeous looking man Greg could hold his own too they arrived at his house in what seemed like a few minute. He had to be driving 100 mph Leah   met them at the door she didn't inquire about there tardiness she knew it was all India as long as she made it Greg had accomplished one of the hardest last task of the year. Their large basement was set as glamorous as time square it was packed wall-to-wall people of all lifestyles that was one of the things India loved about the best-married couple they were drawn to all the ways of the world. Peter did not waste anytime asking India to dance letting her know he had been waiting a long time to spent time alone with her they ran into each other when visiting Leah from time to time. India never thought twice about him she always thought his small talk was just that he was always telling her she was gorgeous and he always made her laugh and tonight India's new found instinct sound off the alarms Peter had on the right amount of cologne nice all black suit with and a tie.

"So tell me are you supposed to be my mystery man Peter.'

Before he could answer, Dena's loud voice was right behind them and she did not waste anytime.

"Cuz, this is my date tonight T-money.' Dena said

India stop dancing and turned to shake hands she was blinded by the two front silver teeth and the tight jerry curls oh and the blue silk suit India held her comments for now Peter gave a quick handshake then pulled India back close although the music wasn't slow. Dena and her date for the night headed for the bar where Jill and her fly by night date Kermit the frog looking self were filling it up India wondered if she and Dena were in competition for the

 worse date ever India shook her head as she watched Leah and Greg tending to their guess. On the second song Peter had worn his self out he escorted India to two empty seats then went to get them drinks at the bar he was convinced this was he and India night and India was convinced she was fine and single. Jill join ed India she was being a little stand offish tonight that was unusual,

"So what's going on where is your mystery man tonight." Jill said

India pointed over to the bar where Peter was standing waiting on their drinks."

"India you don't let white guys let alone Peter what's that about?' Jill asked

"I guess Greg and Leah didn't want me to be alone and I never said that I do not like

108

white guy, I thought you and Dena knew about this I'm been plotting my revenge."

"India why would I waste such a beautiful distinguish gorgeous man on you ."

"Excuse me." India said

"I mean, you know what I mean India you not trying to settle down have babies get married have a real man that would wine you dine you treat like a woman." Jill said

"Jill, slow down its one date." India said

"Look I would love to have a moment with him and give him a wet and juicy New Year kiss."

"Oh my goodness Jill what do I look like I'm to fly tonight for your mess you can have him.' India said

"Please I just need one chance he won't know what hit him.' Jill said

It was obvious Jill wasn't taking India and Peter's date way to serious Jill's been throwing herself at him for years India rushed into the restroom as Peter was making his way back to her Jill was all smiles.

India freshened up and was headed to the large spread that was laid out ham, roast beef, Cheeses, garlic bread potatoes and coleslaw salads and many deserts. Before she could make it to the table, someone took hold of her hand.

"Ms. Lady may I have this dance."

The music was bumping Leah drove India crazy trying to find the best DJ in town Dena and her date were still on the dance floor and India was dancing right behind her Dena had everything going for her no children college education great job. A very nice condo but her choice in men was questionable the gentleman was just about to slide his hands down India waist when a strong voice sounded out he had his hand on the gentleman's shoulder they were about the same height but no where near the same build,

"Excuse buddy this beautiful woman is already taken I'm going to need to cut in." Peter's confidence was definitely a plus but India was not about that type of drama so she turned toward Peter and excused herself from the nice gentleman Jill obviously needed more than a chance. Whitney Houston saving all my love started Peter sang the whole song India was laughing so much he did not much of the words and she was one of her favorite singer's

"Where did you learn all your smoothness Peter I know not from that fancy Ivey league school you'll went too you and Leah or like day and night oh and you know that Jill is very interested in you." India said

"Yes Leah and I have our differences, and I think Kermit is a real good fit for Jill I mean she's a beautiful woman and all but I want what I want."

Greg and Leah finally made it onto the dance floor they were holding each other close as though everyone had left the room Peter mention that he could not wait to find a love as strong as Greg and Leah. He has never seen anyone so in love even though his parent's relationship he thought was written in history as being the perfect couple. When I mentioned them to Peter he wasted no time telling me looks can always be deceiving India knew about that all to well so she cut the conversation real short everyone was out on the dance floor now Jill even more stand offish while keeping a smile on her face talk about looks being deceiving.

Five more minutes until the New Year everyone was grabbing someone and gathering onto the dance floor, the big Television turned to Dick Clarks New Years special Peter had his arm tightly arm India waist. She could not believe how bold he was being she was breaking many rules she was on her third glass of champagne and Peter was trying to give her another the counting began 10,9,8,7,6,5,4,3,2,1 HAPPY NEW YEARS! Peter lips were wrapped around India lips he had her in a dip holding on as tight as he could everyone partied some more India took Jill by the hands and they danced loosening her up a bite. India believed in family and friendship she did not care what anyone else practiced it is what she believed in do not cross her or her family and friends. Four in the morning things were wrapping up only close friends were still hanging around India couldn't take another minute she was partied out Dena left an hour ago she said T-money had another party to go to at 3 am yeah right. India was glad Peter had driven his own car Jill and Kermit acted as if they wanted to party all night and morning Greg and Leah was teasing India about the lip lock.   India brushed it off and said that it was New Years and it was all about happiness everyone was wiped out they all hugged good night

then peter went to get their coats. Jill and her date walked out with them Jill gave Peter a long hug and a kiss on the lips her date must have been mental slow or something because Jill has been getting away with this all night. Peter told her she was being rude but Jill was convinced that India was being rude

 Peter asked India repeatedly if India wanted to go to his place for a nightcap India told Peter she had already went passed her limit hours ago. They were friends and she take it even slower than slow she'd just broken up with Myron hours ago they pulled up to her apartment Peter opened her door India usually had it opened already but she couldn't this time Myron never opened her door or maybe she'd never given him a chance to either. Peter escorted India to the door she fumbled through her purse to find her keys,

"Shit."

"What's wrong India?"

India quickly sobered up when she realized she had the managers key she wanted to let him escort her but she didn't know if she would be up there but naked with her wig still on backwards.

"Oh nothing I'm just dreading walking up all these steps.'

"You know that I would love to carry you Indy."

"Indy.'

"I know how you hate nicknames but Leah says you let her call you that I was hoping I could too." Peter said

"Sure Peter I had a great time thanks for being a gentleman." India said

"Well you're welcome but you didn't give me much choice.' Peter said

Sure enough Ms Shiawassee had the dim light going sitting in her chair smoke filled room she could hear the dog coming around the corner India quickly put the key on the empty hook while backing out the door Peter was so evolved with his macking that he did not even notice how India had to let herself in her apartment she quickly said,

"Thank you Happy New Years."

While walking up the steps India could not believe she would agreed to go to dinner with Peter next week it was late and she knew that was the only way to get rid of him between Leah being her best friend and Jill being head over hills what was Peter trying to accomplish. India was beat, it was five in the morning she turned the doorknob to her apartment then picked up her high heels and clutch purse off the floor after locking the door. India saw that every light in her apartment was on she looked around the kitchen and living room then she walked slowly into her bedroom she closed her closet door

when Myron rushed out the bathroom . He grabbed her by the neck and started to kiss her

so hard she could hardly breath he started tearing at her dress yelling.

"Is this what you gave that white boy slut you gave it to him instead of me huh?"

He threw India onto the bed with his full hand covering her face he was already naked he

was ripping at India stocking she was trying to kick him off but her head was spinning

India pleaded with him to stop she hadn't done anything with Peter.

"What is that the fucker's name you've gone from a dried up virgin to a slut." Myron said

India couldn't even answer she could feel that her tongue was bleeding she tried to force

a word out Myron kept asking the same question over and over he was now on top of her

his hand was over her mouth while trying to rip her dress off.

India managed to bite down hard on his hand instead of her tongue again he jumped up,

"Ouch, shit.' Myron said

He rushed to the bathroom and placed his hands under cold water cursing then yelling his

hand was bleeding he yelled out that India was trying to kill him.

"You going to fuck someone else then try to kill me?"

His hand was throbbing and starting to swell he swore he needed a doctor he continued to

say his hand was going to fall off India put the knife down then put up the phone to call

911 she wasn't going to drive him and by the looks of his hand she knew he couldn't

drive he had to go.

"Put your clothes on Myron the ambulance is on it's way and I didn't sleep with Peter he

is Leah's   brother he dropped me off but that doesn't give you the right to do what you

did I'm telling you for the last time it is over where are my keys and I will be changing my locks. Myron could hear the ambulance he could not button his shirt the blood was coming from the rag he had wrapped around his hand India had bitten him awful bad Myron walked passed India her dress was almost completely torn off.

"Fuck you, you crazy dyke bitch yeah its over." Myron said

He grabbed all his belonging he had left along the way there was a 5 by 7 pictured they had taken at a club one night Myron took the picture and slammed it against the wall glass shattered everywhere.

"Get the fuck out Myron I'm not playing." India screamed

She wanted to fight so bad between her neck throbbing and the alcohol talking India knew she could take him she didn't give a damn he had brought flower and edible panties for the night he took all of it and ripped everything to sheds all over the living room floor. He looked at India with rage in his eyes and she looked at him as though she had nothing to lose. She didn't try to stop him from destroying anything that he'd purchased she just stood with her arms folded feeling the pocket knife she put in her bra her dress was hanging off panties gone, hair all over her head Myron finally gave up on trying to push her buttons the E.M.T's were now ringing India's door bell. Myron jerked his head toward

the door realizing he was still bleeding he rushed out of the door leaving his mess, India locked her door not caring if the ambulance had left are not she went to the kitchen put some ice in a sandwich bag then flopped down on the couch turned on her music and balled her eyes out.

It was 7 am when India's phone rang off the hook India did not answer after the fifth hang up then it rang again she answered and in a loud angry voice India answered knowing it was Myron.

"HELLO."

The voice on the other end of the phone was frantic,

"Hello India is this you?"

"Hello, mom it's me."

"Your sister has tried to kill your father." Sharon said

"My father, mom what are you talking about."

India sat up on the couch trying to clear her vision and thoughts,

"Mom what do you mean did Shay do something to Bobby.'

"Who are you getting smart with India I don't have time for games."

"Mom please calm down what happened where is Shay."

"Shay, what about your father she tried to kill him after all he's done for you'll." Sharon said

"Mom what happen please is Shay alright."

"The police have arrested her I'm going to try to find your father you need to come here right now India you've ignored your family for long enough you left us even after your dead beat father went to prison."

India was so hung over and sore she tried to focus as much as she could she stumbled to the restroom and tried to wash her face with cold water while listening to her mother screaming on the phone. She pulled what was left of her dress off of her and was walking around now butt naked   she didn't even realize how cold her apartment was she placed the cold   cloth on her forehead and leaned back on the couch,

"Mom I thought you said she shoot Bobby mom is he dead why is Shay under arrest."

India asked

"No he's not dead India what are you saying she missed him the bullet just missed his skull it shave the side of his head there blood everywhere how soon can you get here."

If this is not déjà vu, what is this New Year about must be the year for blood everyone is hurt or either bleeding. Tears started to fall from India eyes again they were so swollen that she didn't even feel them,

"Mom was you and Bobby fighting why would Shay do this." India asked

'India how dare you question me this way, I am your mother are did you forget since you've been around all those drug dealers." Sharon said

"No ma'am I'm just trying to understand what's going on.'

After all India was dealing with her own dilemmas and the first thing India had learned over the last 10 years was not to burden her mother with her burdens and she sure could not lean on her father she kept them and her nightmare to herself. Only telling Toshiba along the way she felt she was strong enough to handle anything until she had to deal with her mother.

"India, she told the police her friend gave her a gun and she used it to try and kill her father everything's crazy here she been having sex in the house and doing drugs.

"Drugs are you sure mom."

India your father's not a fool he's caught Shay doing drugs and having all types of boys in the house.'

"Mom ,she's probably just gotten into Bobby's weed they don't consider that drug's even though I know it is but Bobby's been doing it since we were little why would he be so upset if Shay is doing it he's been doing it right in her face just like he did me and."

India could not even say her brother's name it had been a long time she and her mother talked about Ronald together .

"Mom I can't just jump up and leave especially on an airplane I've never even been on one and It's the holidays can't you just tell me if Shay is alright." India said

"Oh you can jump and leave for your father but not for the one's who raise you right India is that what your saying I said I need you here Shay has been taking to the hospital I'm sure she's alright but I'm telling you that I need you here now." Sharon demanded

India and her mom had barely spoken in years she stopped Shay from coming for the summer years ago. She and Shay would talk from time to time she'd beg her to come down   and that she would pay for the trips not realizing the reason's Shay wouldn't come Shay would tell India she was working at some restaurant and doing well in school so India never thought about interfering if thing were going good she realized now Shay had been lying.

"Mom how is Shay doing is she under arrest does she have a bond."

"Of course she'll be arrested the police had to wrestle the gun from her they took her to the hospital to get checked out."

"Mom why aren't you with her she has to be scared straight I'm going to make a few calls what hospital is she in?" India said

"She's gone crazy I need to find your father and make sure he's alright."

India was tired of trying to figure things out and she was getting more worried about her sister by the minute she called Leah she knew she would know what to do she and Greg fly all the time India quickly showered then packed. Leah and Greg were getting ready to drive down to Greg's parents but Leah still took the time to call the air lines then booked and charged India a flight. She wouldn't take no for an answer Leah told India she would cancel her plans India wouldn't hear of it she talked to Jill and she and Jake were more than happy to pick her up and take her to the airport. Jill was ready to question India she wanted to know if Peter stayed the night India's door bell rang she was at the door with her suitcase in seconds down the steps and into the car.

"Hi Jakey."

Her friends kids loved India so much Jake was all smiles trying to reach for India but his car seat was locking him in he started to cry out but Jill drown him out with all of her question India handed Jake a life savers he loved them he started clapping his hands. India blocked Jill out she was driving like she was talking fast, her flight would be leaving in 45 minutes India was so nervous blocking Jill out made it easy she had not taken a breath yet finally she mustard out a word.

"Jill I can't stop shaking I hope Shay is alright our conversations lately have been short I should have know something was wrong I'm pretty sure my stepfathers was drunk and probably whiling out." India said

She would not dare talk about her childhood she only shared that with Leah and Dena know everything of course that is gone on with her father.

Jill pulled up to the airport so quick everyone jerked back in the car when she stopped, "India I'm so sorry I wasn't thinking you have a lot on your mind and I'm being selfish talking about Peter." Jill said

Jill handed India her bags from the trunk telling Jake to calm down through the back window.

"Jill I don't know if I'm more scared of flying or scared that I can't fix things. " India said

Jill reach into the car and into a tan bag in the back seat she hand India three small bottle of liquor she opened one and told India to take a drink that it would relax her this time India didn't have time to figure out why everyone was always trying to get her drunk.

"Doesn't anyone just pray anymore?"

"Dear God bless India so that she can hold her liquor and help her to know that she's a very good sister and daughter oh and God a good friend." Jill said

India didn't hesitate she choked as she almost inhaled the whole amount with one swallow she blew out her breath it was hot on her hand,

"Gosh India you are suppose to be discreet have a little class."

"You carry liquor in the back seat of your car and you want me to have class." India said

Jill gave India a big hug and kiss and told her that one of them should have class Jill choices India they both laughed India blew Jake a kiss and reluctantly walk inside to the airport. She asked the attendant at the counter then quickly figured she should put the piece of gum Jill gave her immediately into her mouth.

The women gave India a strange looked then pointed her toward her destination the suitcase she had was getting heavy she was at gate 20 and she had to make it to gate 32 the line was short India fumbled through her purse. She sprayed her Liz Claiborne

perfume all over trying to keep off any smell that her little bottles may have caused.

India did not want seat by the window she was scared to look around the plane she was

thinking Leah choose the biggest plane on earth a helicopter would have been fine. India

thanked God that Indiana was not that far from her home India finished off another bottle

before someone sat by her then put the rest in her purse. It didn't take long to kick in she

started giggling at the thought of going home a place she'd swear she would never return

to her giggling stopped her from crying. She thought about being in the house going into

Ronald's room and by the time the thought of that had traveled through her memory India

had finished the third bottle and within minute's fear had consumed her then she was off

to sleep.

"Ma'am excuse me."

India opened her blood shot eyes and tried to focus on the pretty long haired and awfully

tall stewardess   she had the prettiest brown skin   she was touching India on the shoulder

India sat up and looked around almost everyone had exited the plane.

"Ma'am are you alright you look sick do you need some help.'

"No, no I just drank to much liquor my friend Jill thought it would help."

"It's not good to drink it could really upset your stomach here let me get you some Alco

saucers you can get a drink of water inside."

"Thanks your very pretty do you like being a stewardess.'

The woman laughed India could barely get out her seat she was being nosey she guess

she was still nervous.

"Yes I do and thank you is someone meeting you." The stewardess asked

This was the first time India realized no one but her mother knew she might be coming and in fact, no one would be to pick her up India jumped to her feet and thanked the woman for her help she exited the plane got her luggage and stumbled to the nearest restroom. She rinsed her face then swallowed the Alco saucers with water from the sink she pat her face with a paper towel fixed her hair she added some deodorant brushed her teeth then changed her shirt. The nasty tablets made her hungry but there was no time to eat India replaced her cherry jubilee lipstick and left the restroom she decided she would go straight to the hospital and that she would call Toshiba from there.

There were several taxi cabs she knew the ride would be long she took out a little bible that she always carried in her purse she read The Lords is Shepherd I shall not want India loved reading from Psalm and Proverbs but it was not easy trying to have happy thoughts. There hadn't been very many made in Michigan other than her prom and graduation and her friendship with Toshiba and the marching band Shay was 18 years old now It was hard to believe she had grown up so fast.

The ride was an hour long to Hurley hospital India was getting tired of lugging her suitcase she would gather Shay if she was still there then go to   the nearest hotel she would go to the house once she knew Bobby wasn't there.

"Excuse me could you tell me if Shayron Bradley is still a patient here?' India asked

"Ma'am one moment."

"She's still in the emergency room down on the first floor you'll see the signs."

India could not believe it five hours later and Shay was still here she was glad she did not have to go to the jail but this was ridicules.

The first nurse India saw escorted India to the area was Shay was they walked around one hundred corners it seemed like.

"She is right behind those curtains ma'am." The nurse said

Shay was sitting on the examining table with a robe that didn't' cover the opened wounds on her legs and arms; She was not crying she was just sitting there looking down at the floor at the edge of the hospital bed. India soon saw why the nurse looked at her the way she did as though India knew what had happened. Shay had done what India had wanted to do almost all her life she should have never left her alone.

"Shay, Shay it is me your big sister."

"India you're here where did you come from I just asked the nurse to call you.'

They hugged tightly India could feel Shay shaking she looked at her baby sister and then at her opened wounds   she didn't want to imagine any longer what happened instead of an officer there was now a case worker she took Shay's story and was still trying to reach a family member the nurse told Shay hours ago.

"India I told you not to leave look, look what that son of bitch did to me as if I wasn't his own daughter."

"Bobby did this to you."

"Yes, he beat me with an extension cord after he found me and my boyfriend in the house he accused us of stealing his weed and drinking his liquor."

"It doesn't matter what he thought he had no reason to ever hurt you this way Shay I'm sorry.'

"I hope I killed his ass I'm so tired of his shit and even more tired of mom taking his shit."

"Shay don't say that your 18 years old you could go to prison."

"India I've been in prison all my life what the hell are you talking about you got out you were with a father that loves you and take's care of you.' Shay said

India did not tell Shay anything that happened with her father she always assumed that their mother would not waste anytime telling Shay she had choice to live with a drug dealer over them.

"Shay I begged mom to let you come live with me   I told you I moved out on my own years ago   I take care of myself your grown now you can come we can get things taking care of and you can come live with me."

Shay gave India an evil look,

"The case worker said I'll probably get some kind of probation for this   because I had a little coke and weed in my system they cant find Bobby or mom she's chasing around town looking for his ass."

"Shay you can cut all that cursing out I'll talk to the case worker I'll asked the nurse to find mom we'll   be alright o.k.'

"Ok I guess you wanted me to end up like Ronald is that what you've been waiting on India so that you didn't have to take care of me either." Shay yelled

"Shay things haven't been what they've seemed for quite some time so please don't talk on things you really don't know about this isn't the time and what do you mean you had cocaine your system."

"Bitch how else was I suppose to live in that God damn house by myself you tell me Miss perfect India I was never fed with your silver spoon."

"Bitch." India repeated

India stepped back she took a deep breath thinking this heifer must be delusional all this way and she calls me a bitch India reached for her purse and pulled out the cashiers check for $2000 she balled it up and threw it at Shay grabbed her suitcase   then rushed out the room the nurse and the case worker tried to stop India.

"Excuse me ma'am are you a relative of Shayron Bradley may we talk to you please."
The nurse yelled out

India didn't look back she ignored them both and quickly got on the nearest elevator to the first floor she walked out the sliding doors there was a man and woma getting out of a cab India asked if he could take her to the airport he told her it was an hour away and would cost her,

"Do I look stupid I need to get out of this place now I don't care how much it cost?'

She handed the   woman her round trip ticket but the next flight would be in two hours so India went across the street to get something to eat at a diner she cried in the bathroom for at least 15 minutes. Then ordered enough food for an army she was hoping to see Toshiba but India could not stay another minute the waitress asked repeatedly if India was all right.

India didn't have an answer so the woman stopped asking she looked over at the pay phone at least 100 times but couldn't bring herself to call her mother she had the cab driver ride past and there was a for sale sign in the yard. When she talked to her mom a few weeks ago to check on Shay her mother haven't seen Shay all day but didn't mention anything about the house being for sale India left the waitress   a nice tip then gathered her things and left to get on her flight.

It was   midnight when India arrived home   she jumped in the shower got into bed and turned on her small radio than cried   she didn't care what Shay did with the money she wasn't going to be blamed another day for anything that wasn't in her control India tossed and turned for hours before she fell off to sleep.

Two weeks had passed India never told Dena and her friends how horrible her break up was with Myron only that it was definitely over they were so glad that they really wasn't concerned with any details. She also told them that her mother had over reacted that's why she did not stay long and that Shay would be getting help with a caseworker. Once again, they always took India for her word they never pried that is why India loved them so much it was the girl's night.   Things were getting back to normal especially without Myron he's called a few time only to tell India he was going to sue her for biting him and to call her a "crazy bitch".   India's getting to the place where she laughs she told him she was going to change her number and he has not called since it was becoming obvious that Dena was rubbing off on Jill since they have become friends.

They were capping on who's man was the worst New Years Eve Leah   liked going to sports bars since she's become a married old lady but India insisted on letting lose at Club Martini it was a new club in the area. She had heard a lot about it Leah arrived just in time for the conversation about Peter India had to talk over the music with her tight jean and silk shirt that hung low in the front she and Leah already discussed it she has no problem with her and Peter taking one day at a time.

"I told you once were just friend's we went to a nice restaurant that one of his friends owns we did a little dancing and then he took me home we talk on the phone he's a very nice guy." India said

"Boring, that man is fine and makes nice money and that's all you'll did Indy I've taught you way better then that." Dena said

"Dena if I did anything that you told me to do, I am never going to get a man."

"You can't be serious India." Dena gave her a look

"So you're going to waste a perfectly good man India?" Jill said

"Jill we can't very well be in love after a few dates." India said

"Why not."

"Ok guys can we please talk about something are at least someone else." Leah said

Yeah I've had enough drama from Myron I'm just relaxing when Mr. Right come's along I'll know." India said

Jill bit her tongue, the music was bumping the Club Martini was nice the dance floor could fit at least 100 people there were red booths and mirror everywhere. It had two floors and two DJ's they ordered there drink India order a strawberry daiquiri she had one of the best at the restaurant she went to with Peter he came over to make some at her apartment while they ate pizza.

Dena finished her Hennessey and was out on the dance floor dancing with two guys India decided to join them and then Jill came over. Leah just shook her head she wasn't big on dancing their was a cute guy that started dancing with Jill he looked like he came straight from his office he had on a three piece suit and had John Travolta moves down packed.

India danced for two songs then back to her seat she ordered another drink then told Leah she was going to the restroom India got to the top floor and as soon as she spotted the restroom there was a tall guy coming toward her. He smiled he had light skin and was very tall slim built a straight up pretty boy almost as pretty as India when he got close enough he asked India to dance he had hazel eyes India was turned off to pretty boys they didn't fascinate her one bit.   He didn't wait for India to respond he took her by the hand and out onto the smaller dance floor where they were they danced through 4 songs he complimented India on her dancing skills she didn't return the compliment although he was definitely the center of attention   on the dance floor.   India had to go to the restroom he waited then followed India downstairs to where her friends were women were staring India down as they cut across the dance floor to the booth where everyone was sitting when they got to the booth a woman walked up grabbed and hugged   Phil then quickly walked away. They had finally exchanged names   India was in the middle of introducing him to her friends he invited everyone to breakfast Leah had to get home and Jill had to pick up Jake Dena never turned down anything free.

He had them laughing until 3 am in the morning they exchanged numbers and everyone drove off in there own cars Phil called as soon as India got into her apartment they talked until they both fell asleep on the phone. One month later they were inseparable the gang wasn't having it India was always at the clubs and not being on time for school Leah had to cover for her four times since she and Phil met.   India was in heaven she did not have time to have nightmares or think about her sister Shay bruised and left alone in that hospital nor her mother and he was a refreshing change from Myron.

It was Friday night time for the girls night out they told India they weren't hearing of her not joining them tonight   it's been four weeks and she been out with Phil every Friday and Saturday night. She hasn't been to church on Sunday's and had started hanging out on Wednesday's Phil was a regular most of the crowd came to see him dance he told India that he worked at a bank he had done two years at Michigan State which made him think they had a lot in common. India did not know how he worked hanging out all night every bartender, hostess, bodyguard and women knew Phil India was not use to and did not really like all the attention negative or positive mainly negative she almost had to fight a girl in the restroom at a local Chinese restaurant last week. The girl told India she had better watch her back and that she did not mean anything to Phil that she was one of his dance partners and lovers. India did not of course care she had a lot of fight inside her but not over a man she told Phil about the girl he said her name was Mona then asked India if she did not want them to dance together any more and if she didn't that he would stop India was not the jealous type she did not care she just didn't want anyone thinking that she could be punked so she left it alone.

"Why did we have to meet at Friday's they don't have a dance floor." India said
"Look, I don't know what that thug has turned you into India but as much as you love Greg you sometimes forget were married see my wedding ring I can't hang in clubs like you all of the time sweetie.' Leah said
"Besides I don't think you should be dating him he's a bad influence on you can that shirt get any sexier.' Leah said
"And those jeans any tighter." Jill said

"And that glow any brighter girl you finally knocked those cobwebs out didn't you."

Dena said

"India did you, to him pretty boy.' Jill asked

All eyes were on India the waitress approached the table to take their order Dena always made her wait because she thought she should already know their orders since they come all the time. India had a guilty look on her face not because she had done anything but because she had to lie to Phil about where she was going because it was their weekend and the only plans he thought India should have was being with him. Looking just as good as he does he had started buying sexy clothes for her he told her she dressed like an old lady he said as bad as her body was the only thing that should be hanging off of her was him. This Friday after the club, he planned on tonight being their night India was somewhat glad not being with him she loved to dance but the way the group of people he hung with danced they wore India out she started hanging on the sidelines. However, Phil made sure she was in plain sight he kept his eyes on her he said he has never gotten so close to a woman before. He is usually a ladies man he has never had anyone that asked him what his goals were what he dreamed of becoming all women normally care about was his looks and giving him their body.

"Yes I'll have a strawberry daiquiri some barbeque chicken wings and cheese fries."

India said

"Oh you're going to act like you don't hear us girl.'

Everyone was staring at India including the waitress India continued to ignore them she asked the waitress if she could have her drink a.s.a.p they finally ordered so the waitress wouldn't get fired she did not care   she always enjoyed   their conversations.

"She has been smiling a lot more." Jill said

"Sure have, and dressing sluttish you would never be caught dead in something that hot before India.' Dena said

"Guys I told Phil on our third date that I was." India stopped

"Don't say it please it hurts my ears.' Dena said

"Shut up Dena you should try giving your's a rest sometimes you get enough for the both of us." India said

"What about me." Jill said

"Don't forget me, I work a little something in the bedroom too you know." Leah said

"Look here damn, hell Mary to all of you'll but I like to give the guy a choice I'm not trying to trip or trap anyone I don't have to." India said

"Look India everyone's not retarded like Myron guys tell you they can handle it but in the back of their mind they are planning when and where trust me.' Dena said

Everyone shook their head as they sipped their drinks in unisons,

"Beside he's probably got something as pretty as he is I wouldn't trust him I mean hell give him some but after that I wouldn't trust him for sure.' Dena said

"Dena you should be ashamed of yourself.' Jill said

"Maybe, but I'm not I'm honest.' Dena said

"Yeah sometimes brutally honest." India said

"Good one India." Leah spoke up

"So where does Mr. Don Wan thinks you're at since you're not joined to his hip tonight."

"I told him I was going out and I will call him when ever."

Everyone laughed as the waitress passed out their food looking as though she was mad she had missed some of the conversation.

"Well I did.' India said

"All I know is you better start being on time to work I know that man is not worth losing your career over right." Leah said

'Yes ma'am I will.' India said

They laughed and joked until 1 am then at the end of the night they argued over whose turn it was to leave the tip. Dena always tricked everyone convincing them she took care of it the last time and the time before that Leah had started keeping a record and Dena lost they hugged at their cars and said their goodbyes.

India put her doggy bag in the refrigerator took and shower then checked her messages Phil had left 11 messages India didn't even remember what her lie was she'd told him she normally didn't have a reason to lie he left about 6 message the rest he just yelled out her name and slammed the phone down.

"What the hell is his problem?"

India laughed she didn't call him back she thought she'd give him time to cool off she started to wander if Leah and everyone was right maybe it was a little to soon for a new relationship. They should just be friends but India also liked a challenge just as much as the next person she thought her friends should chill Dena had a different guy every night Leah had Greg and Jill had little Jake to keep her company. She will slow things down but not completely, she turned on the television and   she fell to sleep.

Phil called bright and early to tell India that he's going out tonight and if she wanted to keep   dating him she'd make sure to be at the Club Martini tonight by 8 pm he also mentioned what she should wear India was to tired to respond she was already feeling guilty about being late for class.

She missed some committee meetings at school and she also hadn't plan any once a week specials for her kids at school like she has always done Phil slammed the phone down at the end of his demand. India wanted to work on her lesson plans for school get prepare for the next school week early she had fallen behind enough. After that she would be attending Toshiba   wedding India promised nothing could keep her from coming but she had to much going on to try and be in the wedding Toshiba understood as long as she was going to attend that's all that mattered India   had a week and a half left to get the best gift and outfit. Leah again did reservations she even offered to fly out with her since she was coming right back but India had some unfinished business she was hoping she could take care of while there.   This reminded her she needed to let Toshiba know her arrival time Toshiba answered on the first ring they talked for over an hour India was elated until Toshiba told her she   ran into her mother.   Toshiba asked Sharon about Shay she told her that she has been missing for a month India's heart dropped she was no longer elated but knew she had to get to back home next week she'd already put in for her vacation time at   work she and Toshiba talked another 20 minutes they still had a strong connection. India knew Toshiba had her best interest at heart India hung up the phone it started ringing off the hook India finally agreed to meet Phil that was the only way she knew that would detour her from worrying about Shay. She wouldn't be getting any work done she told him that she would only stay for a little while he acted as though he didn't hear that part and hung up.

India told Dena to meet her there she couldn't tell if Phil had cooled off and she didn't want to be on the side line she wanted to have a good time keep her mind clear Dena was already on the dance floor India could tell by the crowd where Phil was on the dance floor. India was getting good at drinking and finally figured out why drinking was so important to everyone Club Martini wasn't the girl's favorite spot so this would be the first time Dena would get a chance to see Phil work on the dance floor with or without India.   Dena made her way off the dance floor and over to India she took a napkin off the bar to wipe her face,

"Girl I see your man over there on the dance floor ooh he is so fine girl you better get over there and get your man some hussy is all over him look.' Dena said

But India already knew who it was and who he was dancing with so she kept drinking her daiquiri Phil made sure her drinks and anything she wanted   was free and tonight Dena's were too. She didn't feel like explaining that this was Phil's   normal routine he danced the night away and they normally hung out with his sister and her fiancé or his place.

"India what's your problem girl I don't know how you plan on keeping that fine ass man sitting over here with me." Dena said

Dena had brought alone her friend   Kira she didn't care to much for India Dena said she thought India was stuck up the last thing India did was cared that's why Dena still had her tag along sometimes. Dena knew she looked better than her Kira that is why she hung with her   they switched seats after she pointed Phil out to her friend she said that Phil looked familiar she stood up and walked closer to the dance floor.

"Yep that is him he is fine as hell I thought you said you and India were the same age." Kira said

"We are what's the problem.'

"Oh so I guess you do think your all that you can pull them old and young huh." Kira said

"What the hell are you talking about Ms. Thing?" Dena said

India continued sipping on her drink laughing in amusement at the two of them talking about her as if she wasn't there she was also looking through the big mirrors onto the dance floor Mona was sliding her hands up and down Phil's back.

"You know he's only twenty right I don't know how he get's in all these clubs.' Kira said

"What?" India tried to stay calm

Dena and India said at the same time India looked over at the dance floor again then back at Dena,

"Kira you don't know what the hell you're talking about, But he does look a little young now that I look at him from here oh India young tender Ronnie.'   Dena said

India slammed her finished Daiquiri glass onto the bar and headed for Phil Dena yelled out

"It is only a few year's difference girl who cares."

But she started her way through the crowd to confront Phil when a guy grabbed her by the arm.

He just started dancing did not bother to asked her permission this must be a routine at this club in an instant India decided dancing with this gentlemen would be a better choice then acting out of character about Phil's age right now especially in front on Mona . The guy was already sweating as if he had been dancing in the same spot all night so India danced in place nothing fancy suddenly she heard a loud voice and a pull on her arm.

"India."

"Hey Peggy.'

Peggy was Phil sister they normally kept each other company she was nice and expressed on several occasions to India that she was nothing like the other women that her brother dated and that she meant that in a good way.

"I didn't know you where here why didn't you ride with me." Peggy said

Peggy talked as though India was not in the middle of dancing with a guy India knew exactly what she was doing and she kept right on dancing mainly because the guy had not missed a beat. The guy asked her name even though Peggy had said it 100 times "Salt and Pepa" come on loud and was bumping everyone that was not already on the dance floor swarmed onto the floor pushing Peggy off to the sideline she tried to grab onto India's arm but could not hold on.

"So Linda my name is Lamar, who you here with."

India hated when people wanted to talk over the loud music she did not even correct him "Push It Real Good" was all in her head she had started letting lose Lamar put his hand on her hip and yelled for India to work it. That's what she did she started shaking what her mama gave her getting a little out of her character she broke it down and once she made it back up she heard.

"What in the fuck do you think your doing are you crazy.' Phil yelled

India continued to dance turning her back to him without out fail Lamar was still in rare form Phil repeated himself then he finally stopped in between them India continued dancing.

Lamar asked India who he was and if she knew him,

"What the fuck do you mean does she know me, I'm her motherfucking man India come on?"

"Phil go back to doing what you do best you don't own me."

Dena and Kira was trying to make their way through the crowd toward India Phil grabbed India by her arm demanding her to come with him now.

"Let go of me boy."

"Boy, you better bring your ass on girl." Phil said

Lamar forced him self in between India and Phil they were both about the same height but Lamar had about 100 more pounds on Phil, but he was not backing down. Phil reached around and grabbed India again the next thing India knew Dena had busted Phil in the head with boot Phil did not flinch India's shirt was ripped all the way opened. Lamar pushed Phil back as much as the crowd would allow, Phil came right back-telling Lamar to mind his own business Phil threw a punch they were in the middle of a scuffle when the bodyguards finally intervene. One of the bouncers had Dena thrown over his shoulders Lamar put his arms around India and shielded her until they got outside the club. Peggy walked over to India,

"Girl you know you were wrong you know how Phil is why did you do that.'

"Peggy this is between me and your brother and why didn't you tell me he was only 20 years old.'

"That's for him to tell you not me he was just dancing he spend the rest of his time and money on you stupid Bitch. "

"What, you want some girl you better take your ass some where fool.' Dena said

Dena was reaching for her mace India did not want to fight Peggy she liked rather use to like her so she and Lamar directed Dena and her tag along friend to their car.

He asked India where she parked he was parked right in front so he told them to get in his car he would drive them to their car's which were down the street.

They made it to there car's India and Dena was parked directly across the street from each other she and Kira got in the car and did a u-turn and waited for India to get into her car Lamar was telling her he did not want the night to end on such a bad note.

He asked India if she and her friend wanted to go to Perkins India knew that was Phil's spot so she declined and following strangers was starting to become a bad triangle Dena pulled her car beside Lamar's they were now blocking traffic.

"Girl come on I'm hungry let's get something to eat." Dena said

"Look let me fine my dude and then I can take you and your friends anywhere you'll want to go, cool no string attached I promise." Lamar

Dena and Kira was all game once they saw Lamar's friend then heard free food we went to a Perkin way out we were the only people in the restaurant.

As usual late night eating was an answer to anything Lamar and his friend were very entertaining India tried to break a smile between her pancakes and bacon. The night ended and everyone went their separate ways Lamar insisted on following India home she always felt she was tougher than leather meaner than a rattle snake but tonight she did let it all hang loose she stayed calm and relaxed. They parted in front of her house Lamar got into India's car and talked her head off but India didn't mind she was all for it relieving stress and night time wasn't her friend she felt like all she attracted was lunatic's. She no longer felt like trying or crying so she listened she was looking into his deep brown eye's wandering why she hadn't done any harm to Phil she hadn't tried to because all the drama   his madness his obsession with his clubbing and dance partners India was good at going with the flow. But that wasn't good enough for Phil he had to take it a step farther know matter what India did or didn't do it was all about him and his childishness which India will not   get to address with him. Lamar talked his way up to India's door she turned the key they entered the apartment Lamar commented on how clean she was not a stone left unturned India had never thought about her cleanliness before it came natural to her growing up. Lamar stood looking at India for awhile until she realized he was waiting on her to ask him to sit down so she did he watched her every move as she turned on the radio to set a calm mood. India sat next to him on the love seat not knowing what to do with herself she crossed one leg to the other.   Lamar questioned her about her relationship with the dude at the club India did not really want to respond but since he had been so nice, she gave him a brief response.

"I only attract fool's simple." India stated

'How could someone as beautiful as you attract fools?' He asked

  "Simple I guess fool's or only attracted to beautiful women." India said

He stared into her eyes as though he was trying to read her mind no one had accomplish this before and India hated when they tried she hated when people gazed into her eyes she wasn't going to let anyone near her soul ever. India looked away she had a small light lamp that sat on the end table there was nothing good on television but mellow moods on the radio never let her down. India could block anything out with her music she also hated when men thought gazing into a women's eyes would lead to a kiss then sex Lamar once again told India how beautiful she was and how soft the hand that he was rubbing was one more lame comments and he had to go.

Suddenly Lamar jumped up and extended his hand to India the song was slow and sexy one of India favorite this was the right move she needed to relax at least once in her life she stared at him for a moment she thought he was not the finest or the cutest but just ok. He turned around to turn the volume up on the stereo

Luther Van dross "If This World Were Mind" India extended her hand into his and his strong grip brought India closer than close. He dipped her more than once his strong hard chest pressed firmly against India he smell like fresh aftershave his arms were smooth not a hair on them she did like them tall   he did a quick move and his hot breath was mark right on India left ear lobe,

"I want to make you feel good.'

India tighten up she started to pull away but he didn't let up his grip she thought to herself,

See there he goes talking about stupid shit again just be quiet brother I control this she thought to herself I've had a fuck up life, week, day and year and it isn't going to get any better boy did she had a story to tell. She had three different nightmares last night and only 5 hours of sleep she did not need nor did she want to hear your sweet I know how to wind and dine you bullshit from this guy.

India could feel his nature raise he started   kissing her on the neck he didn't say another word she started thinking again what could be better than to give yourself to a perfect stranger no strings or emotions attached India spoke this time.

"Take me to my bed ."

She told him to leave the lights off the night light was more than enough and the covers made him laid her gently on the bed gazed into her eyes then practically ripped her blouse off buttons where flying everywhere stating he would buy her another one.

"What the fuck." India thought to herself

This might knock her up to slut department India tried not to look at his penis he stood and had his clothes off in a flash and India almost screamed. The site of his thing pointing straight for her   India   closed her eyes for a moment she did not even know how he got her pants off so quickly as tight as they were but he did. She opened her eyes again and focus on his chocolate frame there was just enough light to make him look like a male Goddess a non cute male Goddess India did not know what she was going through but she let whatever it was happen. Her panties were half way down he pulled India legs apart and kneeled down she could not see his face any more he tongue was now inside her private lips. The feeling was indescribable she felt her juices pouring like a water fall she got a little frantic when her eye's rolled to the back of her head she didn't like not having any control   it took all she had not to slap the shit out him when he raised up and said,

"Do you like that baby; I'm going to take you to ecstasy?'

She immediately put her hand on his forehead as good as his hot tongue made her heart pump he had ruined the mood she did not want him to finish India kept her composure

and the look on her face must have been enough of a signal. Lamar quickly adjusted his

strong body on top of India's he then cupped her breast gently then licked her nipples like

they tasted like ice cream slowly sucking on each one and India's body was getting hotter

her skin felt moist. He was grinding in between her legs trying to get the perfect fit she

wanted to scream "Look dude just fuck me already"

She started kissing him on his neck she was glad that she and Myron had watched a

porno or two she rubbed her hands up and down his back gently using her nails she was

breathing in his ear then nibbling on his ear lobe. He moaned on groaned he lift his chest

and glanced at India she reached her head up and licked his nipple wet then blew and

them he flatten her with his chest then stuck his tongue down India's throat she forced her

head to   the side while he tried to suck on her neck. She didn't have any more time to

think about what she was doing or if she should tell him that she is a old ass virgin so she

gasped for air as he pressed against her India blurted out without control Lamar looked

startling.

"You do have a condom right, cause I'm ready for you to use it get this over with?' India

blurred out

Lamar reluctantly rolled over and sat up reaching on the floor for his pants he took out

his wallet without saying a word he then produced a condom India thought maybe this

guy is not a doshe bag even though India kept condoms hidden in her closet because she

never knew.

India was not scared or nervous she remember something about a cherry suppose to be popping your first time India looked to the ceiling while he opened the condom. Within second he was on top of her, her legs spread far apart and Lamar's eye's rolling to the back of his head India thought "This dude is tripping what is he doing" He was breathing as though he had a pillow smothering his face he was chanting,

"Oh baby, Oh baby."

He was acting as though he was going to have a heart attack the bed rail   was banging against the wall with force India realized he'd started without her Lamar reached with his hands pulling India hair back she turned her head trying to join in when she saw the condom next to the pillow. She reached over and it hadn't been opened she called out Lamar's name but he'd obvious made it in to Heaven she thought maybe he had two   he started calling out her name telling her she felt so good and that she was so wet.

"Fuck Lamar what are you doing? "

India did not feel much she   couldn't get him to budge she stared punching him in the back he must of thought it was fore play because he   pushed inside of her even more sweat was starting to drop from his forehead.

India yelled for him to get the fuck off of her at the top of her lungs and started scratching his back until he acknowledge her plea he acted dumb telling India he wasn't finished making her feel good she   blurted out was that your finger or your dick.

"Huh, what you say bitch?'

"I'm not your bitch do you have a condom on." India asked

He started coming toward India trying to kiss her and spread her legs apart again,

"Baby I was going to put it on when I bust this big nut don't I make you feel good."

I might be a bitch but you sound like a bitch India jumped up and turned on the light

gathering his clothes telling him to get out and fast she reached   by the pillow and threw

his condom at him.

"Calm down what's the matter with you is this how you treated the dude at the club and I

don't appreciate you clawing your nails in me girl." Lamar said

"Did you come inside me?' India asked

He grabbed her around the waist and kissed her on the stomach,

"I said I would put the condom on what's the big deal we're both grown right.'

India was livid she could not believe his arrogance.

"Please get the fuck out we are done for the night."

He started putting on his pants then his tee shirts staring at India like he was thinking of

doing the total opposite India walked around to the other side of her bed where she hide a

knife up under the mattress he gave her a puzzled look.

"You know what to be so pretty you've got a fowl mouth what hell is the matter with you

why are you freaking out wasn't it good.'

"Good what if I get pregnant stupid did you think of that."

"Pregnant your birth control will take care of that come on baby let's finished what we

started please."

"I'm not on the pill you jerk, you could have a disease or something hell I wouldn't know

because I don't know you."

"What grown ass woman is worried about getting pregnant doesn't take the pill come on

now be for real.'

"A virgin fool." India said

"A what you're kidding me right you're what 22, 23 years old? "

"I'm 26 and you're a jerk I'm not going to keep telling you to get out."

Lamar laughed so hard he started choking he was stumbling around her room trying to find his shoes.

"Look I don't know what kind of joke you're playing or why you're playing but I don't have a dirty dick and the crazy way you're talking I hope you don't have a dirty pussy."

India picked his shoe up and threw it right at his head it missed and shattered her dresser mirror

"Get out before I kill you."

"Look you can straighten your self up or just lose my number I'm out.'

He stepped over the glass shaking his head then left mumbling under his breath India stepping over the glass and rushed to lock her door then into the kitchen to get the garbage can. Her naked body feeling the draft as soon as she kneeled down to started picking up the glass she heard a knock at the door,

"Look baby, my bad I'll put the condom on let me back in.'

Lamar started turning the knob to the front door India wanted to scream out instead she walked into the living room and turned her music up straighten all her pictures of herself and Ronald and Shay then thought how much she loved them. India was hoping she would not wake her neighbors. It took a while to get up all the glass Michael Cooper playing on the radio this wasn't how India had planned things would turn out she waited all this time for this shit she couldn't believe people obsessed over what she'd just experienced. She could see maybe the oral part but "oh my" then the dirty Son of a Bitch doesn't want to wear protection she definitely wasn't ready for that one she couldn't even cry she showered until she thought she was going to pass out. She ripped

off her sheets threw them in the trash sprayed her bed with air freshener put on fresh

sheets. Then in the dark no more night light only light from the moon which she only had

a couple more hours of India kneeled down by the side of her bed and said her prayers.

Thanking God for keeping her safe yet another day from all the madness that life had to

offer she watched the ceiling fan go around and around until she fell to sleep.

India awake glad that it was Saturday the answering machine had just taking a message

India got up to use the restroom and wash her face while the messages were playing.

Phil's voice yelling repeatedly with each message calling India out her name

saying she had better call to apologize before they are completely through India could not

help but to laugh she could not figure out how one after the other after then the other. She

looked in the mirror wash her face repeatedly until she realized there was nothing

stamped   or tattoo's on her   suggesting that she needed damnation in her life.

India erased Phil's messages especially the one about apologizing to him she sat on the

edge of her bed remembering why she could see the wall and not her refection in her

dresser mirror and out of the blue decided it was time to change then she picked up the

phone and dialed her mother again.

The phone rang six times no answer   again   she wanted to let her mother and hopefully

Shay know that she was coming to town and if Shay wanted to come to live with her,

India   left a long message telling her mother and Shay that she loved and missed them.

She would see them soon for Toshiba's wedding and that she had hoped that attend the wedding with her. Then India remember Leah had gotten her plane ticket but India hadn't shopped for Toshiba's wedding gift or something to wear to the wedding India thought that it would be best to make hotel reservations. Toshiba put her in the same hotel with some of her family would be staying she knew most of them so that was great even though she had not seen anyone in quite sometime.

"What in the world is wrong with you India you been moping all week and don't think Dena didn't spill all the bean's on you and that Phil guy I cant believe the way he acted I could just kill him myself." Leah said

"Yeah and since when don't you finish your food your one of the greediest people I know I don't know how you keep that shape of yours?" Jill stated

"Jill hush your mouth ok." India said

"So what happened with dude how long are you going to make us wait for the gossip India." Dena stated

"Look maybe we need to stop having our little girl's night out because you heifer's are getting on my last nerves just in case you'll didn't know."

"How did you and your night and shining armor end the night?' Dena asked

"Nothing happened guy's lay off." India said

"India you mean to tell me this perfect stranger came to your rescue and you didn't give him any who does that?"

"Dena you're so obnoxious.' India said

"Ok guy's give her a break your drinks or getting warm she'll tell us when she's ready right India.' Leah said

"There's noting to tell he followed me home we talked for awhile and he went home that is it sorry guy's."

They were at their favorite restaurant drinking their favorite drinks the waitress all ears as usual.

"Anyway since India's being stuck up I'll tell you guy's my good news." Jill said

India gladly ignoring the stuck up comment that was usually Dena line but she would let Jill have it for the night.

Well to make a long story short, if I can well I asked Peter out last Friday night that's why I didn't go out with you guy's and I put the whammy on him, We spent the whole weekend together.'

Jill immediately stared at India, India gave her the biggest smile that she could mustard up and it was not because she was jealous this is the last thing she wanted to fight her friends for seriously. She was still beating herself up about what she had done with Lamar it made her sick to her stomach the look on Jill's face. India could tell she might not realize it she seemed that she was delighted that India might be jealous India had not had time to answer Peter calls in the last few weeks and she had already told Jill several times that he was fair game.

"That's great Jill you two will make a good couple." India said

"Well I wish my brother would quit trying to date my friends it's bad business I shocked."

"Leah this is not bad business your brother's an attractive wonderful man and he needs a good woman by his side don't you think.' Jill said

It was kind of weird for Leah that Jill wanted to be with Peter knowing that he was attracted to India, India enjoyed Peter's company but she felt she didn't have any right to cock block anyone everyone is   grow.

"Shit he'd better not come my way I'd turn his world inside out and he knows it too I'm sure of it.' Dena stated

 "India when do you leave for the wedding?' Dena said

"Next week thanks to Leah."

"Will this Lamar fellow be traveling with you?' Jill asked

"NO." India said abruptly

"India you have been acting strange and you do have a little glow I love you but I'm just saying." Leah said

India pushed her good plate of food away from her she put her hands to her head and started shaking it in a yes and no position.

"Alright, Ok damn I did it I gave him some there are you guys satisfied." India said

"You damn straight we are now drink some more of your drink and tell us how that big stallion performed, Oh this is good finally something juicy." Dena said

"Well my news is pretty juices don't you want to know how Peter performed." Jill said

"NO" Dena and Leah yelled out at the same time

"Holy shit India, why didn't you tell me I can't believe this you didn't even know the guy.' Leah yelled

Jill was rolling her eyes with her arms folder blowing just a little steam the waitress had sat down in a chair she blurred out that she thought we were always kidding about India being a virgin all this time.

"She waited all this time to give it up to a stranger Lord have Mercy." The waitress stated

"Girl get up and get us some more drinks before you get fired." Dena said

Leah was truly upset that India had kept such a big secret she still had not realized that India was a professional at keeping secrets. India sat at the table with her hands to her head wishing she could disappear she kept clicking her shoes together then repeating "I wish I was home" but nothing happened she could still hear Dena's loud voice and Leah is now whining.

"I knew you were a freak waiting to happen girl so how do you feel did it hurt you want it all the time now don't you.' Dena said

"Dena let India talk please." Leah pleaded

India lifted her a head a little the first face she saw was Jill's she had a blank look on her face and she was the only one that could care less she felt her news was way more interesting yet again India always got everyone's attention it just always worked out that way.

"I'm done talking, I told you we did it for about two minutes it was like watching paint dry and then he left." India started on her new drink

"Girl I will bust you up side the head with this glass full of gin and juice from my purse if you don't spill the beans I mean it India." Dena said

"She said there's noting to tell guys it was a boring night unlike mind   I don't know how many inches Peter got it ."

"But by out second time and he kisses out of this world."

"Jill I could have really done without that information really Peter's my brothers remember everyone seems to forget this you guys are a bunch of drunks I'm leaving."

Leah stated

"Yeah guy's lets go I have to get up early to go shopping and these drinks or makings my

stomach hurt.' India said

India jumped up right behind Leah Dena was hoping they were joking she was really

about to get crazy. Leah was moving slowing also hoping India did not take the leaving

bait but India had her purse in hands and counting her dollars for her bill and her tip.

"You guy's have lost your mind I'm going home to my new man   I'll see you guys

later.' Jill said

"Jill hold on, We all walked out together you know that." India replied

Jill continued to walk toward the front door India was ignoring Dena and her idle threats

with all of her might they had never fallen out before but Dena was trying her last nerve.

India knew that Leah felt as if they were the closest even though she and Dena are family

did not matter to Leah. However, India was not trying to hurt anyone's feeling hell it was

her own life that she was destroying (Jesus). They were all feeling a little tipsy and   Leah

and Dena were walking and talking amongst themselves ahead of India three attitudes at

once was a bite much for India she had just done the unthinkable with a loser and they are

all mad go figure everyone made it to their car.

"Ok guys group hug at least I had to get up early to shop then I'm off to the wedding I'll

miss you guy's." India said

"Well it's not like you offered for any of us to go." Dena said

"Look guys, Can I get just a little break here I mean this is my life that I'm ruining not

you'll damn as soon as I get back we can civilly get together but like I said two minutes dry paint not much to tell." India said

No group hug Jill pulled off first then Leah and Dena all with their nose up India didn't have the time or energy she would handle things once she got back it was stressful enough going back home let alone trying to   pampering three grown women.

"Toshiba the wedding was so beautiful."India said

"It would have been even more beautiful if you had been in it Indy, I'm sorry we havent had much of chance to talk. How was your first time flying I thought about you all night I remember you said you'd never get on a plane." Toshiba said

India choked up alittle   on her champagne this was indeed her second plane ride and it was just as bad as the first which Toshiba know's nothing about and to have worried all night all my so many secrets sometimes India has to look in the mirror to know her own reflection.

"Oh Toshiba you shouldn't be worrying about me the night before your big day don't you ever tell me that." India said

"It's ok Indy I worry about you all the time actually because of your so called busy schedule that you put before me I had to go off and get married so I wouldn't be so lonely.'

"Toshiba." India said

"Ok I won't beat you up any more but you make it so easy I love you and now you have God children and a new brother in law."

"Sweetie this is your day I promise I am going to do better I am so glad you found a great guy to be your childrens father and your husband." India said

"You can have the same thing India if you ever give anyone half the chance and half that you know what." Toshiba said

"Tosh, we really need to talk but again this is your day we will catch up I promise.' India said

They were both trying to hold back there tears some from childhood memories some from time passed some from the mere excitement of being together again. It took all Toshiba's will not to focus all her attention on India during her wedding they smiled and teared up the whole ceremony.

"There you guys are you two have all night to talk about those ugly prom dates you'll had in high school later."Toshiba mom said

"Mom please." Toshiba said

'Come on your husband awaits I already gave India a piece of my mind if she stays away again she will not live to tell the story right Indy.'

"Yes ma'am right.'

'"Now you two lets go it's time to do garders and India it's time for you to caught bouquet."

"Mama Watson I am sure there are a lot of exciting women here that would love to caught that bouquet.' India said

Mrs. Watson pushed India out on the floor all the women were pushing each other India thought   they'd better stop pushing her then someone elbowed her in the back. As soon as India turned back around after giving everyone dirty looks the bouquet smacked, her right in the mouth that made her immediately put up her hands it was official. She had caught the bouquet now everyone was giving India dirty looks she wanted to hand it to someone else but Toshiba was so happy she and Mrs. Watson were jumping for joy. India could not disappoint them not today immediately after   India took had her second drink she started to get antsy about her mother and Shay they had not arrived. Mrs. Watson said she saw Sharon at her church her mother said she had received the wedding invitation and would be attending the wedding India had also left several message she went straight to the hotel to keep her reservations   when she arrived because she had not been able to contact them.   India put the bouquet on the bar and order a strawberry daiquiri the bride and groom were dancing to "You and I" By Stevie Wonder

India felt a soft touch on her butt when she turned around it was Toshiba's cousin Leo.

"Now that you've caught the bouquet its official were getting married. " Leo said

"Well one thing is most certainly official you still don't know how to treat a lady do you now touch my butt again and I'm going to kick your butt all up in this church." India said

"Still mean and evil as hell India, but fine so very fine."Leo said

"Beside's I thought you were already married or did you forget."

India took a sip of her drink Leo moved in so close India could barely move he put his hand around her waist when she tried to back away.

"Such beauty shouldn't go to waste can I get a hug I know where your staying do you need company for the night?" Leo asked

"Leo, Leo"

There was a faint voice getting closer and closer Leo's eyes widen like a toddler that has spilled milk he let India's   waist go and jetted India laughed to herself she didn't even look back she kept drinking until she heard clapping which meant the dance was over. India walked back into the hall and headed toward the happy couple they were about to be seated to eat they went all out roast or chicken even salmon baby potates fresh cut green beans, corn or wild rice or baked sweet potatoes dinner rolls so soft just amazing. Dinner was brought out to each table their cake was a three-layer cake biggest to the smallest it was all white even the flowers that laid around each layer India make it over to them just in time.

"Well Ed and Toshiba I'm so glad I made it to your wedding it was just what a workaholic needed." India said

"Im so, so happy to finally meet you I heard nothing but good things.' Ed said as he gave India a warm hug

"Same here Ed nothing but good things but since it's getting pretty late and my mother and Shay didn't make it I was wondering if you guy's could open up my gift I got some things for the kids also."

"But they can open their's up later because I was going to stop by you know to check on mom and Shay I hate to run but I've been calling all week." India siad

"India we understand of course we can go to the back room over here I know you have to leave out tomorrow it means a lot that your here India." Toshiba said

India the newly weds a big hug they all head for the back room India had gotten her gifts from the car hoping they would agree to open them because India went all out for their happiness and for making up for lost time.

"Oh my word India how did you do this it's beautiful.' Toshiba said

Ed was just looking in amazement India had the Christmas picture they had sent of them painted into a portrait 11x14 inches and it was framed in sterling silver. India had the art teacher at school do a small one of herself he use to own a art gallery but lost it during his divorce he'd told India she'd loved it but until she saw it she couldn't believe how amazing it looked herself and the frame just topped it off they looked almost live on the picture.

India started crying as soon as she got into her rented car she kicked off her shoes and drove barefoot she hated that she had to leave the wedding after letting so much time go by but she couldn't leave this time without working things out with her mother and sister. India pulled up in front of the house there was a different looking car in the driveway

India sat there with the car off looking at the house it looked the same and India got the same vibe. India wondered if the inside looked the same India finally got out and knocked on the front door over and over until the knuckles hurt she got into the car and decided to drive to the area were Toshiba said was a know drug area looking for Shay if was official she had changed in the worst way.

India drove around for hours asking the safest looking people if they knew Shay they all only want whatever money India had to offer. It shocked India when everyone said they did but they had not seen her that day India's gas was getting low and her stomach was growling. She drove around to one of Shay's childhood friends Rita she said she had not talk to Shay since she went off to college last year she said she begged Shay to go with her but Shay told her she would never have a future. No matter what she tried India didn't let the tears roll down her face until she drove off it was now 11 pm India still hadn't eaten and the gas light had officially came on. India went to the hotel she tired to order some food as good as the food was at the wedding India couldn't eat cheese burgers was all they had she ordered then took she entered the fully furnished bathroom then took a hot showered. India lay in bed eating her burger and fries wondering if Toshiba and her new husband were on their way to Hawaii yet. She did not want to think anything negative about Shay she has been praying and she could only hope Shay remembered to do the same. On the other hand, her mother would have to come to her own senses one day and realize who should be the mother but India loved them no matter what she knew in the morning her life would once again end in Michigan and she would be back in Indiana.

It has been five months since Jill and Peter have been going out, and without warning, they had moved in together after only two of those months that was usual for Jill she was known for moving a little fast. With men but India could no longer call any kettles black Jill has been complaining lately about how they never go anywhere together and how she has been paying for most of the bills even though Peter makes good money. Now she wants to talk and get advice from India of course India came right over after work.

"He said he shouldn't have to take care of someone else's kid he doesn't even pay Jake any attention but he adores his niece and nephew I don't know what's wrong.' Jill said

India gave Jake a big hug and kiss then in a whisper India reminded Jill he should not listen to grown folks business. Jill took his hand and directed him to his new room and of course Jake did not want to leave India presence and she once again had to promise she would tuck him in for bed it was a Thursday night and neither one of them could afford to lose any sleep. India has been tutoring three days a week after school plus on two committee groups. Jill was not working full time she was trying to finish getting her degree in Phyiscal science she dropped out after Jake's dad left when she got pregnant and now that she has decided to live in a big two bedroom fancy condo her life has gotten a little more expensive.

India declined a glass of wine so Jill made her a hot cup of tea and herself a big glass of Chardinay they sat down by the beautiful fireplace the apartment was beautiful. There was not much furniture Jill's old place was full of toys in the living room for Jake because she only had a one bedroom apartment it was huge though.

"Well from what you've told me that doesn't sound like Peter, have you tried to talk to him do you think that maybe you guys moved in to soon what did Leah say?" India said

"I can't talk to her and get a bias answer and no   I don't think we moved in to soon I knew Peter before you did I love him and he loves me.' Jill stated

India shifted her body   she was now sitting on the love seat   she gave the best smile because she knew that Jill would be calculating her every move even still she and Jill before her infatuation evolved with Peter now turned   to obsession   Jill and India were and are the best of friends.

"Jill I was just doing what you invited me over here to do which is to help and try to make some sense of this I'm here for you and besides Leah knows her brother better than the both of us." India said

"Well I don't know why we can't keep your precious friend Leah out of this India I know that she and Peter are close I'm not trying to come between that.'' Jill said

"Ok now you sound crazy, you and Leah have been friends for   a long time long before me and I'm not worried about jeopardizing that but you should really get her opinion I would want to know if he's Dr. Jeckal or Mr. Hyde

"You weren't saying this when the two of you were dating.'

"Jill for the one hundredth time Peter and I are just friends I'm not going to keep justifying that to you I can't tell you what habits are   normal or not normal for him. He's a wonderful guy as far as I know but if you know different then you know different Jill it's all a matter of how your going to handle things doing what's best for you and Jake." India said

"So you don't know anything about him being violent." Jill said

India stood she put her tea down and walked over to Jill she was admiring the fireplace when Jill started to cry. India put her arms around Jill she no longer knew the right or wrong thing to say Jill completey broke down they sat on the sofa Jill's hands were shaking India took her drink and sat it on the end table.

"Talk to me Jill I'm here for you." India said

"You're right I should handle this on my own.'

"That's not what I just said Jill has Peter hit you is that what you're saying.' India said

Jill was pacing around the house picking up Jake's toys walking in and out of the kitchen this time holding the bottle of wine.

"If I told you would you promise not to tell anyone neither of the girls?' Jill asked

"Why do you want me to just handle this with you we need all of us at   one time Jill this is serious he has no business hitting you.' India said

Jill wiped her eyes and stared straight into India's eyes still with contempt in them she had more to say.

"India you may not be serious about Peter but he was serious about you and I knew that but I thought he was over you so I fell in love with him anyway. He always talks about you he even has pictures with the two of you on his manal in his condo."

India looked around then she looked up on their manal she knew that they took pictures at the New Years Eve party and he had someone take a picture of them at the comedy club that they attend but that is what friends do.

159

"Jill I still don't understand why you think this all has to do with me Peter's had lots of women in his life what do you want me to do kick his ass because I will do it if that's what you want me to do.'

Jill laughed she didn't stop India gave her a blank stare she wandered if Jill was having a break down or if she had finally come to her senses India was hoping for the second option.

"India I think Peter's in love with you and there's nothing that I can do about it and believe me I've tried." Jill said

"Then why would you get involved with him just so you could blame all this shit on me Jill this isn't funny I'm really trying here I really am but your making this very hard you want to file a police report what do you want me to do." India said

Jill blurred out her answer because she knew that she could be a better woman to Peter she didn't care if she was hurting India's feeling she just wanted her out of Peters life she didn't even at this   point know if she meant her life too. That is exactly how India took it she was gathering her things to leave when she remembered she had to give Jakes a hug and kiss goodbye.

She walked right passed Jill toward Jake's room when the phone rang Jill quickly answered it she heard Jill say Leah's name. She continued to open   Jakes door surprised to see him still awake she hoped he didn't hear any confusion but he was all ears with his Disney movie.

"Hi Auntie Indy hug please."

"You knew I wouldn't forget didn't you hugs and kissing." India smiled

"Yeah India stopped by to see Jakey you want to talk to her hold on.' Jill said

India gave Jill the (if looks could kill) look why would she tell her not to mention anything then tell Leah that she was there knowing that would be her first question. India grabbed the phone then her jacket and purse Jill whispering under her breath about India not mentioning anything India had brushed Leah off after work now she knows. India confirmed their ladies night out she told Leah she'd see her in the morning at school then hung up even though she acted as though they had a regular friendly visit India said goodbye then left Jill waited on Peter for hours he did not came home for two days.

The ladies decided to meet at India's house instead of the sports bar the air was a little uncomfortable Jill didn't   want to discuss specifies around Leah she just continued to say that she and Peter were butting heads about everything. When Leah and Dena could not pry anything out of her once India was done cooking home made Lasagna and tossed salads   they started passing the wine then they started in on India about Lamar.

"So Indy you never told us what happened girl you know you and slick Rick come on girl details and we don't want to hear about paint drying either." Deana said

"Yeah I have not been able to pry anything out of her either." Leah said

"So the wedding was beautiful." India said

"Girl that was ages ago why do you keep playing." Dena said

"Because I don't speak any other language so repeating myself over and over gets alittle frustrating you know he is history." India said

"India everybody's history to you."   Jill said

"You guys aren't,   I would think you'll would be a little more appreciative." India said

Jill was busy stuffing her face she loved India's cooking   no one really noticed she was not being herself probably because she hasn't been herself in awhile now she was drinking and eating and eating and drinking. Dena finished all the garlic bread like it was the last supper she enjoyed acting like she had   no manners to be so educated she propped   her feet on India's   living room table.

'India he was your first how are you going to pretend that this is nothing.' Leah said

"Watch me." India said

"And Ms. Jill on the other hand you just need to chill and quit trying to smother a brother you know.' Dnea said

"You don't know what youre talking about Dena so you chill and Peter is not a brother." Jill snapped back

" He is Leah's brother   and well from the looks of India I think he might want to be." Dena responded

Jill jumped up knocking her rum and coke on the floor breaking the crystal glass that was in her hand she almost cut herself trying to gather the glass and spilling the drink at the same time.

India told her it was all right then covered the spill and glass with a dry towel then she swept it up into the dustpan with the broom.

"See all gone no worries let me pour you another drink." India said

"Here let me India you don't know what your doing honey rum and coke not coke and rum." Leah said

As Leah handed Jill her drink Jill jumped back up and rushed to the bathroom crying almost knocking down the drink again. Leah tried to grab her by the arm Dena turned down the music she was thinking finally she knew whatever this was this had to be good. India flopped down on the couch then picked up her cooler and started drinking looking up at the ceiling fan going around and around she didn't feel like concerning herself with anyone else's shit today. Not this not today then Jill and Leah came out the bathroom Jill wiping her nose and shaking her head yes to whatever Leah was saying Leah was tearing up also she was just sensitive that way.

"Jill I was only kidding.' Dena said

They both sat back down on the couch both picking their drinks up at the same time.

"Well India and I were discussing if I should leave Peter."

India didn't budge even though Jill was throwing her up under the bus once again Jill was becoming a pro at this game India will be glad when she gets things straighten out.

"Jill what are you talking about when were you guy's discussing this obviously private and personal matter?'

"What's up is he is hitting you Jill is that dirty mother***ker hitting you." Dena said

"Dena that's my brother you're talking about there has to be some kind of mistake right Jill."

"I had a boyfriend that liked to hit on women Jill's mood swings the way she's been quiet and distant what else could it be. Dena said

India had switched drinks from coolers to Dena's Henessey it was almost gone one sip and India was now choking off her first glass. Still admiring the ceiling fan with her legs crossed swinging her top leg up and down listening to As The World Turn Jill's style.

"I'M PREGNANT." Jill blurred out

All eyes were on Jill standing in front of them all in the middle of the living room the waitress at the restaurant would have definitely been fired tonight it was a good idea to meet at India's. She was thinking she was hoping that mixing her drinks had her imagining what Jill just said to no avail she had heard her right.

"Oh shit I didn't know that one you got me on that one Jill.' Dena said

"Quiet Dena.' Leah said

"Excuse me, You left Greg at home remember."

"Pregnant, Jill first you accuse my brother of being an abuser now your pregnant India why didn't you say anything." Leah said

India looked at Jill who had her head down she knew this would be a problem and she knew Leah would come to her.

India tried to stand up she flopped back down then rocked herself back up to her feet she walked around the cock tail table toward Jill she shook her finger in her face then toward Leah.

"Leah we are all grown and it's never my place to pick what someone wants to keep secret Jill chose me to confide in I didn't choose her now I'm not on this mess."

Dena took her bottle of Hennessey from next to India then   turned the music all the way off she was standing against the entertainment center smiling and drink one glass of Henessy after the other One Live To Live didn't have nothing on this she was thinking out loud.

"Jill what are you going to do." Dena said

"I don't know what would happen between Peter and me but I'm keeping my baby no matter what he says."

"What do you mean whatever Peter says you guys did discuss having children before you got pregnant right? Leah had broke her silence

"Leah everyone's not perfect like you and Greg ok."

"Well what has he said about it Jill?" Dena asked

"He said he doesn't want any children at least not with me." Jill said then started crying again

"India will you talk to him for me?' Jill asked

"What did you just say?'

"Leah I'm not trying to cause confusion between you and your brother I know how close you guys are ok." Jill said

"So India decided she should handle what is going on between you and my brother." Leah said

"Look you bitches are getting on my last nerves now you can eat and drink or drink and eat if you want to do anything else you can get out.'

She walked over to the radio and turned it to the maximum the bass was bouncing off the walls LL cool J (Rock the Bells) was playing. India made a plate of Lasagna she said back on the couch and ate looking only at her food. Leah's feelings could not be more hurt India has never acted that way toward her. Tears were in Leah's eyes she didn't know if it was because of the "B" word or Jill endless stories Dena had never been out done but tonight she was she didn't say another word all she knew was India wasn't getting a hold of her Hennessey ever again. Leah and Jill finished eating and drinking Leah glancing at India repeatedly, Jill was not sure if letting this situation go this route was worth it right now.   India didn't feel like nor was she about to apologize to anyone not now not tonight it is what it is for now they continued for hours until noting was left then the night had to end.

A few weeks had passed Leah, India barely spoke at school they hadn't had lunch together, Hello, and goodbye was all that they could mustard. Jill called India repeatedly waiting for her to agree to meet with Peter India had not responded Jill had burned her bridges and was now on her own nothing had gotten better between Jill and Peter. India had started missing her friends she had not been feeling well she was tossing and turning about her life she and the girls so she called her friends to reunite. No club no dancing no men just the gang it was time to work things out they were all she had and she knew that she is a very important part of theirs lives.

India prepared homemade pizzas and   barbeque chicken wings   only wine was allowed she had tap water for Jill she had rented several movies (Low Down Dirty Shame) had become one of India's favorites   (The color purple) was second . The music was always present Phyllis Hyman (Living Here Alone) India felt that was to sad even though she loved her singing with a passion.   Jill arrived first then Dena, Leah was an hour late Dena never hesitated with   her eating habits her plate was full she also decided to bring her stash of Hennessey in her purse even though it was forbidden India could tell she had started drinking before she arrived. She didn't have any question she was calm talking about some new guy she'd met at work India changed the music to Michael Copper (Dinner For Two) that was as mellow as India could get Michael had it going on in everyway no matter what song he was singing.

Leah entered the room immediately stating she could not stay long she said that she and Greg had plans but she did not want anyone to think she was holding a grudge so she flopped down on the couch. She turned her nose at the music that was playing she didn't know anyone past Prince and Michael Jackson Jill and Dena had to fill her in India normally did none of them could keep up with India's selections Leah wanted to hear Cyndi Lauper with out hesitation India granted her wish the day was about her friends Leah knew whom ever she would name India probably had it so she had to put her attitude in check. Madonna or some Pat Benatar than back to Club Nouveau no one could make up their mind either way the mood was set. Leah asked for a drink India handed her a glass of Chardonnay she immediately asked if that's all India had everyone must have taken India's request as a joke she felt hard liquor had maybe a little to do with all the confusion.

"So Jill, have you decided what you're going to do about the baby?' Dena asked

"I've already told everyone I'm keeping my baby that's no longer a question to be asked." Jill stated

Jill started going on and on about how she did not want to raise another child alone and she was desperate for Peter to do the right thing. She did not address India this time for a response even though she knew India had talked to Peter about the situation Leah spoke up.

"Children are a blessing from God Greg and I prayed to have healthy and happy babies and that's what we were blessed with." Leah stated

That comment hit India hard she went into the bathroom to gather her thoughts she splashed water on her face then wiped it away with a dry towel she went back into the living room again but she could not hold back her tears they started uncontrollably.

"Dag India, I thought we were working things out why are you crying sweetie come sit down you need to stop passing out drinks and have yourself one come sit down."

Dena said

India started laughing and crying at the same time she was trying to clear the trash off the living room table but there was not any so she started picking up plates of food that was still full. Everyone was grabbing thier plates from India's busy hands she really did not want to drink anything even though it had been weeks she felt her stomach was still recovering from throwing up the Hennessey she had drank. She walked over to the entertainment center all eyes followed everyone knew she had something to say Jill was hoping that she would talk about Peter and share some news about him wanting their baby.

"Well I know I haven't started drinking yet but I feel like I should confess you'll mean a lot to me even though I don't always express this to you guys I love you a lot." India said

"What is it India tell us please were listening." Jill said

"Peters going to counseling and you all will stay together for the baby and if he doesn't then you will dismiss him, I'll show you how that's done.

India saw Leah's look of discuss so she walked over to her then bend down and took her hand tears still covered her eyes.

"You were going to be pissed if she told you and you were going to pissed if she didn't trying to fix a completely messed up situation so did I get it right so far."

India paced back and forth turning the music up then down smiling at everyone   she starting adjusting her strapless shirt then she walked over to   the living room window the sun was shining bright the weather was a perfect 72 degree

"I want you'll all to know that your very good friends Leah since we've met you and I have been really good friends pretty much   like sisters, But there is something's I have to handle on my own something's my guardian angel can't hide me from something's she you just can't do for me you know." India sat down in a kitchen chair

"India what are you babbling about we've all got each other's back through thick and thin." Dena said

"There is some truth to that." India said

As she took a sip of her champagne,

"Ok Indy calm down your starting to scare me now." Leah said

"Well did you'll know that my father will be getting out next week I was suppose to be all counseled out by now but no India knows best right.'

"So your saying uncle Steve is getting out early huh." Dena said

"Apparently it's called early release isn't that wonderful.'

"India that's great new why does that have you all bent out of shape?" Jill asked

"Because I guess you'll think your tears and problems are more important then mind sometime."

"We haven't said that India, No were near that in fact." Leah said

"I'm 29 years old and not only does no one know me but I don't even know myself I've done an awful thing."

"India snap out of it, I'm pretty sure with you it can't be all that bad tell us." Dena said

"You're a great person to and it's never too late for counseling."

"Don't say everything will be ok because if you say that I think I just might scream." India said

"I wasn't going to say that.' Leah screamed

India's loud voice went silent she was staring up at the ceiling fan again she didn't know why it calmed her she just knew that it did that's why she had one in every room she would have one in the bathroom if it wasn't so small.

"India say something to us," Dena said

India stood holding her glass of champagne it was spilling out of her over flowed glass she did not care she had a point to make and it was time to make it.

"That bastard put his thing in me without a condom I trusted that he would put one on he promised before he started we would be secure but he kept it in his hand he never put it on when I realized it and demanded that he stopped he called me a nasty whore." India said

"So what are you saying India he didn't wear a condom lots of guys will do this you have to watch them put it on I should have told you." Dena said

"That my exact point you guys can't safe me I have to learn things on my own rather it's the good or bad"

"Don't sweat it girl a lot of guys do that you just have to be careful betrayal is a powerful thing." Jill said

Dena reached to hug   India but she leaned back against the couch out of Dena reach

then India held her head down as if what she hadn't said would destroy her life her

innocence she put the couch pillow in front of her as if it could protect her.

"That Bastard." Leah said

"Yeah it sounds as though Peter isn't the only head that needs to be spit its ok India

nobody's perfect and you don't have to try to be all the time your human." Dena said

"Human is that what they call it, I jumped in bed with a stranger when I missed my

period I went to the emergency room   and the first   the doctor said I had indigestion

maybe my bowels were stopped up by the time I was   released he came back in the room

and said I was pregnant."

 "I called Lamar from the emergency room   upset and crying he said I'd better call the

dude that was trying to whip my ass because I wasn't going to be trapping him with

another man's baby.

"He said that he knew I was a whore and It   was a shame I did not know who the daddy

could be then he hung up the phone. I'm not so perfect after all huh." India said

"India, oh my.' Leah said holding her hands to her face

"Don't say it Leah." India smirked

"I'm just saying you didn't have to go through this alone.' Leah said

"She said it anyway." India mumbled

"Your probably right Leah but I can't tell you' all everything that I have locked up inside of me I took care of it though, it's done and I've asked God to forgive me at first I didn't know that he ever would. But I have prayed and now learned   that when you ask him to forgive you and you believe in your heart that you should be forgiven. Then   he will now all I have to do is forgive myself I've never been good at that." India said

Dena reached over to India and tried to hug her she wouldn't budge then Dena kissed India on the cheek and wiped her tears from her eyes then told her everyone has things that they have are need to ask forgiveness about.   It was not anyone's place to judge India she reminded her that no one would ever turn their back on her that was the most sensitive thing Dena had ever said.

India noticed that Jill was crying uncontrollably she couldn't console her or give any words of encouragement as she usually did. The situation just was and all that she had to give she was sharing with her friends an unspeakable sin that she never ever thought would enter her already horrid life.

"How can I face my kids at school everyday knowing what I've done I've always tried to live right have moral's be a good daughter sister and friend my best friends in Michigan love me unconditionally I guess I'm just tired of everyone thinking that I am or that I'm trying to be perfect that has never been the case my tolerance level just works different then anyone else's." India said

Leah gave India a look she didn't like the best friend comment even though to India she had two and Leah would just have to except that Toshiba knew her dark secrets and Leah was there to help her hide them. India firmly stated she no longer wanted to discuss the situation about her father or her procedure it is done and over it could not be changed she looked at each one of her friends.   Then at her cousin their eyes were piercing, she then went to the radio and turned up the music Patti Labelle was singing (If you do not know me by now). That was one of India's favorite song's that she felt was written just for her Jill knew now that she couldn't confide in her friends or her man's sister she knew that Peter would be at their apartment waiting for her to come back with the news of having an abortion . She decided to keep quite she kept eating until India passed out on the love seat she had not slept in days.

A few weeks went by India did nothing but worked then came home she was trying desperately to stop beating herself up but she started to believe she is going to need a lot of help in doing so she put her papers for her lesson plans on the end table. Then finally decided not to just erase the messages on her answering machine without listening to them there were two from her aunt she sound upset so India sat down on her bed then called her back.

"Hi auntie, I'm sorry I haven't returned your phone calls. India said

"Well like I've been saying on that dag on machine of your's she is here and she has been here for several days I've left you many messages to call me.'

"Auntie, I'm sorry I've been busy with the kids at school who are you talking about who's here.' India said

Your sister Shay who in the world do you think I'm talking about you never call or come to see me I am talking about Shay.' Auntie Virginia said."

"Shay, Auntie Virginia are you sure how did,"

"Am I sure I am not senile girl just because you'll never visit unless your mom's in town don't mean I don't know my family she has been here in my house."

"Ok Auntie I'll come right over to get her.' India said

"That is what I'm trying to tell you India she is gone she left a couple nights ago and there is some money missing out my wallet she's on that stuff you know a lady at my church son's on that stuff real bad I know the signs. So you be careful if you see her you hear."

"Yea ma'am I'll pay you back just let me know what she took Auntie and I'm sorry for how my sister has acted.'

"Not your place to take the responsibility of another adult I'll see her again I'm sure and the switches in my back yard grow as long as a hot summer day I'll take of it myself just wanted you to know."

"I love you auntie and I'll be by real soon I promise." India said

India hung up the phone and sat on her bed mind wondering all over the place she put her hands to her face shaking her head back in forth how was Shay in town how did she get here why didn't she come straight to India house why didn't she call. Guilt followed her all through the house she started cooking spaghetti garlic bread then some strawberry Kool-Aid. Then India took a shower she didn't know what to do with herself there was a knock at her door then the phone rang at the same time India decided to answer the door first it had to be one of the girls. They did not wait to be buzzed in she opened the door without hesitation she had not looked into the peephole   asking who it was .

"I said who is it?"

India looked through the peak whole and could not see anyone the light in the hallway had been blown out for a few days she keeps forgetting to tell Miss Shiawassee or what ever her name is Miss Spooky India started to ignore the knock but he or she persisted.

"If you don't answer me you don't get in alright."

The last thing India wanted was one of her ex trying to finish what he could not when he had the chance. She was about to go sit down on the couch when a voice on the other side of the door answered.

"It's me India."

"Me, who." India yelled

The voice was faint and weary India couldn't keep her thought together she was tired and needed to gather her thought about what her auntie had told her she looked through the peephole once more only seeing a blur when the voice said.

"It's your baby sister Shay."

India hesitated she was thrown off guard she thought she had time before this moment happened time to gather her thoughts prepare but in an instant she realized she only had seconds. No time to prepare what she was going to say how she was going to apologize for the time lost discipline her for disrespecting their auntie her hands started to shake as she unlocked the door at the sound that became so familiar to her from days past.

India opened the door and there she was so unfamiliar to the familiar thoughts that were racing through India's head. The door was opened wide there she was standing in India's door way looking like she had been through the storm and through the rain almost as though she had been homeless for a life time. Shay had her arms opened wide she smiled with excitement they embraced then Shay walked right passed India into her apartment she looked around the living room as India closed and locked the door.

"Hi big sis, what you been up to?"

India didn't know what to think Shay hadn't been to her apartment since she was about nine years old she had no idea how Shay could have found her place alone Shay shook her head in approval .

"Nice I knew it would be I've pictured your place a thousand time's you know its been so long after I bummed a ride to vine street after leaving Auntie's house I found my way I know I was surprised I remembered too." Shay said

India took her book bag and told Shay finding her way was good but that she had better leave her ways at her front door India gave her baby sister some clothes then a rag and towel for a shower. Shay eat while they talked for hours Shay admired all the pictures as though she was surprised they were still in tacked

India hoped Shay reminiscing stayed cordial India had always talked about Ronald since Shay was too young to remember him she always wanted Shay to know him in memory and pictures.

"India you always say that you and Ronald was close." Shay inquired

"Yes Shay I've always told you that because it's always been the truth why do you keep asking me the same thing."

"I was just asking Gosh, I was just wandering.'

"Wandering what Shay?"

"Why did he want to kill himself is all?'

"For the hundredth time the reason Ronald killed himself had nothing to do with our relationship you were born he loved you too."

Shay was finished with her second plate she drank some of her Kool-Aid then continued to ask uncomfortable questions.

"India did you try to save him?"

"Shay if he wanted me to save him he would have told me his plans if there was a plan."

"Is that why you couldn't save him?' Shay asked

India jumped up from the kitchen table she wanted to just flip the table over but instead she gave her sister words. India pulled her t-shirt over her head and through it on the floor.

"Shay, Look at me please tell   me what do you see is there an S written on my chest huh, do you know my name is India not superwoman when are you and our mother going to realize that?"

India was shouting to the top of her lungs walking around the table watching Shay's face for any response.

"Huh tell me do you see one I'm not a super hero far from it I'm a person just like you I make mistakes just like you I was raised by Sharon just like you and I'm telling you once and for all I will no longer defend myself you can take that are leave do you hear me."

India slammed her hands on the wooden kitchen table her face in Shays face looking right at Shay.

"I said do you hear me Shay?"

Shay did not say a word still drinking her Kool-Aid eyes widen she just shook her head up and down. India told her to clean the dishes then she went to her room and slammed her door shut she turned on her small television set and turned on her clock radio she laid in her bed feeling her pressure rise her mind wandered until she fell asleep she didn't wake until the next morning.

India jumped out of bed in all the madness she had not set her alarm clock listening to music she focused on the time showing on the clock she had 45 minutes before she had to be at school she opened her room door making sure she hadn't dreamed yesterday. The couch was empty she walked around the corner to she if Shay was in the kitchen she wasn't there she went back in   the living room she looked in the closet where she had put a pillow and blankets for Shay to sleep on the couch. Shay's book bag was gone and India's front door was unlocked India cursed aloud this was unreal she did not deserve this India showered then left for work. She didn't get a chance to eat breakfast so by the time lunch came around India told her student's she was starving one of her students offered some of his packed lunch India thanked him but declined she said it was meatloaf day in the cafeteria and she couldn't wait.

India normally waited for Leah but headed for the cafeteria without her she did not know if it was her nerves are if she was really staring. India stood in the cafeteria line with her tray meatloaf mashed potatoes no gravy buttered corn two slices of white bread and a cup of ice tea she was fumbling through her purse after the cashier rang her up. After a few minutes India finally looked up at the cashier and smiled

"Looks like I seemed to have left my cash at home that's not like me." India said

The young lady was new and it was obvious she didn't like her job she told India she needed to wait on the people behind her if she didn't have any money she should step aside and that it was almost time for her break too.

Drama was right up India's alley at this point but she didn't have it in her so she closed up her purse gave the cashier another smile then left her tray and drink at the register than started to walk out of the cafeteria she ran right into Leah.

"I figured you must have been starving to leave me so where is your food sweetie." Leah asked

"It's at the register it seems as though I've left my money at home.' India said

"So you can't wait on me you know that's not a problem you just left your tray what is this about.' Leah said

"Well I didn't know until I got to the register Leah are you and that cashier working together.'

'India don't be silly let's sit here.'

Leah paid the cashier than walked over to India who was still standing angrily she handed her the tray of food still hot then Leah went and ordered the same only adding the gravy she

asked India what was going on she told her that she had been confiding in Greg about the distance that she noticed between everyone. Greg mention how long it has been since India had been over she told India that the kids Ezra and Leann really missed her and that made India realize it has been awhile but not intentionally she assured Leah that she would change things back to normal

"Well, Dena's in love I do know that." India said

"Again, who's the lucky fellow?'

"I forget this ones name something or another.'

'What about Jill?" Leah asked

"You're going to have to found out about that one on your own Leah."

"I was just wandering if she was still confiding in you about my brother is all."

"Leah, Shay's in town."

"Shay when, where is she how long has she been here why didn't you tell me I would have invited you two over introduced her to the family.'

"Leah, Leah it's not like that she came in town or rather I found out she was in town yesterday she came over and it just crazy.'

"I'm sorry India if I always seem to pry it's just you are my best friend and I'm always concerned when you don't seem happy. You've been looking for Shay and wanting to be a big sister again I just hope and I'm not saying you wont but I just hope you'll let me share your family   too.'

"Of course I will you are in for a surprise I wont get into detail right now." India said
They finished eating India gave the cashier a dirty look before leaving the cafeteria they
headed back to their classrooms Leah holding her head down. India knew she wanted to
talk more about Jill but she was not going to, besides she did not know anything new.
Leah was going to have to take India's advice and call her friend India rushed into the
classroom when the bell rang she yelled out to Leah that she owed her $5.32 Leah looked
at her confused then went into her classroom.

By the time India got home she realized where her money had gone she had three
messages none of them were Shay two were from Jill she was almost demanding that
India come over or give her an immediate call Jill would have to wait or come to her
senses and handle her own life. India started calling around to family when she got
home their uncle Devin told her he had not seen her and that his birthday was coming up
India of course agreed to come to his party. Since she never had any explanation why she
had not seen them mainly because they always wanted to talk about her dad that was the
first thing her uncle mention her father being out of prison. India did not respond she

knew that he had to stay at a half way house for a few months and he had told her that he would be moving to California.   India ended the call she didn't know if she wanted   to kill Shay are to make sure that she was alright she looked through the yellow pages looking for shelters angry because no thefts would living in her house. She wrote down a couple of numbers then decided to look through the purses she carried days ago in case she left her money in one of them. However, all she found was a   business card with a cellular number on it and the name on the top India had kissed the paper leaving her lip print.

"Noel, Noel Harmen first and last name what in the world. "

India had no idea how long she had the number or when she even had time to run into a businessman the last time she looked was at school all the teachers at school were married or gay. She was sure this apple didn't fall far from any tree she quickly forgot what she was doing   once she saw that she had kissed the back of the card she sat down on her bed turning the card back and forth smiling she didn't know why and she was starting to get on her own nerves.

She decided to pour herself a glass of wine turning on Prince "International Lover" turning the volume to the max on the radio she sat in her love seat and exhaled surprised that she was even able to do that as tense as she had been all day. What was it about this person this number India's record of accomplishments made her leery which did not mean anything trouble could find her in her sleep. India went out on a limb she had nothing to loose she insisted on having 10 minutes of an illusion just 10 minutes to believe she had a life maybe he could be someone with whom she needed to let off some steam. She dialed the number on the card and held the phone to her ear then acted as if her wine was kryptonite India sat back and waited for an answer on the other end.

Jill left work early even though she had a client to meet for a sell on a condominium in a new suburban area she was trying to catch Peter at home it seemed that since she had not had an abortion he only came home when he knew Jill and Jake had left. Peter was in the shower Jill followed the sound of running water until she saw the shadow of his body inside the shower glass doors. Jill stood their within minutes the shower doors were opening steam cover the bathroom he wiped his wet face with his hands then reached for his towel,

"It this what your looking for I've been wandering if you still lived here where have you been?' Jill asked

Peter took the towel from her and started to dry himself he walked over to the sink and started putting toothpaste on his toothbrush then looked over at Jill.

"So did you get it done?' Peter said

"Let me see didn't' I mention the last time Peter I'm too far along it to risky, and I'm not doing it I not killing my baby or myself."

Peter finished brushing his teeth then rinse with mouthwash he wrapped his towel around his wrist then followed Jill into their attached bedroom.

"Peter I want you to want this baby please.'

"Damn it Jill, I told you I didn't want any kids you knew that before we even   got together you remember in college when we tried this for the first time you said   you were on birth control then have you every even been on the pill."

"Of course I have what are you saying.'

"That was not my baby either," Peter whispered."

"I'm saying the same thing that I've been saying I'm not ready to get marry and I don't want any children what part of that sentence do you not understand   Jill." Peter said

Jill understood   him every time since college she knew how he felt about this and how he felt about that he's always been precise with every detail of his life he and Leah she has known that since the day they met   but she wanted to be the woman that would and could change that he was the perfect man in every way in Jill's eyes and anything he does not has which is not much his family does. Jill's mother passed away while she was in college her father married 2 weeks later then moved somewhere in the world Jill acts as if she doesn't know his where about. She has decided she wanted the family Peter and Leah has and as for him not loving her right now well Jill could deal with that she figured with some convincing that it would come later.

"Peter I'm not trying to trap you it takes two to make a baby I didn't do this on my own even if your never here.' Jill said

Peter pushed both his hands across the dresser knocking over everything that was on top of it his face was now red his jaws was tightening and all he wanted to do was get out of there he turned to look at Jill he started to laugh.

"Jill the baby isn't even mine so you can stop playing your games because nothing will come out of this."

"Peter you're the only one for me no matter what you say this is your baby that we are having."

Peter put his under garments on, grabbed his clothes, and started walking out of the room mumbling under his breath.

"Peter your not walking out on me and this baby I'm sorry for getting pregnant if that's what you want me to say.' Jill said

Jill picked up a shoe and threw it at Peter it did not faze him she ran up behind him and pulled his hair then started grabbing his arms yelling and screaming at him.

"Where are you going your acting like a coward?" Jill said

Peter pushed Jill onto the couch then started out the door he was half dressed Jill grabbed him by his pants. Peter pushed her hands away causing Jill to jerk back she reached at him again causing his pants to come undone Peter grabbed hold of his pants and again started for the door Jill started scratching at his back with her nails . He turned to her without saying a word he smacked her across the face causing her to fell to the floor.

"Jill I've asked you not to put your hands on me I am a grown man   I am not your son Jake so let me leave before this gets way out of hand do you heard me I am not your coward I am a man." Peter said

He slammed the door as hard as he could then he stopped when it shut guilty about striking her he took a deep breath then continued on his way leaving without any of his belongings that he had intended on taken with him.

India and Noel had been talking on the phone for two weeks they talked for hours on her break and on his lunchtime even through the night, there were good morning calls. Both of their schedules were normally full he reminded India that they had met at a Chinese restaurant and that   he was at a business meeting and that   she had told him that she had just gotten off work. She had decided to stopped at her favorite   Chinese restaurant   that Jill had brought to her and Leah's attention it was two minutes from the school and right on the way home. Noel noticed her at the   counter he was coming back from the restroom he walked up to the counter and introduced himself India wasn't flattered or amused she told him her name he quickly offered his card after noticing his party waiting patiently at their table. India gave a fake smile and put the business card in her purse he looked like a model out of the G-Que magazine but all India needed was more drama after Lamar she was on sabbatical for life   she changed her purse the next day and never gave the   black stallion another thought.

"Huh computer programmer for one of the bigger companies in the world owns several properties with a long time friend right that equals drug dealer or user." India thought aloud

India was suppose to call Noel back when she got off work tonight she was still thinking about how he had said he needed more time to figure out rather India had a sense of humor or was just down right rude. Especially since she had taken his number and never called, he did not have a problem with telling India how beautiful she was also how unapproachable she had made herself. But it was something about her arrogance that lead him to want to get to know he her had no intentions on rushing things although they had several common interest like music Noel's collection went from Jazz to opera to the Blues artist India had never heard of. They shared a common interest for Phil Collins most women he knew never seemed to know who he was are how as amazing of an artist he was to music he thought women did not care about the importance of a live band and Phyllis Hyman the conversation was non ending.   India considered it all Noel which was drawn to India's love for music they also had a love for family and their friends he didn't care or at least he said he didn't care about having children and India has never wanted children either. Although she did not give all that information to him his voice was smooth mesmerizing in fact he was patient with India's uncontrollable sharp tongue. She tried to gather her words when speaking, but her tongue always worked faster then her brain process it had been several days and still no sign of Shay India's long talks with Noel got her through. Even though she told him, little if nothing about her life personal life only about her students the loves of her life Noel enjoyed sharing with India. He didn't noticed the distance that India had been portraying with any knowledge of her private life at first India came home and instead of calling Noel as she had promised she showered then ate then started on her lesson plans. Although she had already finished it she decided to change a few activities for the kids she had added music to their everyday activities and several of her students have entered in voice lesson or they have started playing instruments. India finished her homemade burger and fries she was about to turn in when she heard a firm knock at her door.

"Who is it?'

India had not left the couch she had washed her hair then decided not to blow dry it so it was all over her head she was wearing a white tank top and some gray sweats. This should not be happening why weren't they answering India she thought she should get a big dog maybe a Rottweiler to chase all the stupid people that knocked on her door and then did not give her a response .

India uncrossed her legs put her papers on the couch then got up to answer the door she looked through the dark peep hole she pulled her head back and quickly brushed her wet hair back. She was upset that there was no answer the intensity made her nipples stand at attention she tried to take a deep breath and suck them back in they wouldn't budge.

After she opened the door, she folded her arms in amazement.

"Noel what are you doing here, how did you know where I lived and did you forget how to dial my number.'

He gave her a big smile that made India nipples press harder against her arms he let himself inside India's apartment India locked the door and turned with her arms still folded. She gave Noel a strange look she was dying to look in a mirror how dare him break a cardinal rule call he should call every time before coming India didn't give a damn how fine he was are how smooth his skin looked. His strong arms bulged out of his black fitted tie shirt with nice fitting Levi's (Lord is this man bow-legged) this is so unfair.

"Well I couldn't wait any longer to see you and since you didn't call as promised I didn't have any time to waste on the giving you a surprise." Noel said as he glanced around India place and at her tightly folded arms.

India brushed passed Noel quickly she brushed her hair back again as her back was turned to him she didn't know how silly she would look if she grabbed a jacket so she didn't her back still turned she pretended to straighten things on the end table not realizing that this view was just as uncomfortable as   her front.

"Noel I'm pretty busy right now and I wish you wouldn't just drop by that   is very typical of a man what is this some kind of booty call or something."

It was in that instance that Noel realized what qualities that India possess and it definitely was not a sense of humor. He looked at India as though her head had fallen off her shoulders then he went into his back pocket and came out with a white envelope and handed it to India then walked over to her front door and began to unlock it.

"I'm sorry if I inconvenienced you it wasn't my intentions I just didn't want these to go to waste can't win them all right India have a good night.' Noel said

He slowly closed the door behind him India just stood there confused she looked at the envelope and after opening it her bottom lip felt like it had fallen to the floor Noel had written a little note for India.

"I wanted to invite a friend another rain check for the two of us a special someone."

Just in case India was not home he had plans to leave the envelope under her door. He had given her two front row tickets to an Anita Baker concert India could only whisper,

"Anita Baker"

There had been so much going on India had forgot that she was coming to town India looked through the peep hole knowing she wouldn't see much then she opened the doors and rushed down the seven steps then looked out the hallway window Noel was pulling off quickly. India slowly walked up the stairs into the apartment she felt foolish for the first time from her actions the show started in two hours the only person India knew could handle that short of a notice was Dena. She quickly grabbed the phone then dialed her number some strange guy answered India just looked at the phone then put it back to her ear he was telling India that Dena wouldn't be back from her business trip until 11 pm. Then that he would be picking her up at the airport India knew Leah couldn't go because Greg didn't get home on Thursday's until 10 pm and Jill was definitely out this was the first time India thought that she might need to broaden her horizons with her   group of friends.

She flopped down onto the couch right on top of her school papers she felt   defeated she tried to convince herself to go by herself and then how this wasn't her fault then she ended her thoughts thinking that she was just plain damn crazy. The price on the tickets were $95 India had never been any where like this by herself but she couldn't miss this opportunity she put on some black dress pants and a white blouse with ruffles in front trimmed in black then she brushed her hair into a bun and curling the ends. She fluffed the curls around gave herself one long flipped curl that hung in her face. She applied her lipstick while trying once again to convince herself of some devious reasons as to why Noel could not attend or have just stopped by. Yet still wanted India to have the tickets "Stop being silly India and get going" She couldn't believe she was doing something like this which was   what she thought was daring she didn't want to drive not knowing how the parking downtown would be so she called a cab and had it scheduled for after the concert also.

When India got in at 11:30 pm she quickly called Noel to tell him of her excitement if her voice would allow her too she sang every song she also wanted to apologize for her rudeness then thank Noel for the tickets. He didn't answer India was hesitant but left a message on his machine repeating what she was thinking and ask if he would call when he got a chance. India said her prayers she was definitely powered out she instantly fell to sleep at the wonderful memory of the loud music still ringing in her ear.

A few days had past India still hadn't heard from Shay or Noel she'd had a brief conversation with her father last night then she called her mother before she left for work she was thrown off from the call when her mother answered but was glad to hear her voice. India asked how she had been she did not ask why she missed the wedding she let her know that Shay had been in town Sharon was a little short with India. Telling her that she hadn't seen her father and that she had gotten a job and has moved into a small apartment no other explanation or comment about Shay being in town so India didn't tell her that she was missing Sharon told India to get her sister together than ended their conversation.

India continued with her busy life she had learned not to question things that she already knew she did not have the answer to she was meeting Dena Saturday morning for a little shopping. They arrived at the mall at the same time Dena jumped out of the car glowing and all smiles they walked into the mall Dena wanted to go straight to the Zale's counter then yelled out,

"Girl guess what." Dena said

"Dena you know I hate the guessing game just tell me." India said

"India, take a guess for me girl.'

India looked her up and down the silly look on her face gave India a stomach cramp,

"Ok you're pregnant.' India said

Dena stepped back from the counter with her hands on her hips,

"What in the hell kind of guess is that India.'

"Calm down you forced me to guess now your mad give me a break." India said

"Alright you were right you're horrible at the guessing game so I'll tell you I'm getting married and were moving to Atlanta." Dena said

"With who girl, your talking crazy."

"With my man, Victor.'

   "Yeah sorry, you guys have been seeing each other long enough for me to have known the answer to that question or his name.'

"Funny India its been two long months and   I'm head over hills India   so the two of you have to meet we can double date" Dena said

"There is not going to be any double dating and where in the hell is your ring."

Oh, my goodness India it has been like only a week how did you fuck up this time this guy was a gem. Dena said

They both started looking at rings the sales person had asked them three times if they needed help they hadn't yet noticed .

"So your just going to automatically excuse me of being the one that has   done something some family member you are it's great to know how you really feel."

Dena finally acknowledges the woman standing over them and asked to see a 2-carat wedding ring she was admiring the ring on her finger holding it up in the light.

"Why do you think I'm looking at rings India, alright now I'll play your game what has happened in just a weeks time ."

"We will talk about this later look for your ring you are not buying it yourself are you.' India asked

"No silly he told me to pick out what I wanted and I wanted you to share this moment with me but your about to mess it up now help me pick out a ring and tell me what you did now."

The story was so unreal India had to show Dena the stubs from the concert tickets to ensure she would believe her before they left the mall with six bags between the two of them. Dena told India she would be moving soon and if she did not apologize to Noel for acting like an ass hole she would never talk to her again. This went in one ear and out her other

India got out of the car and walked around to her trunk she stopped at the grocery store after leaving the mall. She was juggling the bags when she noticed Shay sitting on the wall under a tree she stood up and rushed over to India when she saw her than helped her with the bags her eyes looked swollen she was crying her hair was all over her head and the clothes India had given her looked like they were 10 years old she could see Shay's hands shaking she wouldn't look India in the eyes. India did not have the heart to turn her away she unlocked the downstairs door then said nothing Shay started slowly following from behind. India gave her some sweats a rag and towel and pointed to the bathroom reminding Shay to wash her hair India yelled out that she was not going to put any of her possessions away that this was Shay's last chance. They ate and watched television India didn't know what to say and she didn't want to say the wrong thing she knew the streets were doing way worst to her sister then any words of wisdom could do so she would wait until she got a call back from a counsel she had talked too yesterday it was getting late.

Dena stopped over she had not seen Shay in years they hugged Shay said she was tired so India and Dena went into the kitchen closed the door and finished their talk Dena of course was shocked that Shay had returned India got the wine glasses.

"So where is this Victor dude?" India said

"He's in Atlanta right now he is an up and coming R&B slash rapper his sings on a couple of people songs now he wants to start his career he's been recently signed with a label in Atlanta."

"What about your career you're doing very well Dena." India said

"I've already started transferring, my company has a partner company in Atlanta it is all working out we have even found a house India."

"A house wow as long as things are in place and this opportunity is good for the both of you then congratulations."

They hugged as tears fall down both there eyes they made a toast Dena whispered to India that she needed to be very careful with Shay she could tell that she was really out there especially by her being so young. Dena told her the things that drug addicts would stoop to India whispered back she had already found out and that she has to agree to get help in order to stay. Dena was having a small wedding at a local hall India was going to be the maid of honor and Victor's brother would be his best man no bridesmaids or groomsmen just a very small but elegant wedding.   They talked until 11:30 pm India watched Dena through the window as she got into her car.

Shay was knocked out on the couch India got a bright idea she grabbed her purse then locked her front door praying that everything would still be in her purse she hopped in her car then gained some inspiration from her Whitney Houston tape as she drove off. Before she knew it she was in front of Noel's condo for some reason the first thing that they had done was tell each other where each other lived. India was standing at Noel's front door it is amazing how brave wine can make a girl feel she thought to herself, "What the hell am I doing the same thing I just chewed him out for, oh my goodness this is so not me."

India turned around and started down his steps and back to her car when she noticed a man walking up holding a blockbuster bag he did not look crazy.

"Excuse me sir may I use your phone."

India couldn't believe what she was doing now she was approaching strangers the man looked her up then down then he smiled,

"Sure a friend of Noels is a friend of mine he's home though his car is right there.'

India followed behind him not knowing how he knew who she was trying to see the condo's were all attached simultaneously India waited in the doorway until the man invited her inside. He turned his television on put his movies down then asked India if she wanted a drink she declined while he handed her the phone he stood right in her face she turned her back to the man and then dialed Noel's number she could feel the older

man staring her down but the wine she had drunk had her mind buzzing. Noel answered on the

third ring India hesitated then responded to his sexy hello

"Noel, it is me India are you busy?" India asked

"It's midnight I just finished some computer designs I am tired and need to lay it down what's up."

Noel said

Trying to keep his cool although he was just as excited at the fact that India's took the

initiative to act as though she cared,

"Well is that a yes you're busy or a no you're not busy?" India said

She quickly thought that this might be the perfect time to show her feminine side if only she could

quickly figured out which side it was on, she took a deep breath so that her next response would sound thought out,

"India I was only answering your question I'm alone if that's what you're asking." Noel said

Noel wasn't in the move for India's mess even though that's exactly the answer she was

looking for now if he would only take over the conversation it would be all good India

waited for his next response after a few breaths there was silence.

"Hello, Noel are you there?" India said

her strong tone was back,

"Yes India I'm here, you called me remember." Noel said

India clinched her fist rolling her eyes to the top of her head it seemed like eternity and the older

gentleman was now standing in front of her,

"Well I stopped at your neighbor's to give you a call but it doesn't sound like you wanted to hear

from me so I'll be leaving you have a good night Noel." India smirked

She hung up the phone and tried to keep her composure she adjusted her hair from her

eyes and gave the man a sneaky smile letting out a little laugh
.

"Thank you sir this was very nice of you to do, sorry for any inconvenience." India said

She shook the man's hand and slowly walked out of his front door than quickly moved toward her

car the gentleman had a confused looked on his face he was thinking Noel had to be out of his

mind if he did not want such a fine looking woman, he watched the pretty young thing

making sure she made it to her car along with other reason's.

"Next door, India what are you talking about?"

Noel hadn't realize that India had hung up he could hear high heel shoe's clinking

outside Noel quickly made his way to the window that faced the parking

lot and saw India briskly strutting in the night Noel quickly grabbed his rob

he opened his front door then rushed outside. India pretended as if he had startled her but she

knew it was Noel she may only attract fools but India knew she has what men want she just did

not care if they got it she started walking rapidly to her car but Noel was already at her car door

India started waving her hands around.

"Noel I'm sorry for bothering you it won't happen again trust me." India said

Then she started fumbling through her clutch purse to find her car keys her body stumbling back

and forth,

"India calm down." Noel said

"No you calm down." India said

"India have you been drinking."

India tried to push Noel from in front of her car he didn't budge he grabbed her by the

arm and looked her in her eyes India would not give any eye contact she again tried

to push Noel out of the way he did not want to disturb the neighbors so he threw India over his

shoulders and started inside of his condominium. India immediately resisted she demanded that Noel put her down when all the alcohol rushed to the top of her head she stopped

kicking and tried to hold on to his silk rob her hand's were slipping when

Noel turned fast to close his front door. She was sure Noel was going to let her head bust right

into the wall her red silk mini skirt was so short she could feel the air go right

up her bottom Noel walked right passed the couch and was heading for the balcony

unsure to India that he wanted to close the glass door India's stomach was turning she

started kicking again.

"What are you doing put me down damn it." India said

"I should throw your ass off that balcony." Noel said

India lifted her head as much as she could regrettably then shouted,

"Then do it, go ahead Noel." India said

she was hoping her drinks were going to stay down and that her head would stop spinning Noel

made another sharp turn toward his bedroom he threw India down on his

warm bed the sheets had to be expense because they felt like pure cotton but felt like silk at the same time.

"How much have you had to drink India?" Noel said

"Are you calling me a drunk." India said

"Oh you'll know when I'm calling you something trust me." Noel said

He held her down by her arms as gentle as he could,

"Don't worry about how much I've been drinking I'm grown." India said

"You sure aren't acting like it India." Noel said

India tried to push Noel out of the way but when she felt his bare chest she melted   she was

not going to be defeated.

"Let me go Noel move out of my way like I said I'm sorry for disturbing you." India said

"India I'm not letting you go anywhere not until you calm down." Noel said

Noel put his weight on her slightly pressing his bare chest against her India was breathing heavy

the room was still spinning and she did not really want to get back behind

the wheel India noticed that her hands was still against Noel soft silky chest and they were

shaking a little, she looked up at him and sure enough, he was looking her straight

in her eyes which made her uncomfortable because there was not many people

that she trusted. She focused back on his chest his robe was hanging off

his broad shoulders his leg was straddled on top of her a little and   she could feel through his

satin pants that he was at full attention the room had stop spinning and the

alcohol had settled back in her head she guessed   because before she knew it she had
wrapped

her hand around his freshly shaved head and was pushing his

head to meet her lips he tried to resist but was not doing a good job their lips met and they kissed

so passionately, that India wanted to take up kissing as a hobby from now

on she was about to kiss him again when he abruptly pulled away.

"India you've been drinking don't do this please." Noel said

Noel looked at India with such force and intensity that she melted she tried to pull his head down

again as she felt his manhood moving and getting bigger words started

flowing from her mouth.

"Noel I'm sorry for the way I treated you last week I know it was rude and you didn't deserve for

me to be rude to you." India said

India started kissing him all over his chest licking his nipples Noel would wait for this day

as long as it took, he did not imagine it going this way

India was moving her hands up and down Noel's back and squeezing him for dear

life softly digging her short nail into his bare back.

With all the strength Noel could mustard he spoke with his mouth so close to her ear the vibration

from his deep voice gave India chills

"India, India baby we need to talk." Noel said

India returned the intensity,

"Noel I know what I'm doing make love to me."

India had no Idea who she was right then but she wanted her to stay for a while she started

nibbling on his neck and through his heavy panting he stopped again to speak.

But this time India knew what she wanted and it was him she pretty much knew what he

was going to say and she felt like coming clean with everything the

reason why she always acts so cold the conversation quickly spanned through her mind,

"Oh by the way Noel the reason that I seem fucked up in the head is because,

I can't forgive myself for my brother's death and it tare me apart everyday I

pretty much cryed myself to sleep at night."

"Oh and my mother resents me and my sister, my sister hate's everything about me and she steals and

prostitutes for drugs Oh and let me not forget the last and first man that I become intimate with

got me pregnant."

"He then called me a whore and you will never guess how I resolved that issue so Noel could

you love a horrible person like me."

India snapped her thoughts back fighting back the tears that were forming in her eyes it would

be so nice to get some of this off her chest what it would be like to lean on

someone for a change feel free from some of this but she knows it is too much baggage

because it's to much baggage for her to handle so she went for plan A there's

never been a plan B forget about it sweep the drama back to the back of her mind India spoke.

"Noel I'm sorry I won't treat you rude again, I know that I've told you this before and I know that I

told you that I loved music and that is why you brought me over the tickets

although I don't know why you brought them so late but I'm sorry."

Woops India thought the last part just slipped out,

Noel sat up and spoke back in such an alluring tone
.

"India one of my partners was taking his wife but they had a family emergency with their son who's

away at Michigan State College, I have talked about you to them

and our interest for music Tom said we were the first people he thought about and this dude has

four brothers and two sisters India I was so excited to get to you."

Noel's gave her a cold look India could not feel any worse and the only way she knew

to fix this was relax and let go she put her hands on his face,

"Will you forgive me?" India said

She reached up and kissed him and held the kiss until she could no longer hold herself up he put

his hands on her she let go and asked again,

"Noel I want you to make love to me."

He was not going to risk another fight or any more rudeness from her but he could no longer resist

he attached himself to India as though they were one his lips were all

over her, he sucked her neck so hard with his full lips that the burning sensation drove India crazy

she could do nothing but moan he cupped her breast perfectly in his

hands she ran her nails up and down his back with more intensity her return of pain was bitter

sweet to Noel she was kissing him like no other. Noel was circling his tongue

around India's navel, she felt his tongue moving further and further down her body stopping to

kiss every inch of her; she quickly opened her eyes once his hands reached down India's leg then he was gripping his strong hands around her ankles spreading her legs further apart.

Noel whispered to India that she tasted so good while he had made it down to her inner thighs she

balled her fist and thought to herself to just relax India it's to late to turn back now

the next thing she knew she had an arch in her back that made her feel like a ballerina she

looked above her head trying to found something to stop her from

screaming out once she felt his firm wet tongue playing around on her clitoris she could think of

nothing so she

grabbed a pillow and bit down. Until that was not enough, she tried to push Noel away but he

was like a two tone truck so she put her nails back into his back which

made him spread her legs further and further apart until she

could not take his twirling tongue licking in and out of her walls the more she motioned

back on the bed the deeper his tongue went inside her she could hardly

recognize the sounds coming from her mouth she called out his name then looked down at him

and he was looking right at her reaching for her breast she could not take

anymore she put both her bare feet against his shoulders and forced him off of her, his tongue

was still lingering out his mouth, he stood to his feet by gripping India bottom

he slide his face tightly in between her legs to finish the job India was now up in the air sitting on

top of Noel's shoulder she held onto his head for dear life which was very difficult since he was going to town. India screamed his name so loud she was embarrassed

finally Noels knees got weak he laid India back onto the bed her eyes almost popped out

Her head when she finally looked at his big chocolate manhood.

"Oh my God I hope he doesn't think I'm putting that in my mouth." India though

They had briefly talked about sex He had told India that he has been celibate for seven months

the only thing India shared was that she didn't like giving or receiving oral sex but since India's

high-pitched moaning was out of control this probably meant

she didn't know what in the hell she was talking about she was stuck she thought she could

handle   a night of passion but he was a real man and his only mission was to please India while

releasing

seven months of frustration India took a deep breath Noel did not say a word if she

was not ready he was not going to force it even though it would take everything he had to stop.

Noel walked over to his small stereo and turned on mellow moods then came back over to

her   he knew what turned her on she was completely naked on his bed he reached down for

India's hand he bend down and kissed it and then her cheeks. It was then that she realized that he

was not going to be anything but respectful suddenly she did not want anything more but him

she took control gripping the large erect substance into her hands trying not to seem

like an amateur India closed her eyes and hoped she

did not forget what the porno's had taught her

she knew to think of it as a banana on a stick just don't bite into it and

know when to let go if you did not enjoy fireworks and India was scared to death of fireworks

And shooting stars Noel had her hair gripped so tight she had to force her head back and forth

he was now moaning even louder then India his eyes were rolling to the back of his

head he could not help it he was moaning her whole name,

"India Hype, India Hype"

India remember   she needed to keep her

mouth moist and that she did India really liked bananas obviously

Noel   had enough looking down at her taking all control made him want her more he back out and

gripped her under her arms and through her onto the bed

Noel reached into his night stand and took out a condom India laid down on the soft bed she

spread her legs apart then hoped she was tall enough to ride   this ride.

At three am into the morning Noel and India had made love over and over Noel's forcefulness

He made her aware each time he climaxed India was so wet she does not know rather or not she

Would have want they called an orgasm that did not specify this on the VHS tapes she was not

Prepared did she already do it,   she knew that there was a difference in meaningful sex, fucking

and making love

She now knew the difference in the three you can do all three but it means nothing if your not in Love, lesson learned.

Noel continued to lick and kiss every inch of her body and she did the same by four am Noel started dozing off he had her wrapped so tightly under the covers it took India quite awhile to settle her breathing and to calm her body she could do nothing now but lay still while he was kissing her neck over and over.

India looked up and into Noel   eyes were closed she thanked God she quickly realized that she would never get settled in   so she decided to try to leave as lifeless as her body was she had not thought this far ahead once again she covered herself with the cover and sat on the edge of the bed looking around on the floor where all her clothes were scattered she was about to get up when India felt a strong grip around her pulling her back in Noel covered her back up with the covers. He looked down at India a tear fell from his eye India immediately became tense she looked away Noel turned her face back around to his big beautiful light brown eyes staring India down,

"India I've fallen in love with you I feel so crazy because your so over the top I've never meet any one like you since the last time I saw you I do not mean that in a good why if you do not mind me being honest it's a must for me I can't stop thinking about you but you won't let me in and I hardly know anything about you other then you are a wonderful teacher, your beautiful and

your eyes are hypnotizing I know that you are a good woman I can feel that. "Noel said

He wouldn't let her face go her eye's were wandering around the room then focused back on Noel

She has only told so much about herself she tried to interrupt because she

knew that this man could be in his bed with any women that he wanted.

"I've told you practically everything there is to know about me and now that we've made love I

won't accept anything less for you, India I've wanted to hold you in my arms since we met I know

that your smart mouth is just a front, let me in baby I promise not to hurt you." Noel said

He stroked her hair even more mesmerized than before they got started,

"Don't worry I won't let you hurt me Noel, This is fast for me I need more time I'm trying really I
am

it's just not easy for me I don't believe that there is love at first sight it's just plain old attraction."

India said

He reluctantly kissed India on her forehead he knew that loving someone he barely knew was

risky but he couldn't turn back if he wanted to he sunk down and laid

his head on India's fast beating chest. Ignoring her coldness and as much as she wanted to leave

India   didn't move she as a matter of fact could not   move   Noel's strength was apparent

and for the first time in a long time she was too tired to fight

to tired to be smart mouth   and to tired to worry about having nightmares. India was just tired so she just laid there   letting Noel   hold her the way he wanted to hold her

India opened her eyes to the bright sun shining oh so bright to her eyes

wandered around the unfamiliar room, Then she sat up so quickly she almost lost her

breath she jumped out of bed so fast when she tried to take a step it felt like her body had been

tackled by an entire football team in a game she had obviously lost her head was throbbing she

slowly bend down and looked under the bed for the rest of her clothes then she sat back on the

bed she wanted to cry so bad she couldn't believe she'd let her guards

down like this India learned as a little girl there was no such thing as a white picket fence that the

generation curse knew her name she continued to look around the room when she

turned to the empty pillow where there was a note folded with her name on it inside it read.

My sweet India good morning,
you were sleeping so beautifully
that I didn't want to wake you and
I thought that it would be a good
idea if you were still in bed when
I returned home. I had to go to
the office for a few hours I have made you some
eggs, toast, and I hand washed
your undergarments and blouse they are hanging in
the bathroom.

With love Noel,

After reading the letter for the third time especially the part about the underwear she'd hoped that

he didn't think she would ever return that favor India got up and

got dressed she made the bed grabbed the eggs and exited India was

in a daze the whole way home but she quickly came back to reality when she got home Shay was

stretched out on the couch and dirty dishes were on the coffee table

India slammed the front door closed. Shay jumped up and turned to look at India then rolled her

eyes.

"Where have you been all night your phone drove me crazy that dag on counselor man what are

her hours." Shay said

"Excuse me, you're not the only one that knows how to disappear Shay."

"Gosh, I guess you woke up on the wrong side of somebody's bed." Shay said

"I woke up just fine Shay until I saw you still sleep with dirty dishes in my living room."

"Do you have clean clothes for this evening?" India said

"I'm twenty India." Shay said

"I'll take that as a yes now get up and clean your mess."

India went into her room and locked the door because Shay had a habit of just walking in she sat

down on her bed and wrapped her arms around herself India had never felt so good she pictured Noel and chill bumps were all over her arms she took off her clothes and

took a long shower she thanked God it was Saturday she dried off and went to

warm her eggs sprinkling cheese on top of them. India went back in her room locked her door

she ate then decided she would return two phone calls one was to Jill.

'Girl where have you been all night was that little devil lying to me were you at home." Jill said

"No Jill I was out and hello to you too." India said

"There's only one place you could have been tell me the dirt." Jill said

"How's Jake Jill."

'He's fine now the dirt please."

"How's the baby.' India said

"India don't do this to me I hadn't had any excitement in how long."

"I'm sorry Jill but I'm tired you should call Leah, I'm sure she has something exciting to say you

two need to talk you both love her brother." India said

"I know but Peter isn't right I'm not going to take it any more if he doesn't love me or

want our baby so be it." Jill said

"You need to work this out for the baby's sake Peter's probably scared having a baby is a big

deal."

"Right take up for him India I'm not surprised. " Jill said

"Jill I'll call you later."

"Sure you will Ok India bye."

India knew the way her body felt she needed more sleep she had only seven hours before Shay's

meeting that was the only way India would let Shay back into her

home. She had to promise to get into a drug program then get a job she really lucked up because

she had done some stealing while she was missing in action and now has a misdemeanor on her

record. India committed herself to going to the first two-hour meeting she did not realize it would

be so soon and on the weekend less than 24-hour notice, the woman did just what she said she

would do working hard at saving addicts. The woman that runs the meetings seemed to be

on her stuff India returned her call and confirmed that she and Shay would be there

the woman let India know a little bit about the program. She felt it was beneficial to get

To know at least one family member of each of the addicts.

India was going to get Shay the help she needed then work on her own life if she still had

one when this was over India's nap did not do her   the justice but she got up and got ready

for the meeting. At the meeting everyone had to introduce him or herself including any family or

friend's of the patience.

Mrs. Turner had been clean for fifteen years and is married with one son she had

spend   two years in prison and made everyone clear that she had been there and had done that

Mrs. Turner made it clear that no patient was to date anyone inside the program.

If the patient fails one drug test or missed one class which were six days a

week for anyone that didn't have a job they couldn't even be late because if they

did Mrs. Turner would kick them out of the program. They would go to the bottom of the list, which

were months long the counselor decided five minute's into the meeting that she was going

to be Shay's sponsor India noticed Shay was the youngest. That made her case the most severe

most addicts didn't hit rock bottom until they had been   doing drugs for longer then Shay had

even been born. Some needed to do in patient care, which India could not afford Shay

couldn't have had a more bigger attitude but India didn't care Mrs. Turner's attitude was even

bigger and wiser that is exactly what Shay needed. Because she would probably die

at a very young age without the program on their way home India reminded Shay that if she fails

she would not be failing her she will be failing herself.   Shay opened up and told India that she

was ready to do and have better find a cute guy that has lots of money India looked at her baby

sister who is just as beautiful if not more then India she saw the innocents in her eyes for the first

time in a long time she gave baby sister a smile India said that once things started going well that

they would start a new relationship with their mother.

India was exhausted Shay went straight to the refrigerator and India went to listen to her

messages, Leah had called along with Noel India did not want to call Leah because

when India wouldn't talk to Jill the other day. She finally told Leah everything which made her fly the coop Leah was mad at everyone for keeping information from her she was convinced that Peter wasn't a violent man. And that he would never asked Jill to had an abortion but Leah and India has been friends for to long to let this get out of hand India called her.

"Hey girl, I need to see you." Leah said

"Leah, I'm real tired can't it wait."

"Well I guess I can tell you over the phone I just wanted to apologize for the way I've been acting lately I know I've been a Bitch." Leah said

India did not say anything.

"Hello." Leah said

"Oh are you waiting on me to respond." India said

"Ok, ok India I know." Leah said

"Have you spoken to Peter?" India asked

"No he's on a business trip and won't be back in town until tomorrow he won't know what hit him when I see him India he'll be lucky if Jill lets him anywhere near the baby."

"I just didn't want things to go any further Jill's been dealing with this alone." Leah said

"Well Friday night is coming and we've missed the last two ladies out so were on." India said

India started yawning repeatedly

"I heard you've been spending nights out, No more secrets India is it that hunk Noel." Leah said

"We'll talk Friday I've been at the AA meeting with Shay for over two hours." India said

"Oh   she started the program that's great Dena's called me with her new info she's leaving India

we all really need each other right now see you Friday."

Shay wanted to use the phone, India thought about calling Noel but she was so tired she told

Shay to let her know when she got off the phone India got under the covers

and was out like a light she slept   straight   through Sunday.

India's alarm clock rang it was so annoying that India knocked it on the floor she was once again

 well rested twice in the last week she did not get a chance to clear

 her throat when her phone rang.

"Hello India."

"Yes."

"It's Noel is everything alright?" He asked

"What do you mean?" India asked

"I've been calling you since yesterday   and last night your line was busy all night I was worried."

Noel said

"I, I must have falling to sleep early I had a long day." India said

"Well you phone was busy I stopped calling around 2 am." Noel said

"Shay must have stayed on the phone all night I'll have to talk to her about that." India said

'I got your message but I got caught up with Shay and her meeting remember I thought I told you

she came back the other day I had to find her a sponsor, I have been trying to find her a job."

"I wasn't aware that your sister came back." Noel said

"She showed up the other day I hadn't had a chance to get things together yet. "India said

"I thought I would see you when I got home I tried to make you as comfortable as possible."

 Noel said

"I know Noel that's not it I had a wonderful time and I was comfortable I guess I didn't realize how

tired I was but I was going to call you."

"I understand India, I don't mean to complain I'm very close with my family also but we just

experienced a very intimate moment I just feel like that calls for a little more consideration a quick

phone call anything."

The words Noel was speaking sound foreign to India she was use to doing things when she

 wanted and her way beside's she didn't do anything Noel didn't say another word he was already

 on edge for having such strong feeling for India he was thinking that he should jump ship. He

didn't care at this point if he drowned he was in love with a stranger whom seemed like she

does not give a damn about anything. India was also quiet she didn't know what to say she

considered what she should had done the next day how important her actions should have been.

Was this some type of test she taught school not attended school who does he think he is her

self consumed attitude kicked in. Noel had enough of the silence he could feel his emotions

were to the top he had fallen for this woman but he felt as if maybe what she needed was not him.

217

"India I've got to go to work I'll call you later if I get the chance have a good day."

Noel had ended the call India heard a dial tone she slammed the phone down onto the receiver,

"Shit I can't do anything right.' India yelled out

She realized it was now Monday morning she had went over to Noel's Friday night.

She was completely frustrated with herself she knew she needed help understanding a serious

relationship she knew Noel was a great person are so he seemed should she even bother

India got out of bed showered then left for work. She did what she does best act as though

nothing had even happened Leah called Peter's office right after work to see what time his flight

would arrive, Leah rushed to his apartment she knocked and was about to use her keys when

Peter opened his door Leah brushed past Peter bumping right into him.

"I see you made it home safe so that I could kill you." Leah said

Peter closed his front door and walked over to give Leah a kiss   she did not realize until

today that he'd kept his old condo she'd found that out through his secretary

"I've missed you sis can I get a hug." Leah said.

"Oh I'm not here for a social call big brother did you think that I wasn't going to find out Jill and I

are friends."

Peter poured himself a drink then walked over to Leah again and tried to give her a kiss she

slapped him across the face almost making him spill his drink her body started shaking. She and Peter has never so much as raised their voices to one another,

"Sis what the hell is this about tell me.' Peter said

"Jill said you been abusive to her you have hit her while she was pregnant Peter how could you,

you could have hurt your baby how would you like it if Greg hit me ?" Leah said

"I would whip his ass sis but Jill's not carrying my baby Leah." Peter said

'Look there's no excuse for losing my temper but I've told Jill along time ago that we should slow

down even separate and the next thing I know she says she's pregnant."

"Peter she told me that you choked her one night you just came home from the night club and you

 choked her why?' Leah didn't' wait for an answer

 "Then after you find out she having your baby you abuse her"

Leah sat down on the couch clinching a pillow looking to her brother for answers any answers.

"Leah I have tried to leave I tried to walk away every time if I   had been drinking that is what she is

not telling you when the arguments start.   I leave but she gets in my face talking about how I do

not love her and Jake she's right I mean the kids a good kid but it's not what I signed up for all the

nagging and lying I'm sorry I put my hands on her it will never happen again that's why I left for

good sis,

Peter's voice was getting louder and   louder

"Leah look I'm tired I had a long flight we can talk about this at another time."

He turned from the kitchen to look at Leah who was crying her eyes out,

"Leah this has nothing to do with you, you've done nothing wrong me and Jill don't belong

together simply as that now I've apologized to the both of them she and Jake, Leah I'm going to

take a shower."

Leah jumped up from the couch and yelled at Peter she wanted to address the situation right now

Jill had been thinking about calling the police.

"You have a baby coming and this is more than a woman nagging at you I know you."

Peter had a smirk on his face Leah was following him from the closet to

his suitcase then she grabbed his arm to stop him

"Look Leah let it go I mean it." Peter said

Peter took the whole suitcase and throws it in the closet then slammed the closet door.

Leah was a little startled but she kept her rage going insisting that they talk she picked up his

phone and called home to let Greg know to start dinner and start the kids homework

"Leah what did you do that for I'm not going to deal with this and I've told you Jill is not carrying my

damn baby.'

"Yeah right I would be the first to know if Jill was sleeping around."

"And you've been hurting a lot of people and I think that deserves a little bit of your time you take

advantage of my love for you and treat my friends like dirt."

"Leah look please listen to me you don't want to go beyond this point if Jill wants to bring me up

on charges then so be it I deserve it for not walking out the day she told me she was pregnant

when I know that, I cannot have any children but I have not taking advantages of anything."

"I've only tried to protect you Leah that's all I've done so please I'm sorry will talk later."

"Peter you need counseling I'll go with you any time you hit a woman especially pregnant

 something's wrong but together we can fix this I love you."

Peter stood up and poured himself another drink of vodka

"Leah we can just sweep this under the rug just like all of our other family secrets."

Look Peter I am trying not to drink before I have dinner but you are making this hard let's talk

tell me why you've done this and why you keep saying you can't have babies since when, since

why."

Peter laugher got deeper and deeper he walked over to his fireplace and started a fire he felt

a draft Leah was even more confused then when she had arrived at his place. She was getting

angry again Peter's face had turned beet red he was still laughing as he finished off his drink then

 walked into his kitchen to put in a frozen dinner, he yelled out to Leah to see if she wanted one.

"Peter you know I don't eat that crap were is the woman that cooks and cleans for you."

"I have to find a new one Jill fired Rita for some reason or another I have got to get her back

though ."

Leah looked at Peter then took him by the hand she rubbed her hand through his hair like she use to when they were kids . Peter pulled away shaking his head

"Sis it's getting late I really need a shower I just know I can't have kids to answer your question I'm

a little angry you don't believe me and I'm not a woman beater I promise." Peter said

"Then tell me why you've done this Peter why?" Leah's voice was getting   louder

"Because, because your fucking father molested me, Yeah is that what you want to hear why I

 can't get alone with any women other then India now I'm never going to have a chance with her."

Leah was fumbling around trying to pour her a drink she dropped her crystal glass when she

 jumped at the loud sound then stood still.

 Peter rushed to help her pick up the glass Leah yelled at Peter he put his hands to his head the

look in his sister's eyes he never wanted to see he walked into his dining room and punch a whole

right through the wall   his fist was still in the wall   when he noticed   Leah crying uncontrollably as

she   was still cleaning up the glass.

"That old as bastard I'm glad he's dead all his awards his achievements the way mother use to

cater to his ass as if she did not know." Peter's said

his drinks had gotten to him his hand was bleeding and

his knuckles were swelling he was losing the feeling in his hand as he poured another drink then

poured his sister one too as he looked over at her fragile face.

Leah rushed to the kitchen and picked up the dishcloth she emptied the ice tray into it, Peters

head was spinning and his words got worse.

"Peter don't you dare say that, mother, there's just no way no way she would ever hurt us I'm
sorry

Peter I'm sorry if our father hurt you," Leah rushed over to him

Your hand let me help you." Leah said

His hands were flying everywhere blood dripping onto his expensive white carpet,

"If, sis you say if, our father hurt me just like your fucking mother hurt me and you say if."

Leah reached far and smacked Peter across the face with all of her might she jumped back

quickly surprised at her behavior she instantly wished her husband was there

"You see now, you see how easy anger can make you violent that bastard told me if I told anyone

that he would go after you too and I was not going to let that happen, hell sis I think we both need

counseling but you go first." Peter laughed

"Peter this isn't funny I didn't mean it that way I'm sorry I didn't mean that of course I believe you

that's why you were always so sad I did everything to cheer you up nothing I did

was enough Peter believe me we didn't know?"

"Leah I know that you didn't know I did everything to prevent that."

He started pointing his finger while still trying to stop his hand from bleeding Leah tried to help
him

again he continued to push her away.

"But that bitch that evil bitch she knew I came in from playing outside one day and our parents were in the basement arguing like they always did once she found out she told him that she'd found a pair of my underwear they had blood in them."

Leah covered her ears she fell to her knees crying uncontrollably Peter walked over to her and pulled her hands from her ears. He was yelling at the top of his lungs throwing his vodka glass against the wall Leah jumped to the sound of the crash.

"You take your hands off of your ears you said you wanted to know you wanted to hear this so you listen I took your pain my pain and your mothers pain she knew Leah, God damn it she knew

"Ok Peter mom knew, I believe you just stop don't say any more your hand you need a doctor."

Peter fell into the wall his body sliding down slowing he put his hand to his head and noticed the blood still dripping from his hand the wall held him as he kneeled. Repeating that he was glad that the son of a bitch was dead and that he has been to his grave site many times to spit on it he was watching Leah's reaction, she could not say a word her heart was sinking as she was trying to help him stop the bleeding. She got him to his feet and into the bathroom she rinsed his hand He finally let her wrapped it with the towel then she got some more towels and wrapped it some enough to put more pressure on it Peter sat on the toilet crying Leah kneeled next to him they cried until they started to smell the TV dinner.

It was burning Peter told Leah that he was going to take this secret to his grave until he had realized

how it was haunting him it was something he thought about something   that India said to him no

matter how many times you sweep you are always going to leave a little dirt on the floor even if

there is a rug to cover it; he said

he never thought that he could love but at the wedding India was so beautiful and confident she

always has something profound to say.

Have your ever noticed that about her Leah   she didn't know were her brothers mind had

wandered she just nodded her head. He told Leah if he is going to continue in this world

That he needed two things counseling and India Leah was putting pressure on Peter's hand he

his finger's   were now swollen.

"Peter I knew that you had a crush on India but."

"Crush Leah don't be silly, we are not kids any more I knew she was special the moment I saw her

we talked the night of your wedding we connected instantly talking about things

that only people that have known each other for years talk would talk about."

" India knew secrets from both sides people think because they have money and big houses that

they can hide behind their

secrets but some how some way they surface I am a prime example. I am going to talk to her

about getting therapy there is   no need to finish mother off telling her this madness."

"Come on Peter lets get you to the hospital." Leah said

India had Shay write a note about everything that she was to do to bring and keep her life in a

better place she was going to   stay and get clean find a job and then her own place if she steals

even one penny from anyone   she is gone. India told her she needed to also attend church,
which

one would be her choice they attended church's together St. Marks a small but nice church

Shay seemed to like Paster Weber their choir was awesome. Shay and India were baptized

before they left home India thought doing that together would help them to never allow their

bond to be broken.

India's still waiting to get back the bond that she never thought could be broken she and Shay

have been back and forth all day Shay was getting calls night and day she told India she is

meeting people everywhere the bus stop on the bus India was also angry that when Shay

answered the phone she has not been taking any messages when the calls are for India

Shay just tells her sister that she does not know who but that someone called. India has asked

repeatedly   asked if Noel has called Shay said she is not sure then laughed under her breath.

"Shay I don't want any stranger's in my house and I mean that meet them somewhere else, I
don't

Even know when you have the time to meet any one any way." India said

"If I pay rent why can't I have company, don't be mad at me because your man broke your heart I

heard you crying in the middle of the night you do that a lot you know." Shay said

"First of all you don't pay rent, second it's none of your fucking business what I do in my room either let the machine take a message or you take the message can you understand that."

"Oh my goodness you're always up tight I said he called once the other day and when I do start paying rent you need to get it together." Shay said

"Then you'll be getting out."

India went into her room and slammed the door the sisterly love was taking it's time to surface she

was watching television putting the outfits away that she had brought. She wanted to slap

Shay her mind was racing she felt that Noel already judges everything that she does or does not

do and now that India has asked

Shay everyday if he has called she followed suit India turn down the television then picks up the

phone then hangs it back up wandering what she should say, she was horrible at lying and even

worst at being compassionate she did not even have anything to lie about she kicked off her

shoes then sat back on the bed she took a deep breath and

wandered why this was so hard for her to figure out India figured that she and Noel just maybe

they couldt be friends nothing last forever her room door

opened.

"Oh he said when he's not at home you can call him on his business phone."

Shay closed the door back quickly when India looked at her with vengeances a call and a message

wow India thought about how long they were going to make it living together India thought about

talking to Shay about her nightmares but she didn't want it to turn into an argument or give Shay
a

chance to unload her wrong doing on her.   India is trying to be patient especially since Shays
first

week was really ruff for her the second night she had to go to the emergency room she begged

not to be put in the treatment center over night the counselor and doctor decided to increase the

dosage on her medicine it had Shay going she was up all night talking on the phone and watching

television.

India was use to piece and quite now she wanted to cry she was startled when the phone rang

Shay

yelled out that she had it before India could make a move. This time she remembered to knock

but still opened the door before India could tell her to come in India decided to blame it on the

medication until she would not be able to it any more.

"It's him I think, do you want to talk or have me take a message." Shay said

That was it India reached down and picked her shoe up off the floor and stretch it behind her she

jumped up and released the shoe with all of her might it brazed the back of Shay's head.

"Don't come in my room again until I tell you too." India yelled

She slammed her door   India took a deep breath then picked up the phone this time she sat

in her chair and put, her feet up on the foot stool to relax herself with no time to think she spoke.

"Hello"

 Shay put the phone on the receiver   then there was   silence India

exhaled again.

"Hi India it's Noel how are you."

"Umm I'm good I was just about to call you since Shay just gave me your message a few minutes

ago." India said

"Oh, ok I know that we ended our last conversation on a bad note I just wanted to talk about that."

Noel said

"What is there to talk about we are just friends right."

"Ok I wasn't ready for that one umm I don't know how to answer that I wanted to actually get

together not talk over the phone I also wanted to invite you to my niece's birthday party Saturday

how about we meet up Friday."

"Well I'm meeting my friends we can just talk now Noel I hope you don't think that I just jump

into bed with everybody because I don't." India said

"Where did that come from India, I've have not accused you of anything." Noel said

He was trying hard to keep his composure but of course India was making it extremely hard and

since she   had no ideas who was controlling the talking for her the conversation was another disaster Noel cleared his throat several times.

"So are you feeling guilty what made you said that India."

"I just wanted to make it clear I know how guys are especially guys like you."

"Now what the hell is that suppose to mean, Look India I'm at my office still, this is not the time for

this conversation   ok." Noel said

"You said you wanted to talk then you don't, go ahead get back to work Noel goodbye."

Those word destroyed the whole mood and were left at that destroyed,

India made sure her outfit was hot to death she could not wait for school to end as much as she

loved her kids it was Friday night and she just got paid Ms. Thing was single and ready to mingle

Dena needed to be picked up since the night was especially for her going away slash

 engagement party Shay wanted to come but India only said no once she arrived at Dena's house

9 pm sharp jeans tight and a red back out that revealed much of her cleavage Dena had on a

short gold dress to die for and the shoes to match she had brought her fiancée over to India's that

Wednesday for dinner India told her he seemed very nice he was short but seemed nice he

surprised Dena with the ring that she and India had picked out at the jewelry store now India said

that   he would gain points for that because she was beginning to wander, he was back in Atlanta

and would not be back until later on that night.

"Dena why do you always have to get started before the party I mean really." India said

"Mind your business this is grown folks business you want some." Dena said

"Girl I'm driving do not make me hurt you.'

"Oh like you hurt Noel every time you talk to him." Dena said

"Now why did you have to go there we are supposed to be celebrating right."

"India I'm about to be gone hours away I can't trust Leah and Jill to fix you up and I just can't work

miracles you need to get a hold of yourself that man has it going on from head to toe and back in the day you know all I cared about was the head but we are getting older now you should want to be happy cousin, really will you at least think about it settling down please?"

"Dena are you lighting up marijuana you're the one that needs to get a grip put that out."

"Here India that is the reason your always up tight because you won't try this it's nature.' Dena said

She was a little choked up India tried to take it from her and keep focus on the road Dena blew some in India's face to distract her India rolled the window all the way down.

"Now see that's just ignorant Indy." Dena said

"Put it out girl, we are going to smell like that and you blow that in my face again and there won't be a damn wedding."

"Smelling like what, India the earth dag I'll put it out." Dena said

They arrived at Choy's a Chinese restaurant next to the QVC outlet Jill and Leah drove together India couldn't figure that out but was glad Leah hadn't told Jill anything other then Peter was getting help.   And taking care of herself for the baby should be her only concern hanging with Jill without her being able to drink was going to be interesting she was feeling her dress out really Nice.   Leah had on some dress pants and a spaghetti strap top with a short black jacket they all joked as though things have been good they missed each other they only had to wait 15 minutes for a table.

"Let the drinking begin.' Leah said

Everyone was getting along good everyone took turns rubbing Jill's stomach except India that's

when she started drinking.

"Who am I going to inhale the earth with?" Jill said

"Well the next time you will be able to smoke I'll be back for a visit." Dena said

""India said that your guy is the best and that ring is beautiful." Leah said

Dena flashed her hand around the table it was sparkling for days she got so excited talking

about the place they had found and how his sister had decided to move down to Atlanta too
India

almost dropped her drink when she thought she saw a man

that looked just like Noel she put her hand to her chest as though it had stopped.

"India who is that.' Jill noticed

India looked at Jill crazy she didn't noticed that anyone was paying attention to her

"I have no idea why."

"I thought your eyes were going to pop out your head." Jill said

"Funny Jill."

"I'm glad your in such a good mood though I missed all of us so much how is Jakey.'

India had to change her thoughts quick how could she react that way over a man she is
convinced

she should only be friends with (Lord) how does James and Florida Evans do this she was not

trying to figure it out they drank then ate   and ate then drank. Jill had several sparkling waters
she

was more than happy

She had never experience this not drinking they couldn't figure out if they were trying to bring the

sun up until the manager politely told them the restaurant had already closed a half an hour ago.

They wouldn't be able to leave a cheap tip this time but they were prepared the food was great

and Dena was happy that they had not watered down the drinks India never notices. The waiter

watched as they stumbled to their cars they gave a group hug then left promising to call each

other   once they arrived   at home. Dena talked a hole in India's head   going on and on which

reassured India that she was

truly, in love they made it to her house then Dena reminded India of her promise India reminded

Dena that she had not promised anything. Then drove off she was driving for about 10 minutes

when she realized she was in the area were Noel lived she looked at the car's clock 2:59 am by

3:10 am India was pulling into Noel parking lot. No calls no anything feeling to the top of her
game

whatever level that was India sat in the car for a few minutes "Stephanie Mills" The Power of Love

playing on the radio. India knew she did not know anything about love or having power over it,

oh how her heart felt tonight when she thought she saw Noel in the restaurant she was going for

It she took off her high heels. So she would not break her neck then slowly walked up his steps

The night air was taking the moon farther and farther away it was shining full. India rang the door bell   when the sound from the locker sound it echoed in the night air. India was not paying

attention she was all warm inside

about to ring bell the again, when she looked up Noel was at the door giving India one of

those looks she was use to giving to people she smiled then walked inside luckily he was tall she

 fit right under his arms   holding the door if he wanted to be with her then he wouldn't be here with

another woman at the same time but India was thinking if he knew any better, he would have

another woman and run as fast from India as he could ,because she didn't know what she was

doing.

"Hi, I know it's late but,"

"It's not just late, its morning and it's down right rude what are you doing here." Noel said

"I came to see you of course no need for you to be rude."

"India if I wanted to be rude, Look I'm asking a simple question do you have an answer." Noel's

voice got a little louder

"Well do you feel better after saying that I was in the neighborhood and I stopped by that's all I

wanted to know what time your niece's party was?" India said

India was standing with her arms crossed and patting her foot, Noel was rubbing his face India

could not believe how good he looked his silk shirts fit just right he decided to close the door and

turn on his lamp on his end table his condominium was nice he said his niece that he has raised since she was 5 years old. She helped decorate Noel's place he still had albums in their original

covers   they were all kept well and for playing

in mint condition stacked on a wall with a built in book shelf his sofa's was Italian leather a

butter pecan color he had expensive art and beautiful vases with a chandelier at the top of his

staircase that lead to his room.

"You act like you didn't even hear me when I invited you now you come over in the middle of the

night I mean morning to ask me now you want to talk India have you been drinking again?"

"What does that have to do with anything what time is the party."

"India the party starts at 7pm and it has everything to do with it I had to get up really early and I

just got back into town three hours ago."

"So you wouldn't been able to meet today any way you had to go out of town so what's the big

deal.' India said

"Ha ha India are you playing with me is this some kind of joke are there TV camera's or

something."

Noel continued to laugh which upset India to no end she did not know what to say she wanted

to curse him out how dare he laugh at her she thought as good as she looked she grabbed her

purse off the table then walked toward the door she tried to push Noel from in front of the door.

"Noel I'm not going to keep chasing you I've had enough of this shit I am leaving can you please

move?"

"Now you want to ask, a minute ago you were trying to push me out of the way in my own house."

"I know whose house this is Noel, you don't have to worry about me again excuse me."

They looked at each other India had a tear in her eye and she couldn't hold it much longer she was use to making herself invisablel but when she would get past angry tears would always follow. She turned away he turned her back she hesitated but looked back up at him his eyes looked as though he could save India's soul but she knew that could not come true Noel was not sure still trying to find the same look in India eyes she did not want him to see what was inside of   her the   emptiness. So she rubbed up against him then pushed her lips against his

for an automatic kiss he slowing put his hands to her face he asked why she was doing then she rubbed through his soft hair then his felt his skin she kiss his lips and their kiss became intense

Noel pushed away from the door

then picked India up they were all over the couch when India almost kicked over his vase he jumped up to catch it as it was spinning he took a deep breath then up on the couch.

"India I think you need some water to bring down your high. "

"But I'm not drunk."

Noel was already in the kitchen before India could blink she jumped up and followed he needed time to think about what he was doing and whom he was doing it with but he had ran out of time she was behind him at the refrigerator door.

"Here drink this.'

"I don't want that I want you."

"Are you like this when you haven't been drinking?"

"I don't know probably not, all that matters is right now.' India said

Noel picked India up and slowly placed her on the counter he slowly moved between her legs unbuttoning her shirt and slowly pouring water on India from her neck on down the water was cold. It made her shiver he unfastened the one snap in the front of India bra he could see her nipples were on point through her red lace bra the water was sliding down Noel bent down and started to lick the water off of India the warmth from his tongue. Made India's blood rush through her vein's she hold on to Noel tight until the ride was over Noel carried India upstairs into his warm bedroom he had his ceiling fan turning slowly just the way India liked it he carried her into the master bedroom then into the bathroom that led to his walk in shower with stain glass doors. They steamed within seconds the smog filled the large bathroom India was enjoying herself he washed her entire body from head to toe including her hair then she did the same they finished they laid in his bed King size bed India just closed her eyes neither one of them said a word. Noel had India wrapped in his arms so tight she had to keep adjusting her head she thought she could do her usual watching the ceiling fan turn around and around but she couldn't sleep the moon light was shining through the big picture window. India didn't know what it was but she couldn't sleep all of a sudden tears started rolling down her face she finally got one of his strong arms free from around her the tears became so heavy that wiping them away no longer helped thoughts were racing through India's head something's she couldn't even decipher. She tried to take deep breaths but that made the tears came even harder she felt almost like she was about to lose control she slowly wormed her way out of his arms glad that he was a sound sleeper. India rushed into the

bathroom and rinsed her face with cold water in the dark hoping that it would help calm

her from whatever her mind was erupting. She left the bathroom and quickly gathered her

clothes and put them on she looked over at Noel he had not moved she looked around in

the dark. Looking for something to write him a note with she didn't take long looking she

didn't want to wake him up so India grabbed her shoes and rushed down the carpeted

stairs like someone was after her she looked for her purse then she left his house barefoot

locking his bottom lock behind her.

India called Noel as soon as she woke up he didn't answer she was going to leave a

message but Leah called on the other line she wanted to know if India had spoken to

Peter India reminded Leah that she was going to stay out of things. India had advised

Jill as best as she could thinking to herself if Peter lays another hand on Jill she needed to

have him arrested. She reassured India that Peter had started seeing a Therapist they hung

up and India headed out Dena was leaving in two days and India had to meet the person

who was renting them the hall for the wedding slash going away party. Shay put the

phone down and jumped off the couch then went to the door she looked out the peep hole

the manager had finally put lights in hallway. Shay did not hesitate opening the door even

though all she was wearing was a tee shirt and her panties she looked at the man and after

he asked for India. She knew actually who he was she directed him into the apartment and said she would check to see if India was at home because she wasn't her keeper Shay had already watched India leave out. All most an hour ago she knocked on India's closed door then opened It and walked inside as though India was there she walked into her bathroom that was inside her room look in the mirror and quickly looked through India's drawer for some lip gloss. Then glossed her lips and went back into the living room Shay closed the door back and told Noel that India must have stepped out for a minute and would be right back she walked over to the end table and bend down so that whatever wasn't already showing to Noel would now be

 completely she slowly stood back up looking behind her for Noel eyes but he was looking down at the floor even as he talked.

"Well since she's not here I'll just come back.'

"She must be expecting you because she doesn't like unwanted guess so you might as well wait for her unless your uncomfortable being alone with me. Shay said

"Your right India doesn't like surprises so I'll call her later.' Noel said

He quickly head for the door Shay rushed behind him then in front of him before he hit the door they were so close Shay could feel his breath on top of her head she looked up at Noel lust written all over her.

"I know my sister's jive self isn't half the woman that you probably need for a small price I can give you what I know she is not she is to perfect to be a real woman."

Noel took Shay's hands from his chest and firmly moved her from in front of the door he had no idea what or why this was happening but he wanted no parts of it.

 "Young lady I'll call your sister later."

Noel left without another word Shay laughed it off he was not fooling anybody she went back to watching television and talking on the phone,

Dena's wedding party went off without a glitch she and Victor looked so happy he catered to Dena the whole night they weren't going to have time for a honeymoon by their life was destined for fun and excitement Leah and Greg brought them china Jill purchase them double spa visits at a hot spot in Atlanta. India   brought them a new dinette set for their kitchen she couldn't think of anything else Dena had a small dinette set India spend a pretty penny a week had past and   much to India's surprise her mother had left a message saying she'd be in town for her brothers birthday party. She said that she and Shay could come if they wanted the call distracted India she missed Dena already but her happiness was more then enough for India to try and move on with her life she promised Dena she would try harder to make a life for herself stay out of the clubs unless Dena was in town. It was Saturday and the only thing on India's mind was making it to Mindy's party Noel's niece   she convinced herself she should be there no matter what she showed up a half hour late. India had to pick up her gift and it took two hours to pick it out the way Noel went on about her she had to be special India picked her out a designer purse a Louis Vuitton purse India didn't even have one for herself she didn't care about name brand only nice things.   India was not sure about it because it was an expensive gift but she brought it anyway had it gift-wrap and ended up at Noel's door an older woman answered India shook her hand and told the woman her name.

"Hi my name is India I'm here for Mindy's party."

India's hands were shaking she couldn't remember the last time she'd attended something by herself   she remembered it was Toshiba's wedding this was nothing like that the condo was full of people and after the woman directed her in she didn't see a familiar face Noel was no where in sight India tried to mingle. She hopped out the chair and stood to her feet when she saw Noel enter from what she remembered to be the kitchen. She started over his way he stopped in his tracks when he saw her she smiled and gave him a big hug he stepped back from her then gave her a look as though he did not know her India took a deep breath and gave him a respond.

"Hi Noel, your house is full I didn't know it would be a party like this where is your niece Mindy I have a gift for her."

"India what are you doing here.' Noel said

"What do you mean you invited me Noel why would you say that?" India said

She had a confused look on her face even more confused then Noel's look he grabbed her gently by her arm and directed her into the downstairs bathroom once they were both inside he closed and locked them inside.

"What are you doing here?"

"Ok Noel I give, why do you keep asking me that how many niece's do you have you invited me to your   nieces birthday party and I'm here, I know I'm a little late but why are you tripping I'm mean really?'

"You leave my bed in the middle of the night after you swear you were ready for   a relationship, but my fault I should have known that alcohol speaks for you."

"Ok I'm not sure why you think I deserve that I was going to leave you a note but I couldn't find anything to write with it was dark."

Noel walked closer to India he did not trust himself at this point a week has past his thoughts were racing he was now convinced that she was playing him and any guy that would allow her too to do so. India could see the smoke coming from him eyes but she had done the right thing she called him first thing the next morning she had no intention of explaining her emotions because she still didn't understand them herself all she knew was she felt like she wanted to be with him.

"You know I am done chasing you India I've had enough this is not some kind of one night stand I'm tired of trying to get you to see this really I am, what are you trying to do to me." Noel said

"I'm not trying to do anything Noel, I called you the next morning I tried to do the right thing I just could not stay the night you were sleeping so good I did not want to wake you that is all.

"I'm not playing any games nor am I trying to hurt you and I'm not playing games with anyone else I told you that."

"Then what are you India who are you do you even know.'

Without just cause tears filled India's eyes she did not know how to respond she didn't swear to him a commitment but she did promise to try and she felt like that is was what she had been doing. With being at the party dealing with Dena leaving then Shay the fact her mother was coming when they have not had any type of relationship in God knows how long. There was no excuse but at this point in her life that is what controlled her life she did not know how to include Noel India looked down at the bathroom floor it was polished extremely clean she could almost see her reflection once again she was focus on the wrong things she tried to open the bathroom door to leave.

"Here we go India's big escape should I take the door off the hinges for you or would opening it for you be enough?'

Noel's voice was loud and by this time India only wanted to respond with violence she wanted to whip Noel's ass right now and at this point, she always felt she would win but leaving would be less dramatic and would not ruin his niece's party. She knew the way he talked about her that she was top priority right now and she had no intention's on ruining that it was the first thing he shared with India the night they talked about how he has been taking care of Mindy. The majority of her life Noel's sister Olivia had Mindy while she was in college she attended Harvard University for law in her third year of making straight A's she met Mindy's dad. He was in his last year before graduate school an Italian guy with strong values he had deep brown eyes with dimples in his smile Olivia had not dated but one person in college. Since she had started at Harvard they broke up because he did too much partying Brian did not do anything fancy just be himself that is what Olivia liked about him they met in study hall. He was also in law he spoke to her the first day that he saw Olivia her silky brown skin was irresistible to him he told her that he could get any girl. But he wanted a girl with confidence that did not need to show it he loved her natural brown skin and silky black shoulder length hair. Even though he knew he, could never take Olivia home to meet his parents even though she also came from an upper class family her father owned his own construction company until he merged with the fourth largest company. That was in the south even though her mother didn't have to work she became a proud pediatrician but her parents had struggles but would settle for nothing less for their children other then a college education she wanted to make use of their sweat and tears her parents are now both retired.   Brian was head over hills after a month of dating after the third month of dating

Olivia was overwhelm with studies she never drank nor did drugs but trying to keep up with the first man she thought she loved. She surrendered when Brian offered her valium then she agreed to acid and then came   cocaine she didn't know what hit her she was far from home so it was easy to say she couldn't come home and that everything was fine. She would say that she had a class or she needed to get a paper done everyone had always been so proud of Olivia they never thought a thing their fifth month of dating and drugs she found out she was pregnant. Olivia went to tell Brian at his dorm she did not think to knock she just walked into his room when she entered she saw three women on top of him. Then she noticed his roommates laughing   she yelled out his name he turned around and offered for   Olivia to join them Olivia ran down the hall and out of the building, she never told anyone. Brian ended up a few days later in jail something about possession of controled substance his parents told him that they weren't going to spend another dime on Brian unless he went into rehab this would be his second time. Since his junior year in high school, he did not tell Olivia one of the women he had been dating along with her had told Olivia that she had been kicked out of school also while dating Brian. Then months later Olivia could know longer take care of her appearance she was now living in a shelter she did not know what she was going to do. She felt that she could not tell her family that she was having a baby by someone that   did not care if she or her baby existed although she had stop using drugs even though she wanted to do drugs everyday. She did not have a plan she promised herself for the babies sake that she would not use any drugs while pregnant then she went into labor at the shelter at 8 months an ambulance rushed her to the local hospital. They rushed her into the hospital labor delivery they asked her if she wanted any of her family to be with her, she gave them her parents contact information. But only in case of an emergency Olivia delivered her baby the baby was 4 pounds 2 ounces and two days later after the nurse put the baby back in the incubator Olivia asked if her baby would be healthy and if she would be alright the doctor reassured her that the baby was a healthy happy beautiful baby her lungs and heart was doing fine. Later that day Olivia got dressed and walked out of the hospital's front doors three days later they used the emergency contact information and Olean and her husband Neil along with Noel were there immediately taking the baby. They did not even know existed they hired a private investigator to find Olivia never looking in a place that a dope fean would be one day the investigator walked right passed Olivia. Giving out flyers with her picture on it the detective handed her one and never looked back she was no longer the high school beauty prom queen that covered the flyer. Noels parents kept The baby they named her Mindy after Olean's mother for her first three years then Olean got down sick Noel stepped in even he had been close all along he saw after his mother for a week then he drove back home and has taken care of his niece every since hoping and praying for the day he could do the same for his older sister.

India jumped when she heard the knock on the bathroom door it was hard as though whoever it was had been knocking for a while.

"Noel are you in there, your dad and Mindy are on there way up they are getting out of the car." Mrs. Olean said

"Ok mom be right out is everything ready."

"Well no thanks to you this last half hour get out here son use it later.' Mrs. Olean said

Noel could know longer respond to India he had to gather his composure she looked down at the floor she walked around him and gathered some tissue. She pat her eyes saying nothing she could not walk past all those people now if they see her coming out of the bathroom.

"If you want me to leave I will without a scene I don't want to upset you any more." India said

"I can't deal with this shit right not I'll leave out first you do what you want." Noel said

The lights were out the curtain were closed Ned took awhile to get up the steps and his precious granddaughter waited every step they lived two hours away and never missed a birthday he took her too the mall to get whatever she picked out at   tiffany's her favorite store.

"Surprise."

The lights came on India had blended into the crowd thinking how she could escape she maneuver around stopping when she saw Noel's eyes on her she was almost to the door when she bumped right into someone.

"Well hello beautiful girl how are you?" Ned said

"Hello, Um I'm fine."

"You sure are, are you one of my granddaughters friends."

India's eyes widened out of all the people in the room she runs right into Noels father if it wasn't for bad luck she wouldn't have any at all.

"Uh sort of I was invited to her party, here can you give her this gift for me please." India asked

Ned pushed India alone toward the middle of the party were Mindy was greeting everyone mostly Noel friends and   family.

"You can tell her yourself pretty girl, hey princess I found a friend of yours what did you say your name is."

It seemed like everyone in the room's eyes were on India they were all smiles waiting on her response including Noel he was loving this for once India was stuck no where to run nowhere to hide she had to answer this question Noel could see the sweat forming on her brow.

"India.'

"I'm sorry honey what did you say."

"My name is India hi everyone."

India gave a quick wave then walked up to Mindy and handed her the gift wanting to smack Noel for not attempting to save her.

"Did you say India, Hi I'm Mindy I'm so glad you could make it.'

Mindy hugged India for dear life India was patting her back waiting for her to release   so that everyone could get back to the party it seemed like the hug was forever. It's nice to meet you she introduced India to everyone they were confused as to who she was but Mindy knew actually who she was. Noel just stood their ignoring his father who kept asking where Mindy knew her from he told him he'd explain later. It was time to eat and that he needed a drink Ned   agreed they both headed to Noel's stash to make him a stiff one and sneak his father a taster he wasn't suppose to drink. He had some trouble with his heart and Olean would kill him they went out on the deck so that Noel could fill his dad in on the woman that he thought he had in his life.

Everyone ate and drank from the lower dose stash Noel made available   Mindy was acting as though she'd known India all of her life showing her pictures and things that she picked out for the house India followed as Mindy talked and talked   both telling each other how pretty the other one was Mindy looked just like Noel's mom. Beautiful light brown skin Noel had his fathers complexion strong cocoa brown   Olivia had to be just as pretty from the pictures Mindy showed her. India couldn't tell them apart the last pictures they had was Olivia going off to college Mindy was told Olivia left her with them and some day she would find her way home. All she has been through a person would never think Mindy wanted for anything she loves her mother and was glad she was able to be left with the most wonderful family in the world. India never saying a word about her attempted departure it was obvious that Noel had not bad mouth her. Mindy was turning 20 years old Noel couldn't be more proud she had to practically beg so that she could attend where her uncle attended   being so far away they never figured out where they went wrong with Olivia and they were not willing to take losing anyone else. But they never could say no to Mindy so they make a strict list to call every Sunday she and Noel spoke every Wednesday she had to come every holiday and birthday no exceptions. Also three weeks during the summer if she felt overwhelm she would immediately get a tutor no matter the cost and if she met someone she wanted to become serious with they had to under no circumstances know about him and his family. Mindy respected and agreed to their extended demands she only knows her mother never finished or returned from college. She has visit several times and the last time was when Mindy was around 10, she does not remember much other then her telling the family that she was ashamed and that it was not time for her to return they didn't know any other way to protect her.   India excused herself from Mindy to go to the restroom India barely made it before her sadness over came her again she'd never seen such love and even though Olivia has broken their hearts they still love her unconditionally and are waiting patiently for her to come home.

India was amazed how pleasant Mindy was she didn't even know her she's mention more than once she could see why her uncle choose to speak to her the day that they met. And that she knows that their relationship is brand new but just like her uncle Mindy told India she knows she is the one with all the gold diggers he's met in their fancy clothes and nice cars model bodies none of them worked any where though their riches were from the men who cared for them. She says her uncle is a busy well educated man with a plan and he and Mindy needed someone to share their lives with, It totally freaked India out that this young lady almost the same age as Shay and they are like night and day. India couldn't understand how Mindy had so much trust for Noel and her relationship especially since India has done nothing to earn it she looked in the mirror her eyes looking back at her Noel had ask if she even knew who she was it hurt to know that it was a fare question to ask . And that she didn't have the time to answer she freshen up and returned to the party Mindy told India that she wanted to show her, Her bedroom she had   some music that she knew India would love.

"You think we should leave the party Noël might not like that."

"I'll handle my uncle."

Mindy closed the door to her room it was decorated as if she was still 10 years old she said her mother slept with her in her bed and she won't change it until her mother returns.

"I don't mean to bombard you India you've taken a lot of pressure off me since you and my uncle met and for some reason you two have barely spoken lately, And he hasn't introduced you to anyone trust me I watch him like a hawk too I'm not letting you go anywhere   India how can I help.'

If India was overwhelmed with Noel this was round two her mouth could not move,

Mindy was staring her straight in her eyes.

"Lawyer right." India said

"Huh.'

"You must be going to school to be a lawyer or attorney."

"My uncle tells me you don't believe in love at first sight.'

"No Mindy I'm afraid I don't its called lust.'

"What if you hadn't done anything with the person then what is it called.'

"Wait a minute are we talking about me are you Mindy where's the music you have for
me to hear?" India asked

Mindy flapped down on the bed next to India her demeanor became tense she was
looking around her room,

"I love my room what about you India, I love your name by the way who gave it to you
were you born there." Mindy said

"No I'm not sure really my father named me I guess one day I'll have to ask him."

"Well India there is this guy and I've broken one of my families request and it wasn't
right of me to do, I made a promise to my family they love me and they give me
everything that I need my friends that have two parent household's envy me can you
believe that India."

"Yes I can I envy you Mindy, Are you going to tell me his name.'

" I know that your an A student what else could it be if not a guy.' India said

"India I think that I'm in love first sight he's so sweet he treats me special and he wants
to be in my life I just don't know how to tell my family.'

"Just do it you're a beautiful young lady they have to know you were going to meet someone eventually Mindy."

"It's not that simple."

"Why, Is he too old for you what is it maybe you should be talking to your grandparents or Noel this is a touchy one.'

"I know, I know and trust me I don't mean to burden you but you are what we need in our life someone they doesn't think that she has to protect me but could just be there for me talk to me don't get me wrong I know that I can talk to them but I, I."

"I know what your saying Mindy someone like a mother or big sister someone you can share things more than a diary."

They both laughed Mindy gave India a hug tears were in her eyes it didn't take but a second for India to share and relate she wished her sister felt what Mindy desired she knew so well that it hurt her heart Mindy continued talking.

"He dropped out of community college his junior year his families not rich."

"Why did he drop out?"

"To help care for his son he's two years old and Sean is an amazing father India really he works with his father that owns his own heating and cooling business he says when his father retires the business will be his India he's smart he's funny he's ,"

"Hold on hold it, Mindy I think this is something you should be talking to your family about I'm sure they will trust your judgment." India tried to reassure her again

There was a quiet knock at the door then it opened,

"There you are why are you guys hiding up here away from the party sweetie, we haven't met I don't think I'm Mrs. Olean Mindy's grandmother where did you too meet."

Mindy look at India then stood and hugged her grandmother she had not given India a chance to answer her question about why she and her uncle were acting distance but she was determined to have India in theirs lives so she did her uncle's job for him.

"Grandma this is India she uncles friend and he invited her to my party so that we can all meet."

Mrs. Olean gave India a confused looked wandering why she'd just been told her only son had someone special in his life that wasn't like Noel India quickly noticed the look on his mothers face. She extended her hand for her to shake and waited for Mrs. Olean to respond Noel never mention that his parents would be at the party but how could they have missed it India knew as far as his family is concerned first impressions can't be changed

India gave her one of her best smiles she had know idea how to fit in to a family like this let alone begin to blend her broken family aboard.

"Honey in this family we don't shake hands we give hugs.'

She gave India a hug that only a mother could it filled India's heart Mrs. Olean held on until she felt India exhale.

"It's nice to meet you India what a pretty name for such a beautiful young lady I must talk to my son about not mentioning you there has been a lot going on how are you.'

"I'm great we haven't known each other for long only a couple months we both have busy schedules so we haven't gotten to see each other much." India said nervously

"Oh, what do you do for a living?"

"She a school teacher she teachers 2nd grade isn't that wonderful.'

"Miss Mindy I think she's capable of talking herself and how do you know so much about her and Pa and I know nothing."

"Well I kind of did some investigation myself   then I pried it out of him you know he can't keep anything a secret Grandma."

"A teacher huh that's wonderful are you married do you have any children."

"No ma'am and only the ones in my classroom.' India said

"Well do you want to get married or have children?" Mrs. Olean said

"I don't think I want children but maybe married one day when I'm about 50 years old." India said

Mindy laughed Mrs. Olean figured that means India couldn't be after her son for money she was not after her son for anything from the look on his mother's face   India felt like e she should have thought out her answer instead of being so blunt fully truthful.

They joined the party downstairs people were starting to draft off India told Mindy and Mrs. Olean she should probably be heading home too. Mrs. Olean disagreed so India joined them in the kitchen to help clear things away. Ned and Noel were feeling pretty good   which made him relax he was feeling uncomfortable the way Mindy was latching on to India. He didn't want her breaking Mindy's heart too India thinks he rolled his eyes several times at her she mentioned out loud that Mrs. Olean insisted she stay a little longer then she was convinced Noel was rolling his eyes he was thinking not his mother too.

"Yes, young man you have some explaining to do you didn't tell me you were seeing anyone."

"Come on now sweetie, there is a game on and it in the 4th quarter lets us know if you'll need any help.' Ned said

Noel and his father quickly exited the kitchen and India quickly wandered what Noel had told his father. After finishing everything they talked in the kitchen when India noticed the time 11pm. Mrs. Olean said it was well past her bed time but was having a good time she gave India another hug she could tell after awhile that India would need some work but that she could be the one she knew that no one had ever pushed her sons buttons like this woman was doing . It got time for her to turn in Mrs. Olean left out of the kitchen to Mindy and India talked for a few more minutes Mindy told India she would check her uncle. About his behavior India declined the offer to Mindy should enjoy their time together.   Mindy asked India to consider talking to Noel about the love in her life India just smiled as they walked into the living room India announced quietly that she was leaving Ned jumped up to give her a hug he whispered into India's ear that his son was the right one then kissed her on the cheek. India did not respond she asked Noel to walk her to her car he hesitated then started toward the door they were slowly walking to the car not saying a word to one another   he stopped at the sidewalk then India stopped too. When she noticed his footsteps had stopped she turned to face him he was looking good as usually in the moon light. She was repeating over and over in her mind that she should say something she looked up at him he looked away with his hands in his pockets. India walked over to him she reached up and put her hands to his face she wanted so bad to confess to Noel everything she had held up inside for such a long time.   Why she leaves his home in the middle of the night it is because she is afraid to have a nightmare so many things were racing through her mind, she wanted to just run.

"I had a great time, your family is more wonderful then you said they were kind of wandering why we didn't talk much or why you hadn't told them much about me."

"As long as you know the reason India, that's all that matters right I'm not going to force this any more are chase you India and I'm definitely not going to let you hurt my family." Noel stated

India stepped back off the sidewalk then rushed to her car she fumbled through her purse for her keys she looked back over at Noel,

"I'm not trying to hurt you or your family Noel really I'm not and your not chasing me because I'm not running, I don't deserve for you to talk to me this way."   India yelled out

"Then what do you deserve India why did you come just to run away again.'

"I'm not running away the parties over right goodnight Noel."

India rushed off Noel stood their for awhile watching her until he couldn't   see her car anymore then went inside he gave his parents his room he went into his small room were he work from home to set up a fold away bed he was so upset that he went right to sleep.

India's mind was racing she kept remembering what Mrs. Olean said repeatedly.

"Never let your circumstances hinder your ability to live a full life."

India knew she didn't know anything about that are she wouldn't be still having nightmares for almost 11 years ago she wouldn't let her mother are Shay push their guilt trip on her any longer. And she definitely would be able to see that Noel wasn't anything like Bobby, Or was he she's sure her mother Sharon thought the world of him too until she fell in love with him and he started treating her like a piece of trash.

India got home Shay was doing her usually every light on in the house music and the television and unfinished food still sitting on a plate she was on the phone. India didn't have the strength to get into it with her right now she headed for her room and closed the door as soon as she put her purse down and took off her shoes Shay yelled out in a loud voice.

"India some dude's on the phone he says his name is Peter he sounds cute you want to talk to him." Shay said

"He sounds cute yeah Shay I have it hang up.'

"Hello"

"Hey India it's me Peter sorry I'm calling so late but I've be calling all day can I see you."

"I don't know Peter so much has gone on I'm not trying to choose sides."

"It's not like that India you know me I started counseling."

"No Peter I don't know you I would never believe you would beat on a woman then deny your baby."

"India please, please I need to see you you're my only friend right now."

India could hear the desperation in his tone,

"Ok when Peter."

"Right now is good I'm outside your apartment I needed to see you." Peter said

"Peter what are you doing outside my apartment."

"Trying to see you please can I come up is that your friend that answered."

"No she's my sister she been in town for awhile look I'll come down for just a minute." India said

India left out ignoring Shays remark about a booty call she saw Peter sitting in his BMW across the street she waited for the cars to pass Peter was about to get out of the car to assist but she had   already made it across he already had the car door opened. India got inside Peter was all smiles he immediately reached over and grabbed India up into a big hug she embraced him back he kissed India on the lips she leaned back

"Hello to you too Peter it's really late."

"I'm sorry but I had to see you and explain things."

"You don't owe me anything Peter you owe it to Jill she' carrying your child." India said Peter turned to face India he turned his music down he only listen to jazz he said he didn't like getting caught up in someone else's words he took India's hand into his,

"India I'm not a woman beater I didn't just haul off and hit Jill yes I'm a man but I tried to walk away every time Jill, she just grabs me back pulls my hairs slaps me whatever she wants. I'm not going to call the police and say that this woman is beating me I have no right to strike back I know that I guess she was bringing things out of me that could only come out that way did Leah tell you about our talk."

"She told me the two of you finally talked and that it was successful you were going to counseling, Peter no one thinks its ok for a woman to hit a man it's no different both parties are accountable for their actions and are wrong."

 "I'm sorry the both of you had to go through this neither of you deserve it but we don't always get what we deserve." India said

"India that's why it was important for me to see you, You always know the right things to say that's why I love you and I don't want to loose you India I started counseling."

"She thinks I should find a person that I trust to confide it you know a shoulder to lean on not to be holding things inside and you were the first person I thought of you would like her India she is good."

"Well what about Leah you're very close to your sister."

"I love my sister but I'd rather share this experience about the therapist with you I have got a card for you you've been talking about seeing someone." Peter said

"Yeah I did I don't know if this is a good time for me or my pocket book but thank you though Peter."

"Well I could help you with the cost India that's no problem."

"Peter I couldn't let you do something like that I'll keep his card though Dr. Torres huh." India said

"Ok just let me know." Peter said

"So what are some of the things you guys talk about?" India asked

"Well, you of course."

"Come on Peter be for real your not going to counseling because of me."

"That's true but getting to know you and becoming very fond of you I know now that I can love that I want to love and I hope it is with a woman exactly like you if it can't be you."

"But Peter I know that you have close friends I've met them not the brightest group but none the less."

Peter laughed,

"See India that's what I'm talking about you make me laugh I've even cried."

"You were mad that your team had lost the World Series."

"Doesn't matter a cry is a cry and yes I have buddies but again there are things I can't tell them they have their own life's their own wives, girls toys kids."

"You mean that jerk that I met likes girls I couldn't tell." India said

"You are calling him a jerk."

"Duh and he didn't notice me now that's odd."

"India he noticed you trust me but just because he is black doesn't mean anything though he only dates Caucasian women."

"Oh ok now I feel better." India said

"Well, Peter I'm here for you but we've been talking for hours I promised myself Shay and I are going to church in the morning would you like to go." India said

"Ha Ha I haven't gotten that far into counseling yet maybe next time I promise."

"Don't make promises you can't keep I have to go."

Peter followed India to the door,

"May I have a goodnight hug pretty lady?'

"Oh you're going to ask this time and its morning the crack of dawn Peter.'

India fused as she gave Peter a hug as usual he hung on for dear life then he backed up and watched her until she was out of sight waving at the last window India showered and with two strokes of the ceiling fan   she was out.

Mindy refused to leave back for school until India and her Uncle talked he refused to approach the situation head on first   neither saying why   so they agreed to dinner

Mindy's treat they were to meet after work at the restaurant India had a parent conference that ended at 7 pm. She put her dozen red roses in the back seat then headed for the restaurant they had not talked for a week India had her hair done and had a new outfit on she even got her eyebrows arched even though the stylist said they were already perfect. Channel number 5 perfume her tight black leather skirt and leather jacket with a with a white and black poke a dot silk tank top. India spotted Noel's car he stood when she arrived at the table then handed her a dozen pink roses they were both trying to ignore how good the other one looked but their expressions told it all the waitress broke the ice saying that they made a good couple then asking what they were drinking. Noel said ladies first India ordered a Sex on the Beach then Noel order Hennessey and coke they said they would need a few more minutes to order.

"Thank you so much for the flowers so did your parents get back safe?"

"Yes thank you for asking."

"And your feisty niece Mindy?" India said

"Ha ha Noel laughed yeah she is growing into a new character for sure I can see how she's so drawn to you." Noel said

"Is that a good thing or bad thing?' India asked

"I haven't been able to figure it out a man can only take so many beat downs before he's out for the count for good.' Noel said

"What do you want to know?" India asked

"I don't really know right now I mean it is great seeing you but it doesn't seem like your for the right thing India, we are not headed in the same direction you have everything going for you and your building it all just to be alone I didn't think anyone wanted to be alone.'

The first thing India had to get use to was Noel being so blunt a quality they both shared but not received by either of them she was only use to man that were blunt while talking a whole bunch of nothing. Noel was straight forward just like India she knew what they had in common but she also knew their differences.

"I, I want those things Noel I'm a honest good woman I don't set out to hurt anyone I'm trying,"

"That's the thing India what is it that your trying to do you give yourself to me and then you run and then you react to me like I'm the one running what are you running from." Noel was in rare form he was not cutting any corners free from all this madness as good a time as any to escape,

"What do you want from me Noel?"

"Is there anything that your willing to give India because if there is then I want your heart I want your love I want you to be my woman, then my fiancée then my wife the mother of my children."

He finished his drink then ordered another Noel was by far a heavy drinker that was another thing that scared him about India she was bringing out unusual qualities in him India had not finished her first. He stared at India hard and serious he waited patiently for a response for a few minutes.

"Now are you willing to share that with a simply man like me India Hype are or you seeing someone else."

"No."

"Huh, she talks the floor is yours." Noel said

"I want to be your woman but we should still take things slow just because your so bold and out spoken doesn't mean everyone else should be."

"India you know how many times you've told me to kiss your ass or told me the type of woman I must be use to being around be for real."

"I am for real I am just saying I don't want kids ever and marriage is a big step things should be taken slow."

"Ok India I'm willing to take things slow but only with a commitment from you about our relationship your right marriage and kids in a year or two there's no rush for that as long as I no longer have to chase you or pry things out of you."

" I want to know everything about you your mother your father your always talking about your kids at school and your friends I want to know   your likes dislike you have to want to let me in."

India didn't answer his questions until she had finished her second drink and they had started their meal."

"Yes I can give you a commitment   there are things that won't be easy for me to share with you I've been thinking about going to a Therapist."

They were interrupted the man walked right up to India with his fork still in his hand he reached down to hug her then wipe a piece of rice off her lip with his hands.

"Hey babe you're a popular woman more rose's he didn't know your favorite color though is this who you were meeting after work."'

Peter looked over at Noel who's   veins were about to pop out of his head he extended his hand to Noel he wiped his mouth on a napkin then was modestly looking at India for a response without a handshake India picked up her drink and took a sip.

"Noel this is Peter and I'm sorry I   do not know your name ."

"Oh this is a good friend Cindy and this is the beautiful India and her friend I'm sorry what did you say your name is again."

Peter acted as if they bumped into each other but after he brought India a dozen   roses to work after school he said he wanted to thank her for being such a good friend they were her favorite color she thanked him and told him there friendship was for free. While rushing out she mentioned she was meeting a friend at Chow Miens she did not have time to remember the coincidence with all of Peters boldness the woman he introduced gave Peter a strange look when he referred to her as a friend since he has been seeing her for a month.

Noel stood while extending his hand he and Peter were neck and neck 6 ft 2 inches neither budged

"Hello Cindy, Peter is it I'm Noel Hardman India man it's very nice to meet her friends wont you'll join us."

"Man, huh she didn't mention that the other night,   no thanks we're getting something to go so we'll see you guys later."

"But we're already eating   Peter.'

"Not any more let's go.' Peter walked ahead of the his friend

Noel sat back down the waitress was cleaning off some of the dishes he did not wait until she was finished.

"Ok what the hell was that about is he the reason we have to go so slow."

"No Noel it's not what you think Peter is Leah's brother remember one of my best friends.'

"No India I don't know I haven't met any of your friends and how does being Leah's brother give him a pass to be a rude and arrogant ass hole isn't he the one you mentioned hit one of your friends.'

"Sssh, gosh Noel I don't know what was going on with Peter he's been going through something's I don't know exactly know what   though I'll talk to him later sorry.'

"It sounds like you have already been talking to him   more than enough at least more than my roses and his comment about what you didn't tell him the other night."

"We're just friends Noel, and my friends want to meet you that's no problem."

"So how long did you'll date."

"We didn't date we've gone out and hung out as friends like I said.'

"India you've got to be naive as hell if you think that man wants to just be friend with you I mean if you truly believe that then I'm sorry but I'm telling you as a man a friends is not what is on his mind.'

 "Excuse me, I've told him we are friends and he respects that I'm not naïve."

"Look lets not ruin a perfectly good evening lets finish the night showing each how much we missed each please India." Noel pleaded

A week went by fast Tuesday night was suppose to be a late night for India at school but she finished tutoring and her weekly meetings on time that some of the teachers had on Tuesdays early all she wanted was a shower then straight to bed between trying to spend time with Noel which never wanted to come over

to India's house and never giving a reason why.   They had dinner at Leah's house

Sunday with Greg and the kids after church Noel and Greg clicked immediately Leah wanted to marry them on the spot the union felt so comfortable for some reason. India was a nervous wreck because Leah would not let her help cook and because she never cared about what her man thought about her friends and visa versa this time she did. Jill felt fat so she didn't make it India promised to stop by to check on her later the kids were jumping around asking Noel over and over who he was he laughed then they laughed. Greg took great pleasure in showing off his finished basement their big screen television with surround sound a pool table and two big lazy boys he's been waiting for someone to share them with he doesn't have brothers and Peter only watches baseball and definitely wouldn't wrinkle his expensive suits for relaxing. India also invited Shay but she did not want to come she said India has been acing as if she is invisible lately. But India was spreading herself thin a few days later Noel had to go out of town for a week to program some systems for a new company India was shame to say she was glad she could go back to being off balance non centered selfish the works. She brought she and Shay home a pizza for the night sort of a piece offering maybe they could chill and talk. "Shay who is this?"

The guy put his cigarette out in one of India's candleholders while Shay started buttoning up her shirt.

"I thought you weren't coming back this is my friend EJ."

"This is my home I have the key to come anytime and your unbuttoning your shirt for a guy with half a name.'

"India don't start.'

"Wow you said she was stuck up you didn't say she was fine and stuck up.'

267

"Hey don't make me go off on you.' Shay said

"Nobodies going off I'm going to say this in front of you since my sister is hard of hearing no one is allowed in my home when I'm not here is that understood you'll have to get a hotel room where did you all met." India said

"At AA, is that pizza?'

"What, AA how   Shay when he's got a bottle of Hennessey in his hand you'll are not suppose to be dating does your sponsor know about this Shay."

"He got kicked out India, Dag she doesn't have to know everything like you India."

" Oh my goodness well she called me at work today you lied you did apply for assistance so your receiving food stamps seems as though you've been selling them outside the center.' India said

"Key word India outside the center I haven't missed not one of my classes or meeting not one so why is she all up in my business I need a new sponsor." Shay said

The guy sat back ready for a brawl then put his foot up on the living table he lit his cigarette again and blew the smoke up in the air in circles.

"Look dude last time leave and don't come back."

'If he leaves then I leave." Shay said

"Heifer are you being for real you have me spending money to feed you and you're getting $248 dollars worth of food stamps."

"Man I'm out of here baby girl your sis is tripping   I see you later.'

India rolled her eyes at him as he walked pass she repeated her message to him he just nodded his head and continued to walk out the door with the cigarette in his mouth. India waved the smoke away from her face she asked Shay did she need to leave the door

opened Shay folded her arms and flapped down on the couch she did not say a word.

India rushed to open the living room window she told Shay she would give her a time

frame because the only people that would be disrespectful in her house will be her. She

needs to start buying her own food and she then asked her if she was on birth control

Shay yelled out she's grown she did not need India trying to be her mother India.

The phone rang Shay didn't dare answer it she didn't want to talk to any counselor India

went in her room she had not calmed down yet so she let the phone ring for the third time

before she answered.

"Hello.'"

"My goodness I was about to hang up."

"Hi mom how are you."

"You would know if you called."

"It good to hear from you too."

"I thought I would call I'm at your Uncle Parkers for his birthday." Sharon said

"So you're in town now?"

"India yes that's what I said your Uncle sent his sister a plane ticket to come see him."

"Ok I did not realize the date was here already.'

Shay started waving her hand whispering for India not to say she was around she stood

up and started walking toward the kitchen then stopped in her tracks.

"Ok Shay and I will come over is everyone dressed up for the party.'

"Dress how you need to India he's 67 years old he said he told you about it."

"Right give us about a half hour."

"What in the world did you do that for India I'm not going around them trying to be all up in my business I told you to say I'm not here?"

"Girl fasten your pants straighten your hair and lets go mom is here for Uncle Parkers birthday."

"So she didn't even call me for my birthday what do I care about your Uncle."

"My Uncle huh so you haven't been over there to borrow money huh.'

"India you think you know everything."

"No you just think everything is a secret. "

They arrived in a half hour Shay kept an attitude the whole way she slammed the car door when she got out India held her tongue she hadn't seen everyone in quite awhile   and they were going to way in on her too she was sure of it. At first, everyone seemed excited they all hugged Shay gave a fake smile all they knew were rumors most had not seen Shay since she was little. Sharon had already filled everyone in on her divorce and God knows what else.

"Shay you look like you've gain some weight."

"Yes mom I could stand to gain a few pounds."

"Where is your husband at India you aren't married yet.'

"No Uncle not yet."

"India can't think about anybody but herself no man wants that." Sharon said

"That not true I'm seeing someone." India said

"I've never met any man since you left home."

"You saw your father?'

"No uncle not since he moved to California I talked to him ."

Shay walk off she was glad the subject wasn't her India smiled that was true she doesn't know what a good man walks like are talks like she doesn't even think they exist that was most certainly true she certainly didn't have many examples growing up.

"Well I'm looking for a wife it's about time I settle down I'm not getting any younger."

"Daddy you to old to be trying to get you some it's almost time to cut your birthday cake." His daughters started bringing him gifts as she laughed at what she just said he started ripping off paper and throwing it everywhere India asked her mother how long she staying. She was thinking since Noel wouldn't be back until the end of the week even though she was thinking about what she was saying Sharon told her she was leaving back out in the morning she had already been in town for two days.

India took a deep breath then exhaled she didn't say a word Shay had blended back in with the kids in the other room   they were driving her crazy,

"Shay." Sharon yelled out

You don't have anything to say to your mother after me and your daddy gave you everything trying to   raise you right." Sharon said

"Mom I said hi an hour ago I'm here to see you."

"You here to see me are India made you come."

"India can't make me do anything mom.' Shay said

"You right nobody can that's why you're in the situation you're in now."

"Mom this isn't the time please.' India pleaded

"Still trying to protect everyone never did a good job at that you turned your back on your family look at you no man no kids."

"Mother what's the matter why are you so bitter with me and Shay."

"Bitter it that what you call the woman that sacrificed everything for you bitter I called you to come help find your father   see about your sister now your to good for your family right now you disrespect me and call me bitter ."

"Mother I'm sorry I'm just saying we are all here together to celebrate don't be upset."
India said

India didn't know what to say she's never disrespect her mother   their relationship has gotten to this India doesn't know how to bring back something when she doesn't know how she lost it. Tears were in her eyes she wanted to talk to Noel just seeing his face would take away this moment are would it trying to tell him about this mess was started to make India want to scream. She looked over at Shay she was biting what was left of her nails standing in the corner this was the first time India started to see her father in her she was about to lose it she picked up her purse then left she didn't say a word by the time she pulled into a neighbors driveway. To turn the car around and head down the street   she heard her name she looked in her rear view mirror Shay was running behind the car India stopped she had forgotten about her just that fast. Shay practically jumped into the car while the car was still rolling India headed onto the expressway the music blasting tears filled her eyes she blinked them away. Shay was talking but India could not hear a word she continued to drive turning down the music once to tell Shay she needed to find her a place of her own soon as possible.

Three days later India woke up around 3:30 am she could not believe she still had the same headache she went to bed her ring finger had been hurting all day and the tip of it had swelled. India got up to look at it in the bathroom she couldn't figure out how she had hurt it   there was a throbbing pain she ran it under cold water when that didn't help she decided to go to the kitchen and get some ice to put on it. India   made it to the middle of the living room and fainted her fall to the floor was so hard it woke Shay out of her sleep. She thought someone was trying to break in she jumped up off the couch and tripped right over India   she screamed out not knowing what was happening she fumble to get to India's room and turned on the light she saw India laying on the floor Shay stood there in shock calling out India's name when India didn't respond she reached for the phone and called 911.

India woke up in a small bed in a cold room with a strange woman holding her arm sticking a needle   in it.

"What in the hell are you doing, and where in the hell am I this is not   Heaven?'

"Close, sweetie you're in the hospital General West I'm nurse Ryan how are you feeling."

"That has to be a trick question right nurse Ryan."

"Being a smart ass doesn't count as a good sign of health just so you know."

"Ok than I feel like shit why am I here nurse Ryan I hope you'll didn't give me any drugs because I don't want any drugs in my body."

"You past out your sister called the ambulance your blood pressure was 178 over 110 at

273

first they thought you had a stroke when they couldn't get you to come to but your pressure starting to drop at your age you should be no where near a stroke territory."

"Lady I don't know what you are talking about I don't have, Stroke I'm 27 years old."

"28 and that nurse Ryan you'll probably have to go on hypertension medicine but I'll let the doctor confirm that for you.'

"Where is my sister?'

"I'm not sure there is a man I had to promise him I wouldn't leave the room until he came back from the restroom."

"Is it my father?" India asked

"If he is get his number for me because he is fine as wine honey." The nurse said

India was thinking no way she had a cute face kind of favored her auntie on her mothers side but her hands were way to ruff especially for a nurse and especially to be touching India.

Noel walked into the room tall bold and handsome as ever India had no idea where he came from she did not have time to think if she looked a mess.

"India are you ok how do you feel." Noel said

"Noel, where did you come from I thought you were out of town."

"Shay answered the phone this morning and from our conversation I caught the first flight home.'

"You didn't have to do that Noel, your work you said it was a important job for your company." India said

"Nothing and I mean nothing is more important then you India."

Is it to late to still get his number girl?" The nurse asked

"Huh." Noel replied

India and the nurse both laughed the nurse reminded India that laughing was a good sign and the doctor would be in, In about an hour India asked Noel if he knew where Shay had gone. He asked her if she wanted him to call the house India declined he sat down on the edge of the bed and took one of India's hands then stroked her hair with the other one looking into her blood shot eyes.

"Honey what happened your blood pressure was through the roof you passed out and you were dehydrated.'

"I, I don't know Noel I guess the doctor will have to tell me why.' India said

She could not look him in the eyes she did not even remember fainting she did not remember what happen she looked at her left hand and saw a bandage around her ring finger. She was at a lost but starting to remember what caused her delay everything was in shambles she told Shay she wanted her to move out that night they came from the party India had not eaten anything in two days she kept calling her mother but she hadn't answered.

"Well don't think about it we have to get your pressure down."

Four hours later India was leaving the hospital with a blood pressure prescription she was also broke out all over from the codeine they had given her for the headaches   they said she was allergic to them. Noel wouldn't take no for an answer India was coming to stay with him until she felt better he even cancel work for her they told him she should take all the time she needed India fussed all the way to his house. Noel didn't respond he pulled up in front of his condo and carried India inside she said she would stay for a couple of hours and then she would be going home he knew what she had just gone through she wouldn't have the strength to fight. He was right India showered he didn't take a chance going to her house for clothes so he gave her some boxers and a tee shirt once the massager's in Noels shower hit India's body. She thought she was in heaven again the bathroom was full of steam after a half hour India was drained Noel made up the bed turned the music to mellow moods on low. He pulled the shades on the pictured window closed India tried to resist wanting to jump in the big king size bed but was drawn straight to it Noel tucked India in bed while she was still confirming just a few hours of rest then she would be going home. He got her a hot cup of tea with lemon he called his mother while India was in the shower she told him to put a touch of honey in it and to call her back if he needed her. India was out so heavy that she started snoring if she found that out she would be livid. Noel pulled his recliner next to the bed and watched India until it was confirmed she was in a deep sleep he quickly went to see what he could prepare for dinner. His parents taught them well his father always prepared dinner and had Noel and his sister in the kitchen first hand, his mother taught them how to wash their clothes clean house everything necessary to prepare them to be self-sufficient adults sometimes your best is not enough.

India didn't awaken until the next day some of the night she tossed and turned but she was still in a deep sleep Noel thought it may have been the medicine still wearing off they had to give India a different dose of medicine to help the inflammation for being allergic to the codeine.

"Honey sweetie it's me."

India tried focusing in it took a minute the light in front of her was bright she could see red lips moving and white hair then she focus more into blue eyes and a soft voice she began to think she was in the hospital again she sat up in the bed and grabbed the woman by the arms.

"Where am I?" India said

"It's me honey, Indy it's me Leah.'

"Leah where did you come from."

"Getting here was hard getting in to see you now that was harder." Leah said

India got out of bed a little dizzy Leah jumped up and held on to her India continued to walk into the bathroom. Leah stopped at the closed door Leah talked the whole while India used the restroom and brushed her tooth then held a cold rug to her face for a few minutes. She was talking a mile a minute upset with Noel for not letting her in yesterday he told her that India was resting and shouldn't be awaken Leah told India she started to break the door down how dare him and why wasn't she the one that took India home she's her emergency contact. Leah said she's surprise Noel allowed her to come upstairs to the bedroom and then she mention how wonderful his home was and that she could tell a woman decorated Leah said a classy woman must have been his ex girlfriend she had to have been an interior decorator.

Leah was talking so much waving her hands all in the air looking up to the ceiling and around the bedroom she didn't even notice India had come out of the bathroom and was about to put on some of Noel socks she hated for her feet to touch the floor even if it had carpet.

"Indy what are you doing up honey get back in bed please."

Noel put the tray that he was carrying down on his nightstand he asked Leah if the lazy boy chair was all right for her to sit in, Leah shook her head yes and with her arms folded she walked over and sat down.

"Here I got you some tea with honey and scrambled eggs with bacon toast and cheese grits with lots of butter sweetie."

Noel stood there while India looked at the plate of food it was piping hot strawberry jelly in a small bowl India looked up at Noel still not able to speak.

"It's almost dinner time why is she eating breakfast." Leah said

India gave her a dirty look then she took a bite of the toast after he spread some jelly on a piece,

"How long have I been asleep?"

"Well I went downstairs to cook you dinner yesterday after you showered I came back up and you were snore--."

   Noel thought about what he was saying then stopped.

"I mean you were sound asleep I couldn't wake you so I figured we'd start with breakfast and then if you wanted lunch or the dinner I saved whatever you want I'll leave you two to catch up I have a conference call to make is this ok ."

Before India could respond with something off the wall Noel turned up the light from the automatic switch then closed the door.

"So he can call you Indy and what about honey   when did you get all girly like that?"

India could not stop eating if she tried, she was almost finished with her lightly scrambled cheese eggs she offered Leah a bite while ignoring her.

"I thought you and Greg liked Noel you asked him to marry you what happen."

"He locked me out from seeing my best friend that is what happen, didn't I just tell you that how dare him try to take care of you better then he thinks I could he reminded me of Ms. Shawiasee you know the lady downstairs in your apartment.'

"You mean your apartment." India quoted

Leah crossed her arms then looked over at India who had stopped eating and was looking directly at her simultaneously their laughter filled the room they did not stop laughing until Leah said her stomach hurt.

 "How dare he be a good man he might have to be a keeper?"

Tears start rolling down Leah's eyes India took another bite of her bacon then she moved the tray and hugged Leah thanking her for coming which made Leah mad again how would she not she even wandered if Noel had maybe done something. To cause this but her first impression of him had to remain solid she just saw him in action with India's track record with men she didn't blame Leah's concern.

"India what happened?"

"What happened my mothers was in town." India said

"Your mother did you go and get her I just saw you and you didn't mention anything.'

"Leah actually it's a combination of everything building up to everything building up even more   I didn't know she was in town something went down during a conversation and I guess that contributed to my body having enough I haven't discussed it with Noel yet so I don't know where to begin." India said

"The hospital called the house I'm sorry I wasn't there, Greg I could kill him he didn't check the messages how long are you going to be off work I can't take another day without you."

"It's not Greg's fault." India said

Leah started tearing up again then she whipped out a picture from her purse and handed it to India which was back into her plate   she looked up from her plate and took the picture out of her hand.

"Whose pretty baby is this?"

"Guess." Leah stated

"You know I hate guessing Leah just tell me.'

"Ok, ok your right nurse Noel said we have to keep your blood pressure down did you take your medicine."

"Don't say that it makes me sound crazy."   India said

"Girl don't be silly it's your new God daughter that's why I wasn't at home I was at   the hospital all night apparently either Jill or the doctor miss calculated because she just had a healthy baby girl Shantae."

India looked at the picture again and thought maybe the light was not bright enough until tears started falling from Leah's eyes again she kept wiping them away not saying anything just smiling.

"Ok either that hospital gave me something much stronger or Noel slipped me a little something extra because that baby who took that picture they gave her the wrong ones."

"No there the right ones.'

'But she's."

"I know biracial.' Leah said

"What the hell." India said

"Apparently my brother wasn't just the problem in the relationship and he does know what he's talking about didn't give him a right to lose his temper with a woman but none the less he's in real bad shape right now.'

"You've told him." India said

"Told him, He told Jill and I he'd promised you he would be there for Jill during the delivery so he saw his I mean who ever baby come out thank God he refused to cut the cord India that probably would have been yet another scare that couldn't have been heeled."

"Oh my Goodness what is going on?'

"Stay calm I know Jill is blowing your answering machine up she won't tell me or Peter anything the doctor had to tell her twice that the baby was biracial they took a blood test which Peter and Jill had agreed upon so I just feel so bad for not believing in my brother he thinks I trust Jill more."

"Don't cry Leah this is definitely going to take some time to get through just stick by his side we'll be there for him for the both of them."

"Peter called you over and over at the hospital.'

"You didn't tell him I was here did you." India said

"I didn't know why he has been acting a little possessive about you lately.' Leah said

"Yeah but not that he and Noel didn't quite hit it off."

"Yeah he told me Noel seemed rude you know Peter can be a little off the wall sometime Therapy is really doing him good he doesn't talk much about but I take him to his appointment every other week that's my commitment to him he hasn't let me all the way in yet." Leah said

Noel knock then came in to check on them he again offered to make Leah something she only wanted a stiff drink that would have been much better they talked a little longer then India started conveying her need to go home routine Noel called his mother with Mindy on a three way then he gave India the phone. She could not take another mother episode and she definitely did not want to get into what went wrong she nodded her head as Mrs. Olean spoke then India rested another night

India returned to work in three days she'd never missed a day weeks later she was taking down the signs, picture and balloons that her kids made her along with a welcome back cake. Noel brought her roses red ones India was hesitant too introduce Noel to her class she has never presented her prized possessions before to a man she wished he had done like Peter always did and waited until after class. But it was inevitable they loved him they asked him was he going to asked India to marry him and without hesitation he said yes they all laughed some covered their face some covered their mouth India's jaws dropped.

"Noel you shouldn't be telling them those things.' India said

"He looks serious to me.' A student blurred out

India didn't like blushing she whispered to Noel to stay quiet then she got order in the class room she started passing out the vanilla and chocolate ice cream that were having for snack Noel asked the kids if they liked their substitute teacher while India was gone India looked at him and laughed.

"Are you serious?'

Noel put his hand up to the kids to hold off on their answer then he walked over to India and whispered in her ear,

"If they say yes then you agree to go with me to my parent's house next month."

"And if they say no or yes then you agree to meet and welcome Mindy's friend." India said

Noel stepped back then looked at the kids faces he quickly became confident beside India was pushing it he held back a lot due to India condition but he wouldn't when he saw Mindy he shook India's hand.

"Deal."

They all yelled out yes,

"Because he didn't give any home work and they got to talk in line and timothy didn't tie his shoes all day but we love Ms. Indy we don't want her to leave ever again.' Little Me Myra spoke

"Ok you can't be disturbing my kids this way time for you to leave."

"Oh you're jealous are you?' Noel said

"Just a little Mister." India said

"Meet me for dinner tonight."

"Well Leah and I were going to see our new God daughter I really want to see her.'

"God daughter I thought she was Leah niece.'

"Well, I'll feel you in on that later I don't know how long I will be so I'll call you in the morning.'

"Ok baby I'll talk to you in the morning call me if you need me India.' Noel said

"I will."

Noel gave India a stern look then kissed her on the cheek he told the children and Leah bye they all said goodbye in unison then he left with confidence. Leah and India picked up dinner for a from a local chicken place then they arrived at Jill's surprisingly Jill was filed with joy to see them Leah did not feel comfortable going back without India. Jill did not know anything about India's episode and they did not mention it the baby had gotten even bigger. Leah sat down on the love seat India looked at Jill like she was stranger her face and body looked so different if she was not convinced before she was at this date and time India declared that she would never ever have kid's and not to know who the father was this was straight madness beyond believe. Jake was already asleep India went into his room and gave him a kiss he awake out of his sleep the baby had already awaken him an hour ago.

"Auntie Indy where have you been." Jake said

He jumped up and held on to India neck as though it was to safe his life India kind of choke trying to release his grip a little,

"Auntie Leah and I have to work a lot but we love you Jake."

"Mom said you have a new boy toy in your life do you like him better than me." Jake said

India turned on Jakes light and sat him on her lap fixing his hair on his head he big brown eyes staring into her waiting for an answer India kissed him on the forehead then told Jake there was no man on earth that could ever take his place. And that he would always be the apple in India's eye and that Noel wanted to meet him and ask why she loved him so much.

Jake was smiling ear to ear the new man wanted to meet him and ask his secret for India's love oh boy. He told India he needed to get plenty of sleep so that he could think about his answer that he would give her but that first he had to talk to Ezra and LeAnn they all fought unintentionally for India's attention. Jake was excited about his new baby sister he was to young to care about her race India did not know why they loved her so much not because she did not love them. She took her role as Godmother very seriously as she took any role in life India thinks the problem was she didn't see any differences in her roles she didn't want kids. But she was drawn to Jake, Le Ann and Ezra and her Godchildren in Out of town simultaneously because of the role she was given she didn't realize how important of a role she had until this moment hugging Jake made her protective role came into play no matter who no matter what kid adult neighbor, friend or best friend   sister brother etc. India started to tear up she was rocking Jake back and forth she heard Leah and Jill calling her from the living room. She did not stop rocking Jake's 5 year old self until he fell asleep once again amazing herself how comfortable people felt around her even though knowing how uncomfortable she felt with herself. She covered Jake up   then went back into the living room Leah even her being a mother of two quickly say her hi's then her goodbye and that's always enough India always had to go above and beyond without even knowing what she was doing. She backed away from Shantae who was swinging in her swing figuring she would not over due herself with the new addition she just stared at her swinging back and forth in the swing sucking on her fingers her skin a bright tan.

"Dena called earlier she has been really good about checking on the baby."

She looked over at India as she poured herself a light drink the first she's had in months

Jill was glad to see them she wanted a drink all day but she was scared to drink around the baby alone she's been so confused Jill never once thought that the baby wasn't Peters. She hadn't spoken about the issue since the baby was born she told Leah that she'd wait until she and India could come over still not knowing India was hospitalized just thinking Peter was turning everyone against her. He had not seen the baby since she was born and he had no more intentions on seeing Shantae again even though Jill has pleaded.

"Jill take it easy on the drinking were not staying all night you said you would explain once we were all together we have supported you through all this madness and we are here now so tell us what's going on tell us who Shantae's father is because we know now that it's not Peter's."

India sipped on her drink and almost choked up with Leah's confident character she sounded just like she thought she was glad to be able to lay back and see what was going to happen this was not her drama anymore and she definitely did not cause it. This made India happy and sad at the same time she leaned back on the couch and wandered what life would be like without all the drama.

"It's Jim." Jill said

Leah stood spilling her drink all over the dining room table even though she just stated she knew Peter was not the father some how she still expected to hear his name she rushed to the kitchen to get paper towels. Jill stood stiff standing near her fireplace wiping her eyes that were blurring hoping her friends would do as they said and be there for her though this would be a long hard-extended road she was facing.

"Jill who do you mean are you talking about Shantaes father its ok we are here for you and Shantae." India said

"Yeah, even though there are lives destroyed Jill we have to stick together for the baby she has done nothing wrong.'

"Oh and I did Leah." Jill stated

"You bitch, You had a baby by another man while you were with me brother telling us all the while that he was the father are you drunk or being funny."

It was official Leah has definitely been around Dena way to long India tried to say something but her words did not come out or that were not loud enough because Leah and Jill's words were getting beyond hurtful. They were both crying and moving around the room stopping and staring at the baby which made them both cry more and more India did not want to get excited she promised Noel that she would be off the blood pressure medicine before they went to his parents since she lost the beat. She just sat on the sofa holding her head Leah telling her to stay calm Jill asking repeatedly since when did India need validation from anyone.

"Jill I was in the hospital when you had Shantae that's why you couldn't reach me.'

"What hospital why, what are you saying.'

India hesitated she did not want to relive her ordeal and she did not want things to become about her as they usually did but she wanted Jill to know that she had not turned her back on she and the baby.'

"I passed out and I'm temporarily on hypertension medicine no big deal who is Jim and why in the hell did you screw him while you were with Peter I thought you loved him this bullshit could have caused the end of all of our friendship then you betrayed all of us why." India said

"What do you want me to do Ms. Perfect kill myself."

India stood then walked into the kitchen to put her glass away she grabbed her purse then told Leah she was on her own for answers she wasn't about to take any mess off anyone tonight without a fight. Jill walked over to India pleading for her not to go and that she was sorry and that her shame was getting the best of her she had made a horrible mistake and didn't know what to do to fix it she sat back down on the couch asking Leah and India to join her with a brief thought of ending it all   India thought about Jake and the baby then Jill spoke.

"Jim, her father is Jim."

Leah and India looked at Jill then it dawned on them at the same time Jim.

"Are you talking about Peter's friend Jim please, say I'm wrong Jill this can't be true?' Leah asked

 "It just happened Leah, I'm sorry he came over one night to see if   Peter was around he and I had just had a fight because Peter hadn't been home in days I invited him in I had already been drinking and once he came in he started drinking also one thing lead to another." Jill pleaded

"The old one thing lead to another pretty typical Jill don't you say." Leah said

"Wait a minute drunk are not you all didn't use a condom what the hell.' Leah said

"We didn't plan this he left right after and I awoke the next day never giving us another thought.' Jill said

"You know he's married right with two kids.'

"He has two stepchildren they aren't his biological kids but they aren't with his present wife now they are from his first wife." Jill stated

"Really I didn't know that, I mean he's hung around a couple of time even though it was never with the same women but my goodness Jill my brother's good friend crap." Leah said

"All that I can say is that I'm sorry I don't know what else to say maybe Peter and I can work this out some how and raise Shantae together." Jill said

"Are you crazy?"

"India I," Jill stated

"No don't mention my name don't even think I'm about to get into this mess Shantae's here now she healthy and I'll love her regardless but I am not going to try to convince Peter to raise his best friend's baby I'll walk right out of here." India said

The room got quiet the drinks were raised one after the other you could hear a pin drop the baby was rocking back and forth rattler still in her hand.

"Well does he know?" Leah said

"I think Peter told him he called and asked why I wanted to ruined his life and his friendship he wants a blood test before he tells his wife about this we are going to meet next week."

Jill started to cry uncontrollably they both hugged her with just as much emotion they felt every bit of her pain she and Leah go way back and Leah realized ultimately this situation was she and Peter's situation India and Leah agreed to stick by Jill's side that night.

The next morning after calling Noel India found Shay's note that she was staying at EJ's mother's house with him she balled it up then prayed that Shay continued her sobriety then left for work. When she arrived in her classroom Peter was waiting at her desk with coffee and doughnuts and a smile dressed in a dark blue Armani three-piece suit.

"I'm not going to even asked how you got in here and I can only imagine what you're doing here at all this early." India said

"Good morning beautiful, I had to come before your class started and I just blended in with everyone else I stopped by last night and saw your sister leaving she told me what happened with you I wanted to make sure you were alright."

"Doughnut."

"Blended in I don't think anyone else in this entire school could afford a suit like the one your wearing I have been shopping with you remember and good morning to you how are you I'm great Peter.'

"How are you, And I'm sorry about the baby even though you didn't want one and you knew that she wasn't your's that is a lot to handle I'm glad your in therapy are you alright.' India asked

"I'm good I'm just glad the baby is alright and now Jill can get on with her life I'm still waiting for you to start therapy with me." Peter stated

" I know getting into it with your mom hurt you since you have been trying to get back your close bond I know how it feels when your family hurts you India are you still having nightmares."

"Wow my sister Shay sure has a big mouth she doesn't even know you.' India said

"I told her who I was." Peter said

"Oh that makes it all better, Peter I never said I was starting therapy I have the number though remember, thanks for the breakfast class is about to start."

"Ok well I was thinking about getting something for the baby you know a piece offering I don't think I could ever mend my friendship with Jim but the baby is innocent in all this you know.'

"That sounds great Peter and in time you can mend you friendship with Jill.'

"Well how about you come with me help pick something out we'll have dinner tonight."

"Not tonight Peter I'm really behind with my weekly lessons and I'm meeting Noel can I

call you later."

"That's not over yet." Peter said

"Peter that's not nice what do you mean over yet." India said

"Nothing, I'm going to hold you too dinner." Peter stated

"Ok I'll call you by the end of the week I promise.' India said

"Ok beautiful, don't make me kidnap you because I will."

"Don't be silly, Peter goodbye have a good day."

Peter reached over and kissed India on the cheek as close as he could to her lips he

moved back from her slowly staring deep into her eyes wondering what she was thinking

India just smiled then quickly turned around to clean the chalk board .

The next week Jim and his mother entered the doctors office together Jill thought it

would be just she and Jim she didn't invite anyone although her aunt offered she's not

very close with her family. Jim introduced his mother Kim she looked Jill up then down

Jill just looked down at a magazine she was nervous wondering what his mother thought

and how she was responding to the situation.

"Hey baby how are you lets get this done from what my son has told me although he's a lying cheat you don't know this but I have been waiting a long time for a grandchild if she   is ours then it's meant to be."

Jill   didn't know what to say she responded to Kim's hug she instantly saw Jim's mothers smile in her daughter face Jill knew she was a lying cheat also but she knew that Shantae was biracial. And that Jim was the only man that could be her father she was sure of that Kim asked where the baby was she wanted to see her right then look into her eyes. Jill explained that the baby's blood test was already on file from the first blood test with Peter and she did not need to be present she had left her with her aunt.

Two week's later   the blood results revealed Jim was the father his mother instantly became a proud grandmother she had know intentions on missing a beat Jim was her only child and she wasn't getting any younger she was 65 years old and now she had her wish it   was official. Kim agreed to keep the baby while Jill went back to work no charge no questions. Jill immediately took her up on her offer against Jim's protest he didn't have any time to digest any of this he didn't even have time to tell his wife. His mother told him either he told his wife or that she would because her granddaughter would be in their life forever Kim knew Jim and his wife had tried to have a baby. That the doctors confirmed that she probably couldn't have children and she was sorry for that but through Kim's son's stupidity she now has a grandchild since the baby came early Kim brought the crib the stroller the high chair Jim couldn't stop his mother from spending her retirement funds on the baby.

India was getting ready for work Noel has insisted on her staying at his place he walked into the bathroom and took India by the hand she reminded him she needed to get to work and that she was about to be running late Noel leaned against the sink in front of India.

"We need to talk." Noel said

"Noel I have to go you know that I don't like morning talk's can't it wait."

"Well I have been holding off but I think since you've gotten your pressure down that this needs to be discussed first I love you and I just wanted to talk about the nightmares."

"Excuse me." India said

"India, I don't mean to pry but maybe if we talk about this then you would be more comfortable with staying the night and building our future I'm here for you on anything nothing can change that.' Noel stated

India quickly exited the bathroom she was not prepared for this, first Peter now Noel she knew she shouldn't have stayed the night no more medicine to make her sleepy through the night she had nothing to say she didn't want to fall out or argue she grabbed her purse and bag.

"India I'm not going to let you do this don't turn this into a confrontation I'm just trying to help, baby if you don't want to talk to me then maybe you could see a therapist I'll go with you."

"I'm not a child Noel I don't need you to hold my hand for everything I didn't mention anything about nightmares, because I'm fine there is nothing to talk about it has nothing to do with us if we are meant to be then we will be."

"This is about us because now I'm a part of your life and I'm trying to stay with you forever and anything that's meant to be doesn't surface from air you have to put time and effort into anything that is worth having India.' Noel said

India stopped at the front door then looked back,

"Therapy were did you get that idea do I look crazy are you saying you think I'm crazy."

"Don't be ridiculous India you know that's not what I'm saying lots of people get therapy hell I've even had therapy with Mindy for years."

"I guess we should cancel the trip to your mothers you should go by yourself I wouldn't want to embarrass you having a nightmare I was probably having a plain old crazy dream you know normal people have those too."

"You always do this whenever you don't want to talk about things or deal with something, India it's not going to work you've had this nightmares three nights in a row calling out the same name a Ronnie or Ronald."

"Noel I have to get to class my children can't teach themselves I'll stay at my place tonight I'm sorry if I kept you   awoke have a good day ."

"India Saturday's Greg's birthday party we ."

India was out the door she did not look back or respond to Noel's comment,

   India was forced to return Peters calls after her machine had no one but his calls   she had intended on doing so she was back to her usually tired as hell routine she has spent the last couple of nights at her place no Shay no Noel watching the ceiling fan and back up at 3 or 4 am.   She agreed to meet Peter for drinks it was only fair to spend some quality time with Peter everyone else had support around them he deserved it too, Peter was wearing a pair of Levi's and a crisp white dress shirt. India was pretty much dressed the same she put her hair up she wear a pair of black dress slacks and a white silk blouse with a pair of black pumps India arrived 15 minutes late Peter was on his second drink hoping India didn't stand him up.

"Thank goodness I didn't have to call S.W.A.T."

"Peter you're a funny guy you know that, how are you, here you go this is the reason that I am late I picked this up for you to give to the baby."

"But we were suppose to go together what is it.'

"Peter you've been out of town calling me like you were in town so I just took the initiative to pick something up   trust me you'll love it, you always have to pick your niece and nephews gift right what's the difference."

"The lady will have what I'm having Peter strongly told the waiter."

"And what are you drinking?" India asked

"Gin and tonic."

"Ma'am I'll have a sex on the beach please." India quoted

"India your going to have to start living a little sooner then later babe I'm almost sure you need a man like me to show you the finer things in life." Peter stated

"Ok, I'm not sure what you mean by that I'm not from the hood Peter I grew up in the suburbs like you why do you think we have so much in common and by the way you know I'm seeing Noel now."

"Yeah what's up with that guy, why or how is he still around."

"Don't be rude he's still around because he's a wonderful guy.'

"India this isn't like you to be suckered in by a guy now I've been waiting patiently for

you to get rid of this guy as I have with all the other no good bums."

{Laughter}" Peter I've never told you whom to date and you've dated my friend Jill and

Noel is a far much farther cry than the guys I have dated in the past so knock it off what

would your therapist think you sound crazy you want to have all of your sister's friend no

I don't think so.'

"First of all I started dating Jill only to get your attention I didn't realize until after I

agreed to get a place with her that your attention span is really limited by then it was too

late India."

"So how serious are you guys your meeting at Leah and Greg's again this is the second

time be for real twice you've never taking a guy there who is he.' Peter said

"He owns his own computer programming company and he still works as a private

contractor with IBM and I'm going to ignore that attention span comment he's never

been married doesn't have children and his condo is 2 or three minutes from yours."

"But does he know you India?"

"Know me, what do you mean Peter?"

"Does he know that you don't want marriage or children and that you're very capable of

taking care of yourself and the last thing that you need is a needy man."

"He is not needy he's a very confident man actually Peter."

"And Ms India, you have a way of tearing down the best of the best without even batting an eye trust me how many times has he asked you for a commitment."

"How is therapy going Peter, I've been thinking about calling actually I did call but I hung up before I made an appointment.'

Peter's look was alarming he asked if Noel had anything to do with her decision was she trying to clean her closet for this man. India reassured Peter that this was something she needed to do for herself. To assure himself Peter took out his cell phone and dialed the Dr.'s private number and made India's first consultation in two days giving India enough time to change her mind.

"Done." Peter stated

"Peter you didn't have to do that let me handle this on my own ok." India said

Peter put his hands in the air he surrendered then opened the gift India brought it was a sterling silver rattler with the babies initials engraved on it he gave India a kiss on the cheek. She jokingly told him she was going to start charging him, that Noel would not like his open affection that she feels that she really cares for him, and that things were getting serious. He told India that he did not care about Noel's feelings and left it at that they ate appetizer and had a few more drinks then India ended the night. The rest of the week went fast Shay called asking India if she would bring her some groceries India picked up a few things and as she was about to get out of the car Shay ran outside to the car telling India that EJ's mom didn't like strangers in her house. That was fine with India she looked Shay over then asked where EJ was Shay hesitated for a minute then said they had an argument and she hasn't seen him in a few days. She promised that she was staying clean and that she almost got a job last week she knows now that India loves her, she wanted to apologize for hurting her, and trying to push Noel away instead, she gave India the tightest hug it sent chill through India they had not hugged since Shay was little. India told Shay that her sponsor Mrs. Turner could still get her a place in a shelter and that she would take her right now if she wanted to go Shay looked back at the small brick house then back at India and refused. India did not want to leave her but she could not make anyone strong while she is still weak she learned that in one consultation India gave Shay $50 dollars she told her that she loved then drove away.

"Hey, Indy."

India's purse fell to the ground as she was grabbed up into the air literally off her feet she quickly reached back with both hands to keep her sundress from lifting any farther. Leah walked up behind Peter and he was slowing returning India's feet to the ground. The look on Noel face make Leah's face turn she had forgotten to talk to Peter about Noel's coming he had been rattling off about India all day. He had a business meeting in Chicago and was suppose to be flying out in an hour but he didn't care he had to see India and make his last impression on Noel before he left and what an impression he was making on this day. Noel was still standing behind India in the doorway his body temperature was hotter than the 85 degree sun.

"Peter leave India be and let my new brother in law in the house gee what are you thinking."

Leah took that brother in law comment out of her bags of tricks she knew Peter's was being down right rude. Greg had to make a quick ice run and was just pulling up Leah began to exhaled. India tripped over trying to make it through the doorway both Noel and

Peter grabbed to help her keep her balance.

"Man we're going to have to stop meeting like this before one of us gets hurt you know what I mean man to man."

"Right."

"Hey everybody's here good we could get this party started."

"It's can Greg, can get this party started dear."

"Happy Birthday big guy you can open this now are later."

"Come on in everyone what are you'll standing in the doorway for the house is more than big enough Peter's business car had pulled up with a driver he continued to stand in the doorway once he noticed the car.

"Well guys I'm sorry I can't stay for the party Greg I hope you like those gold cuff links and India I took care of 5 sessions for you so you don't have to worry about a thing have fun brother in law."

He pick up his over night bag and didn't look back he waved as he passed a few of their neighbors coming to join the party since Greg was the only child he was elated and ignorant to the character that Peter was playing. But Noel was convinced they were all in on this but he could not figure out why they were so nice. Greg put his arm around Noel's shoulder stated Leah was in charge of making him happy for the day and that they should exit to the man cave. Were he'd left a few of his guy cousins and neighbors to go to the store he stopped in his dining room and looked behind him while he entered into his stash of expensive cigars that Peter had pick up in Spain and given to Greg for his day.

Leah hate any kind of smoking Noel followed Greg downstairs into the basement wondering if anyone else had anything up their sleeves in this house he gave India a last look as she stopped putting. The finishing touches on the potato salad to give him a quick wave and smile hoping Greg would quickly adjust his mind from Peter she waited until t he basement door closed then she followed Leah outside to turn the steaks. And grilling salmon India closed the patio doors behind them she hugged everyone that she knew and waved at the one's she didn't.

"I wonder were Jill is."

"Jill, India what's going on with you and my brother 5 sessions what's that about?'

"I didn't asked him to do that and nothing going on you know that I've been thinking about going to counseling you know I've mentioned it before." India said

"And Peters paying for it no wonder Noel had the look of destruction on his face I'm going to have to talk to Peter I don't want Noel to think were condoning his behavior."

"He seems to think you and Noel's relationship is a joke that's kind of my fault." Leah said

"How and Noel wont think that, I told Peter Noel and I aren't a joke he knows that he's just going through a lot he confused."

"Well when he and I had our talk I should have mention Noel then but everything was so tense and he agreed to go to therapy I didn't know how to tell him."

"Leah I told him I've told him that if there ever was a chance there could no longer be since he was with Jill I will never be with someone that's been with my friend even if she felt like I wasn't the right one for him."

"India I really think."

"There she is well were is the baby." Leah's mother Lillie said

"Her grandmother insisted on keeping them today where the birthday boy."

"Who's your friend Jill and most of the guys are in the man cave."

"Everyone this is William the III."

"Ok nice to meet."

India went back inside to finish things before it was time to eat and sing happy birthday Jill wanted to know what they thought about her new beau India asked stated that she hoped they were just friends the baby was only a 10 weeks. Jill assured them that she knew what she was doing and them not to judge her they both agreed friends don't judge India didn't want t\he night to end Noel getting to know everyone they were the last two to leave   Noel opened and closed the car door for India they made it half way down the street.

"So did you have a good time?"

"You mean before are after you allowed your boy toy to humiliate me."

"Do you mean Peter?"

"India you know exactly who I'm speaking about I guess I'm just the butt of everyone's joke Leah and Greg must think I'm a   fool I just cant figure why in the hell their being so nice to me if they want you with their brother and brother in law."

"Noel there is no conspiracy Leah and Greg love you as my,"

"You're what, India say it,"

"I'm trying to say it if you'll let me and why are you getting loud cant we end this lovely night happy,"

"Happy,"

"Have you completely lost your mind I practically begged you to see someone and not only does your boy toy find out about but he pays for your session he practically loses his mind when he sees you and you want to end this night happy you out of your fucking mind women."

"Oh now your cursing at me."

"Yeah well I guess you're not just rubbing off on PETER huh."

"What are you trying to say Noel he gave me his therapist number months ago we discuss it when we first met I met him for drink he's going threw a lot I just trying to be a friend."

"Bull Shit India pure and utter Bull Shit this mans knows more about you then I do does he know your family and you say you haven't slept with him is that your next confession."

"I 'm not making a confession I'm just explaining how things happened and you met my family."

"I mean the black side of your family damn it look I've had enough I'm taking you home.'

Noel made it to India's house in minutes he pulled up abruptly he didn't put the car in park he told India to get out of the car,

"Excuse me."

"You heard me right India."

"I'm not going anywhere are you coming up you never want to come to my place." India said

He did not say a word he knew saying anything about not wanting to be around her sister would be disastrous plus things weren't good between them so he didn't say a word. India folded her arms and turned to look at Noel he looked straight ahead for a few seconds then put the his Mercedes in park he bite down on his jaw bone he wanted nothing more then to hold India in his arms tonight. But he was not going to be played as a fool he was the one running out of energy he opened his car door then walked around the back of the car India looked up. Noel was at her door he opened the door and put his hands under India and lift her out of the car she gripped her purse he bend down and released India to her feet.

"Your just going to leave me here are you serious, you can't be serious you better not get in that car and drove off Noel."

He didn't say a word he didn't look back he got in the car lock his doors then waited for India to go into her apartment after a few minutes India was still standing on the sidewalk with her arms folded. Noel slowly drove off still with out a word it took India a few for seconds before she realized Noel meant what he wasn't coming back the next day

India was glad summer time was in two weeks she was only going to had 6 weeks of summer school. She started to cancel her appointment with Dr. Torres but she felt going may save some lives because she was convinced Noel was the one that had lost his mind this time.

The doctor was a short and slender man with salt and pepper hair he said he was from India Peter told her that was one of the reasons he knew the therapy was meant to be, the session went well the Dr. refused India's payment offer. Saying the session was paid for the doctor said that Peter only told him that the two of them were very good friends.

India took a long hot bath the therapist gave India some reading material that she was going over how to relax and let go of situation that she had no control over. She put her hand back looking back and forth from the lit candles to the article.

There was a loud hard   knock at her door It startled India she laid there was a few seconds hoping that who ever it was could hear her yelling who is it no one answered and the knock was harder. Upset she was being interrupted India dried off put a tee shirt and then a rob on to answer the door she hated when her neighbors let people in when she didn't ask them to she quickly opened the door. India saw EJ's face sweating then her eyes went down to the gun that he had facing her then back up to his fearless eyes.

"Where in the hell is my sister."

"Bitch don't ask me questions I told you what to do now sit your ass on that couch."

He closed and locked the door then turned the television he told India to get her purse and atm card fast,

"Where is my sister what did you do to her."

"Bitch you say another word I'm going to shut your stuck up ass down for good give your ass some real man hood now go get what I told you."

"India got her purse from hanging behind her bedroom door she still had the $200 dollars that she was going to give the therapist then she grabbed her atm card she didn't want to give him anything without him telling her where her sister was he was acting nervous pacing back and forth across the living room floor.

"Shit, Shit hurry up girl."

India rushed out of the room and handed the money and card to him there was breaking news on the television a bank on 1st and Greenly had just been robbed a security guard has been shot and there was know word on his condition yet. The news reported that the man was a young black male he was were a dark blue shirt and a pair of dark blue jean he was wearing a baseball hat and he is armed and dangerous.

India look EJ up and down he dumped the rest of the things in her purse onto the living room floor he told India to get her car keys and to put on a pair of pants or she could go naked he didn't care.

"I'm not going anywhere with you where is Shay did she have anything to do with this."

He rushed over to India and smacked her across the face knocking her to the floor then quickly telling her to get up and get dressed. India sat up then wiped the bleed from her mouth she looked up at him he had the gun still pointed at her as she got up she thought maybe he'd take her to Shay.

"You're a hard headed bitch and your sister started to act just like you but I fixed that shit is this all the money you've got this won't get me anywhere."

"I thought you just robbed a bank."

The words came before she had time to think about them he punched her right in the stomach then told her to get her phone India was choking gasping for air she told him the phone was in the kitchen. He told her to get it she put on a pair of jogging pants and rushed into the kitchen turning the stove on under the cooking grease she had left in a pot after frying chicken. Then she told him the phone wouldn't reach he'd have to use the phone in her room on the nightstand India stood in the living room door way holding her stomach she was to worried about her sister. Worry about what he would do to her he started yelling into the phone saying where is the bitch how did she get away India's hands started to shake. She knew he was talking about Shay what had he done to her she didn't want to burn him to a crisp until she knew so she left the pot boiling he told whomever was on the phone to leave and take any evidence with him then he hung up the phone. He told India to hurry up he grabbed India by her hair and directed her out of the apartment door he didn't allow her to lock it. India was starting to fear the worst about how this day would end for she, Shay and EJ all he kept repeating was the bitch should have done what she was told if the bitch would have done what she was told. He would be rich on his way to the Bahamas EJ let go of India hair once they got outside the sun was shining bright it the first week of June.

"Bitch which one of these cars is your's."

India pointed to the red car but didn't say a word she didn't know where he wanted to take her and India knew letting him take her wouldn't be good but she couldn't jeopardize Shays safety EJ was fumbling with the car keys. Everything seemed quiet there was no traffic coming from either directions India had seconds to decided if she was going to risk her and her sisters life. EJ had dropped the keys trying to hold his gun on India he told her to pick them up then he heard the words,

"Police get on the ground get on the ground now."

EJ looked at India with fury in his eyes India looked behind him there was men wearing black hats and vase coming from everywhere EJ had his gun pointed at India's chest he told her not to move her he would blow a whole in her chest she did not move she could not move.

"Put the gun down and get on the ground we have you surrounded."

"I'm not going anywhere you son of a bitches I'll kill all of you and this bitch." EJ said

EJ swung India around and put his arm around her neck with the gun to her head now,

"There's no place for you to go so you might as well release her and surrender son"

"Look don't call me son I'm not your fucking son this bitches sister made me miss out on a lot of money and she going to pay for it."

"Can you find my sister Shay Wilcox he's done something to her please."

EJ hit India in the head with the gun,

"Shut up bitch."

"Sir put the gun down nobody has to get hurt here let's end this before that happens."

"Is he dead."

"Who are you talking about son?"

"You know gooding damn well who I'm talking about the security guard you not here for nothing don't play me."

"We are not sure of his condition at this time put the gun down let the women go and we can talk about it look we have snipers on   the roof there is no place for you to go lets end this son."

EJ looked up at the apartment roof he saw the scopes of two gun at each end of the apartment building there was a day care across the street were he saw the end of yet another sniper gun. He took his gun away from India head and point them at each of the gun that were pointed at him then he pointed his gun straight ahead at the men that were getting closer and closer to him and India. India heard one shot then she felt blood splash all over her face the sniper had shot EJ right between his eyes he fell to the ground with his gun still in his hand. India was frozen in place she couldn't move until she saw Shay coming from behind an officer running toward her crying bloody clothes their embrace was surreal they cried in each others arm for what seemed like eternity. Shay repeating over and over that she was sorry, Sorry for ever being with EJ and putting India in danger Ej wanted her to rob the bank. With him when Shay refused, he told her he'd kill India he'd had a friend to hold Shay hostage tying her to the bed in the basement the guy burned her with cigarettes while waiting for EJ to return. Shay hit the guy in the head with an iron and escape running down the street for help until a women finally stopped and drove Shay to a police station Shay explain things to the police officer and told them that they need to help her sister she escape to safe her sister. EJ dropped the money after he shot the security guard that died four hours later EJ died instantly the snipers noticed smoke rushing to the roof the police called for ambulances and fire trucks. By the time the fire trucks arrived they found that India's apartment was engulf with flames the fire fighter put the fire out and told India her apartment was ruined her pictures furniture everything at this point India could only be grateful that she and Shay were alive she would dread the lost of Ronald's things later. She didn't let the ambulance take her to the hospital she make Shay go and told that she and Leah would be there Leah didn't have time to ask India questions. She arrive to see the smoke and India sitting in the back of an ambulance she and Greg took her to the hospital to check on Shay India called Shay sponsor she was at the hospital in minutes. India knew that Shay would have to take a drug test after a two hour wait Shay drug test came back negative she had kept her promise to herself and to India. Which made her eligible for housing at a group house room an board was free they would help Shay stay clean and found her a job and permanent housing. India stayed with Leah and Greg but after scaring them and her god kids to death with three nights in a roll of loud and haunting nightmare India told them she would go to a hotel they insisted that she stay. India was to embarrassed she refused to stay she knew that they were sincere about their invitation but she didn't   know how to explain the nightmares.   They were starting to be about Noel and EJ her kids at school India didn't know what was going on she just knew she couldn't stay another night with Leah and Greg. She loved and respected them but she had to go Peter came in right when India was about to leave and Leah was following behind her pleading for her not to go Leah used her last playing card the children saying they will be hurt if India left.

"India I came over as soon as I could I was out of town babe I'm so sorry were are you going I thought you were staying here is your place ready."

"Hi Peter I'm never going back there, But I just don't want to put Leah and Greg out any more beside Greg's parent will be in town tomorrow I cant keep putting them out."

Leah was very emotional India   had an appointment with her therapist later on that day he wanted to hypnotize India to search for answers since India wouldn't let him in during their last session he even told India she might have to see another therapist if she wasn't going to cooperate.

"Leah please understand I don't want to put you guys out any more then I have I cant keep waking the kids up in the middle of the night."

"Then you should call Noel why go to a hotel they are not safe."

"Leah EJ's dead he cant hurt me."

"Hold on hold on this fool has let too many things happen to you India its obvious he can't handle being your man you're coming with me I have to go back out of town for another week. But I'll be back next Wednesday my condo have secured doors and a doorman that monitors everything your be perfectly safe there lets go."

He grabbed India's suitcase with all of her new outfits and small amount of belongings that she was able to salvage from her apartment.

"Peter that's not going to work India can't stay with you." Leah said

"Why not sis tell me Greg's parents like to sleep in separate room you guys don't have the room I do it's a done deal lets go baby."

"Peter you have to stop calling me that."

"Why your not with that jerk any more I knew It was a matter of time I'll take care of you just as friends India   I know you've been through a lot I'm not trying to pressure you I promise." Peter said

India agreed   even though Leah wanted to call Noel she felt comfortable with India going to Peter's for now India didn't say why she and Noel hadn't talk how could she explain that Noel thought that all of her friends were conspiring against their relationship. She couldn't help that she was closer to her friends than her family but she was determined to change that Dena drove down to check on her she was a full 7 months pregnant. She and her husband drove down but could only stay over night Dena had to go on bed rest   India   knew she couldn't talk to Dena she would only tell India whatever it was it was her fault and to work it out. .   India had even told Toshiba about him she was ecstatic she could not wait to meet him. India hated she's going to have to break everyone's heart eventually.

India followed Peter to his apartment introducing her to the doorman he showed her around his place he didn't have much time until his flight so reluctantly he left giving India his security code.

India showered then left for her therapy appointment she told Dr Torres that she thought about being hypnotized but had not made a decision yet they talked about her relationship with Noel the entire hour. India had not been able to finish the information he had given her they talked briefly about the fire the situation that caused it the doctor asked India how she felt about her sister. Then EJ being shot to death in front of her that made India lay back on the leather therapy chair she closed her eyes and shook her head from side to side then said she had not had much time to think about things. She was very happy that Shay had been scared straight literally and as for EJ, she told Dr Torres she knew that his advice to her was to stop pushing more and more things of importance into her closet. That he is working on revealing to India how full it already was India understood that but couldn't push it forward she didn't know where she would live everything was destroyed in the fire things that she could never ever replace. India slipped and told the Doctor that she was staying at Peter's house the Doctors eyes widened he questioned India's decision to stay with Peter. With her knowing full well how Noel felt about their friendship India reminded the doctor that Noel had turned his back on her the doctor then sat back in his chair.   He crossed his legs and looked at India with a tight face he told her that he usually liked to start from the beginning of a person's life then work toward the end and he has struggled a little on the fact of India making things difficult. He explained to her that he had spoken to a few colleague and they felt like the type of help India needed without her immediate attention to her issues. Therapy would not do her any good Dr. Torres carefully explain things taking her future into her own hands with his helps India agreed again even though she feels strongly about beating herself up. About her past things like the abortion, and so on he told her that she needed to stop blocking her path. India stood up from the hard sofa and asked the Doctor was he calling India retarded are something the doctor laughed for at least a minute he asked India to sit back down then he apologized for laughing he boldly told India that she was a real piece of work with a serious case of self-destruction and that he had no idea where her comment came from. India told the doctor that she was not going to stay and let him insult her anymore the doctor told her that there was not enough time in the day for all of her drama that she needed to sit herself back down. They needed to get down to business if she truly loved Noel she needed to learn how to show and then tell him then he got even bolder he told India that the reason she continues to keep Peters in her life is it allows India to keep Noel at arms length. He knows she isn't doing it on purpose but she needs to know that she is doing this India returned the favor she was now laughing at the doctor she told him the reason that Peter is in her life is because they are friends. That she should be allowed to have friends the doctor gave her a firm look again sitting up in his big leather chair his voice deepen when he told India that Peters intentions were not for friendship judging from what India had already told him. He stated she needed to stop all ties with Peter immediately and that Noel had a right being hesitate and wanting to move forward with

313

her that she has too many obstacles in their way. India disagreed then yelled out that she loves Noel at least she feels that she does the doctor cut her off and asked if Noel knew that and India said how could he not the doctor talk for the rest of the session. He gave her more reading materials he had them in order for each awaited break through by the end India understood what he meant about Peter. She had to get out of denial the doctor told India to write out her thought before she goes to bed to try and pin point the nightmares and to practice in the mirror. What she would say to Noel if she could she went back to Peter's place an older lady met her at the door she talked a mile a minute she had a pot of beef stew for India she said Peter said to take good care of her and since she didn't have any family she was more than happy to help out. India reluctantly invited her inside oh my the lady talked and talked stating that she had a black friend when she was little her she use to come over with her mother to clean their house. The lady said she always liked black people India had no idea where the conversation came from are where it was going India fell asleep a few time. The lady never notice it India could think of nothing but Noel wondering why he wasn't there the fire the shooting was all on the news why wasn't he concern. After two hours the women finally left it was the middle of the day India couldn't think about going to a hotel right now she figure it out before Peter returned India fell straight to sleep on the living room sofa music playing.

Mindy has been calling India over and over she wanted to thank India for talking to her uncle about her beau even though under the circumstances no one had met him Mindy also needed to tell India   about her grandfather. Even though her uncle told her not to say a word she knew her uncle Noel needed India right now more then anything her grandfather had a massive heart attack. He had told Noel at Mindy's party that his heart was starting to give out on him he didn't want surgery and that he didn't want to be kept alive in a vegetative state things didn't look good for him. Mindy told her uncle that something was wrong that India's phone was disconnect Noel told her that he didn't have time for India's shenanigan's right now his mother Olean was frantic that she was losing her husband   Noel told his niece that India's behavior was normal.   Mindy put her summer schedule on hold to be in town for her grandparents

"Uncle what are you talking about India is a gift from God."

"Yeah a rotten one."

"Uncle, India is a very complex woman you have to give her more then a chance she needs to be here right now as a matter of fact I'm sure she would want to be here for you for us right now something's wrong I know it.

Noel hugged his niece tightly he knew the reason why Mindy was trying to hold on to India she was scared for her grandparents and she didn't want to lose the closest thing that she'd ever had to a mother. She's never like Noel's girlfriends and vise versa the women he'd attract didn't care about anything but themselves one of his ex girlfriends faked a pregnancy saying now he would have a baby of his own another told him that Mindy was not his responsibility Noel had to end one relationship after the other and her uncle never knew that Mindy felt guilty about it.

Mindy was fidgeting around the hospital with plans of her own she didn't want to handle the situation on her own so she had not mention that her boyfriend had arrived in Illinois a few days ago to be with her he was staying in a hotel near by. And Mindy was planning on going to Indiana to find out what was going on with India Sean had brought round trip plane tickets for them. Mindy tapped into her saving that Noel and his parents set up for her the day she came into their lives for car rental when they got there and other expenses she knew with the amount of money in the account that no one would notice she just didn't no how they were going to sneak out until Noel came back into the hospital room.

Noel got off the phone with his business partner Javier he was taking care of everything

for the last two weeks telling him he did not know how long he would be away

when he got back in the hospital room. His mother was crying she knew the pain that

her husband was feeling in his heart was far worse then anything his father was saying

Olivia's name over and over. No one knew what to say Olean held his and Mindy's hand

she whispered to Noel that she trusted in God's will but she knew wanting his daughter

here was the reason her husband Ned of 38 years was holding on. Olean let go of her

husbands hand for the first time that day and direct Noel out in the hallway she request

that he try and find his big sister even though all of their interventions have failed this

needed to be done. Noel pleaded with his mother to rethink her request he did not want

her getting her hopes up at a time like this and he could only imagine what state Olivia

would be in but she insisted so Noel complied. He waited until his fathers brother and

sister in-law arrived from Alabama where most of Ned's family were from, Mindy and

Noel didn't like Illinois that much so Noel settled in Indiana once he got out of college. It

was not far from his parent's Noel was ready to carry out his mother's request he left

Mindy in charge giving her a kiss on her forehead.

Noel jumped in his BMW then called the investigator he last hired to find Olivia she was

last spotted outside of Gary Indiana a few hours from where   Noel lives Noel headed that

way. He was having a hard time blocking his thought of India out of his mind if his father

didn't pull through then he would be the man of the family he never intended on doing that alone his father told Noel of his failing health at Mindy's party he told his son that he had no worries and would be leaving him in charge. He was the finest man that he knew and that he knew that India was the one for him they had a lot in common they put their families before themselves. He who finds a wife finds a good thing but with two stubborn people at the table that at some point someone is going to be giving more and receiving less and in the end things will work out for the good.

That repeated over and over in Noel's head and before he knew it he was out of Illinois and in Indiana he headed for the area that the detective got some information from he drove around he didn't see many people out the sun was shining bright he didn't have much time. Finally he settled on a block that had a few people staying close to his car Noel showed the neighborhood people of picture of Olivia the one he took of her the last time she visited. He didn't think anyone would notice her pictures from college long pretty hair thin waist with curvy hips and a smile brighter then the sun the last picture is how they would recognize her so he stood there for hours.

Mindy told her grandmother that she would go to the house to get it ready for the family even though everything was already in order. But she and Sean had to get going before Noel returned someone had to return with good news Mindy was a nervous wreck about her uncle finding her mother. But this was for her grandfather and she understood her grandparents had asked Noel about India he escape reason so far. She and Sean arrived at the airport then rented a car Sean set his watch to the hour they had no time to waste they arrived at India's apartment the only address Mindy knew they rang all the doorbells. The one they rang repeatedly read manager until a woman that looked like her wig was on backwards opened the door a little dog started biting at Mindy sandal. Sean pulled her back a little when the women gave them a mean look and raised her fist at them.

"You two crazy fools the one ringing my bell?" Ms. Shiawassee said

Mindy jerked her foot from the dogs small mouth Sean kicked at the dog then the women swung her cane at them yelling for them to get away from her door. Sean grabbed Mindy by the waist trying to pull her away.

"Ma'am we are sorry but we are looking for my aunt India."

Sean was still trying to pull Mindy to leave,

"Sean no stop we can't go." Mindy said

"I don't give a damn who your looking for she gone no more India the fire took everything they were shooting everywhere around here, now get away from my door before I call the cops they come and shoot you like they did that bank robber you hear me." Ms. Shiawassee yelled

She grabbed her dog up into her arms and slammed the door that was way too much information coming to fast at Mindy she looked at Sean with both her hands to her face. She was walking in circle then she started walking to the back of the building were India living room window was there was a big parking lot full of park cars. Sean followed behind Mindy they walked around a big tree when they saw some men on ladder's climbing to the top of what was left of India side of the apartment building. Half the roof was gone and the apartment windows were boarded up Mindy felt like she was going to throw up she was bend over choking and crying Sean was trying to calm her down.

"Baby, honey calm down please."

"She dead, India's dead Sean oh my God I'm losing everyone oh my God."

"What's going on guy is she alright.' The man said

He was getting out of his car and started walking over toward them with his wife he asked if they needed anything,

We, we just found out about her aunt India." Sean said

He started to get emotional while holding on to Mindy for dear life he wiped his face while the women handed them tissue from her purse.

"Well we know she lost pretty much everything but at least she didn't lose her life I think nothing is more important then that really you need to know that." The woman said

"You mean she's not dead." Mindy screamed

"Why would you think that haven't you'll seen her since the fire."

"Well the lady with the dog in her building said someone was shooting and then there was a fire." Mindy said

"That old lady needs to be put to sleep along with that dog no one knows who's the oldest I am betting on her." The man said

"We've been living here for 17 years we know everything India had some trouble with that sister and her boyfriend he was crazy the police shot and killed him though, India had something on the stove,

"Child it's a long story her apartment caught fire thank the Lord they weren't still in there I'm pretty sure she left with her friends though I thought you said she was your aunt."

"Well she will soon be married to my uncle so,"

"And where was he in all this?" The woman stated

The man told his wife to mind her business,

"Well she left with the young lady that use to live here, Leah   I have a number for her in the house I'm not sure if it's recent but you can try to reach her." The woman said

"Um yes ma'am I'm her niece Mindy and this is Sean my boy um my boyfriend.'

"Well I would love to know how she's doing so I'll go get it for you all just wait right here."

  Mindy and Sean followed, the couple to the front of the apartment building even though they looked innocent they stood there with them.

"Well, I'm almost her niece my uncle Noel is going to marry her I'm sure of it."

The man just shook his head while still waiting on his wife,

Mindy was still shaking all over she couldn't calm down within minute's she thought India was dead now she's been told that she is alive all the while watching Sean's watch for the time they needed to be back in Illinois soon. She didn't want anything to happen to her grandfather while she was on a quest that her uncle had forbidden her from but Mindy knew it was worth it and she would do anything to finish this task. She knew there was nothing she could do to change her grandfathers health but she knew he wanted the best for his only son and she knew it was India, she wiped her eyes the woman stopped in her tracks

"You mean your Mr. Fine's niece I remember now well I hope he has a good explanation for abandoning her." The woman handed Mindy the number

 "With all due respect ma'am I'm suppose to be in Illinois right now my grandfather is seriously ill and my uncle is there rather he's looking for my mother because my grandfather wants her to be with us." Mindy stopped talking

She was getting   a little choked up Sean held her close they both looked at the woman with desperation the woman and her husband immediately took notice. India was one of the best neighbors they had. They were close to Leah while she lived there also India talked about Noel as though he was a super star no one would ever know that they didn't even think he was real until the day they let him in to the locked apartments he expressed the fact that he needed to see the love of his life.

"I'm so sorry to hear about your grandfather so your uncles been caring for his father these last few weeks."

"Yes the doctors are trying everything finding India among some other folks will bring things together my grandfather's wish will be done I'm sure of it." Mindy said

The woman gave them big hugs then sent them on their way. She also gave Mindy her number to keep them posted they would do anything they could for India and Leah. Mindy and Sean said their good byes as they dialed the number on their cell phone a quiet voice answered.

"Hello"

"Hello may I speak to India please?' Mindy asked

"Auntie India I miss you are you with Uncle Peter." Ezra's small voice said

"No, no this is Mindy, I'm looking for India please."

"Mommy someone's on the phone for auntie India I want auntie India."

"Yes, hello who is this?" Leah said

"Hi, uh hello this is Mindy I'm trying to find India I'm Noel's niece please, I need to speak with India." Mindy said

"Hello Mindy, I'm so glad to hear from you but India's not here." Leah said

"What do you mean I need to talk to India please it's an emergency I can't get into details right now can you please tell me how I can find her." Mindy said

"She's staying uh   she at my well she will be right back   is really going through a lot right now."

"Look I'm begging you how do I find her I have to get back to Illinois." Mindy stressed

Leah blurted her address out and told Mindy that she would get India to her house quickly they hung up and Leah immediately dialed Peter's number the phone rang over and over Leah started pacing back and forth.   She was in her kitchen trying to keep the children quiet she didn't think telling Mindy that India was at her brother Peter's would be a good idea she didn't want India to go but India insisted. Leah hung up she thought about driving to Peter's she called out to Greg he came into the kitchen.

"What's the matter honey, who was on the phone."

"I was calling India she's not answering I'm going to go over there can you give the kids a snack or something I'll be right back." Leah said

"Honey, what's going on she's probably out somewhere." Greg said

"I just gave Mindy our address they are on their way over here they think India's here I have to go get her." Leah said

"Honey calm down, sit down take a deep breath who is Mindy and what does she want with India." Greg stated

Leah sat down and took a deep breath then stood back up grabbing her purse and looking for her car keys.

"Mindy is Noel's niece they are looking for India she sounded hysterical she said she had gone to India's place and that she needed to see her it's an emergency so I have to go get her."

"Look Leah India's been through enough you might need to think this through you don't even know what she want's where is Noel.'

Before Leah could answer their doorbell was ringing Leah looked at Greg as though she had done something wrong, nothing he was saying stuck with   Leah sje dialed Peters number again Greg finally left her and went to answer the front door. Greg spoke while standing in the doorway arms folded India was his only concern,

"It's very nice to meet the two of you but India has been through a lot and my wife and I do not intend on anything else occurring anytime soon she mean a lot to our family." Greg said

'Sweetie what are you doing invite them in," Leah said

"I will not until my questions are answered."

"Your name is Greg right?" Mindy asked

"Yes,

"And this is must be your wife Leah.' Mindy said

"Your more than right to be concerned I've only heard bits and pieces after talking with India's crazy landlord I thought she was dead.'

Tears filled Mindy's eyes Sean once again took to her side finishing her sentence,

"Hi I'm new to the family it's sound like a lot has been going on we just want to make sure that India is safe trust me we all want the same thing, We also need for her to know that Mindy's grandfather is very ill and Noel needs her right now if that's possible." Sean said

Leah opened the door she and Greg stepped aside Mindy told them they needed to get back everyone said how sorry they were for each other situation Leah was relieved to know that Noel didn't abandon India. As India thought even though his situation was severe she too knew that they both needed each other they told Mindy that they would found India and if they had to drove her to Illinois themselves she would be by Noel's side Mindy and   Sean left with confidence that raced to the airport   back to Illinois.

Noel was flustered he didn't know what else to do and he didn't want to spend to much time chasing a ghost he's never disappointed his father a day in his life this time would be the first he drove around for three hours straight hoping that his desperation to find his sister for not only his personal reasons but for selfish reason not knowing which one out weighed the other.

This day was one of the hardest in his life he was 25 miles from where he started   and the traveling has defeated leaning against his car an older gray haired gentleman with a older woman   they were walking toward him. Noel   started to get into his car but something stopped him he looked toward what looked like a couple they both had on coats even though it was around 72 degrees he waited until they noticed him.

"Hello, hi my name is Noel, I just wanted to asked if either of you have seen this woman this is the most recent picture that I have of her may I show the two of you?"

Noel felt himself getting defeated and hopeless the closer the couple got he could hardly gather his thoughts he had lost his sister he was losing his father and he didn't know what category to put India into. His hand was shaking as he showed them the picture of Olivia the picture was from the last time she had made her way to his house so many years ago the woman took hold of the picture.

"What you want with her, you some kind of cop or something?"

"No I'm not a cop she's,'

"You know everyone out here ain't lost some people don't want or need to be found you know that son we don't need anyone judging us." The woman said

"Yes I do and I'm not trying to be anyone's judge or jury out here this is my sister and I, rather we love her unconditionally we always have and we always will but right now I need the woman in the picture to put all things aside I need her to forgive herself. Because our father is on his death bed and the one thing, the only comfort that he needs right now is to reassure his baby girl that the door to her home will always be opened."

The woman took the picture from Noel's hand even though she had already recognized her the man smiled he looked Noel up and down.

"Just how far or how much would you be willing to give for some information?" The man asked

"Excuse me." Noel said

The woman quickly grabbed the picture from the man that she has known from the streets for the last thirteen years they met at a crack house and have never left each other's side . This is the only commitment either of them has ever   kept the woman was a registered nurse for twelve years beaten by her husband for nine of those years one night after working a ten hour shift. She came home and refused to clean the snow from her husbands car he beat her unconscious a neighbor found her that night she left the emergency room without thought. She walked away from her husband and their four son's she knew her husband would never let her leave with them she got on a trailblazer bus not knowing were she would end up she never looked back. The man he never knew his father his mother died when he was a teen he was raised by his Aunt and molested by her husband until the age of 16 after his uncle beat him in a drunken rage he left and he has been in the streets every since.

"What did you say your name is son?" The woman asked

"Noel ma'am."

" I don't mean to be rude I just need to find my sister."

The woman took Noel's shaken hands into hers surprised by him not flinching his eyes focused into her weary eyes the man stepping back not aware of what was happening not sure of the woman he thought he knew so well. She did not have a soul or heart as far as he knew but right now at present, she was crying now reaching for Noel's face he did not flinch.

"I know her your sister, she makes sure most people don't use dirty needle's out here

She is a good woman I have always told her she does not belong out here and in return, she tells me the same pisses me off every time." The woman laughed

Hope invaded his heart he hugged the woman holding her tight he quickly released her hoping he didn't hurt the woman she laughed as she noticed the panicked look on Noel's face she pictured him as her oldest son so handsome and graceful even in the worst situation.

"I really have to get back to my father in Illinois I can't stay out here any longer he needs me do you know where I can find her I'm sorry may I address you by your name."

"Not right now son, but soon I haven't seen her in a week or so, doesn't mean anything you go where the wind leads you but I'm sure I can get word to her for you." The woman said

Noel reached into his car the man put his hands up as though he was ready to fight he told Noel he would have no problem taking him to the ground the man's build was solid   for a drug user but his voice didn't follow. Noel was not alarmed he reached into his car and got out the ticket to Illinois that he had purchase for Olivia without hesitation he handed it to the women   she didn't search the envelope she put it inside her coat pocket. Noel was at a lost for words he did not want to offend the couple in anyway.

"Is that a plane ticket for us?" The man asked

"No Jackass it's a ticket for his sister."

The man laughed as he tried to figure out how much a refund would be for a plane ticket the woman couldn't see anything but her oldest son face still hoping that one day he would have unconditional love and come searching for her with his brothers. He ignored his soul mates excitement but what she said in this world goes, she promised Noel that the ticket wouldn't be used in vain Noel gave the women another hug. Then went into his pocket but before his hand came out with money he asked the women would it be alright to thank her with a monetary gift they were the only ones that didn't hold their hands out since he started searching four hours ago. The woman didn't say a word she continued to look Noel in his eyes Noel reached into his pocket   coming out with the money he had left after already giving $400 dollars away with no insight on his sister's where about for today. He handed the woman four one hundred dollar bills hoping it would help lead his sister closer to her journey which is her home. Than   Noel handed the man three hundred dollar bills just hoping he and the woman also had journeys. The man thought for a quick second how it would be seeing his older sister in Ohio   but the moment was just a moment as he took the money from Noel strong hands.

Noel drove off with calmness in his heart he started again thinking of India how she would have handle the situation if it was her sister. Noels phone had not rang since he has been gone as he phoned the hospital to give a quick word that he would be back soon he drove in the directions of the signs for a gas station upon driving through downtown he noticed a beaming sign that read (Tiffany's) he immediately pulled over in front of the store. They have a door man that opened the door and a woman quickly greeted him toward their finest jewelry Noel reached for his wallet seconds after noticing a ring. It was almost as beautiful as India the woman was all smiles as she cosigned that he had chosen one of the most expensive ring in the store. She stated that whomever the woman he was buying the ring for must be a wonderful woman then she quickly swiped Noel business credit card she wrapped the small box in India favorite color red with a small gold bow then Noel was off. It was 4 pm and he would be back in Illinois in a couple of hours maybe less at high speed not knowing how are when he would present India with this ring. But he wanted to show his father and tell him he would never stop being the man he has raised him to be.

India awoke out of her deep sleep in a sweat she jumped off the couch wiping her face with her tee shirt. She instantly heard the therapist voice over and over in her head she was using Peter as a shield she quickly started gathering her things when she got them all packed she sat down on the couch. Then took a deep breath she knew it would be completely rude to just leave like this all that Peter has done even though it has been for his own agenda it still would not be right. India used Peters note pad and pen then carefully wrote Peter a long letter she placed it along with his keys on his dining room table. Then called Jill to say she needed her car which was waiting on her rental car since the new love of her life wrecked her car on their way from a gambling boat.

India was determined to find the love of her life she didn't know how but she was going to be herself she was going to kick his door down if she had too Jill came to pick her up in a flash she was going to say goodbye to Peters neighbor. But half the day was already gone Jill was talking a mile a minute about Jim's mother being such a great grandmother and how she has not had to do anything. They had no problem keeping Shantae and Jake when she and her beau went out of town which no one knew about until she got back {spare of the moment} she said. India did not know where she was going to stay camped out on Noel's lawn she guess but she had to talk to Leah so they drove there first. Leah was coming out of her front door getting into her car when India and Jill pulled up India's adrenaline was running high. She had to share her news with Leah she practically jumped out the car India was finally ready for love she didn't want to hurt anyone anymore. She just wanted to find Noel and convince him that they should still go to visit his parents and commit to a relationship,

"What are you guys doing here, Jill where are the kids, India I've been trying to reach you?"

"Well hello to you also sweetie." Jill said

"I'm just saying I haven't seen the babies in months." Leah said

"They are with Shantae's grandmother duh."

"Again?" Leah said

"I've tried to tell her she doesn't thing anything of it. India said

"India made it around the car finally,

"Coming from someone who has no children.' Jill said

"No that's coming from someone who's never having any children." India said

"Look, this time is about me right now I need to find my man quickly I need some TLC on my fractured bones and a home to stay I need,"

"India, India we need to go inside Mindy and her friend were here looking for you.' Leah said

She turned to go inside and they followed, Greg held the door while helping the women inside asking Jill were the children were she told him that they were safe at the new grandmothers house. On that note he volunteered to take his kids for ice cream things were back to normal since his family had gone Greg told the women bye then pack the kids into the car.

"Leah what's going on, Mindy was here are you sure?" India asked

"India of course I'm sure she looked just as you described her she was frantic she thought, well she thought anyway I didn't get to explain everything   but I did tell her that you were alright because she had to get back." Leah said

"When was this I need to tell Noel that I'll go with him to his parents house I have a couple of appointment to look at apartments, but that can wait so have I been wrong does

Noel still care?" India asked

Leah walked into her living room to pour her a drink then she sat down and take a deep breath.

"Well I'm not completely sure but I'm sure." Leah mumbled

"Give me a drink to, so you don't think I should go with him is that what your saying."

"You shouldn't be drinking are you still taking pain medicine for your fractured ribs India I'm sure he's moved on a guy like that please." Jill stated

while pouring herself a drink

"I poured them into the toilet I didn't like the way they made me feel I hate taking medicine ." India said

"You know how much those things cost I have lots of friends we could have made some cash from those pills India."

"We are not drug dealers Jill aren't you breast feeding you shouldn't be drinking.' India asked

"And that Is why I'm not breast feeding so aren't we all minding our own business, I stopped I mean I dried up." Jill said

"You dried up." Leah asked

"Hello guys you who, I'm over here." India said

"India, Noel's dad is very sick he's been in Illinois caring for him I told Mindy that I would get in touch with you." Leah said

"Oh my goodness Mr. Ned he is sick."

"Very sick India you have to go to them they need you and you need them." Leah said

"I, I can't go in the middle of something like this I mean his family means everything to him I can't interrupt something like that."

"Your not interrupting you will be giving your support India I'll go with you." Leah said

"You're always trying to hold India's hand Leah she is not a baby." Jill said

"Jill I thought we were minding our own business sweetie." Leah said

"Look India I'm sure he didn't know what happened and he needs you right now."

"What about Peter after he destroyed our relationship to be with you, your just going to turn your back on him now too." Jill said

"I can't do this with you Jill I left Peter a note thanking him for everything.' India said

"A note maybe we should try to call him you know how he reacts to things." Jill stated

" I tried calling him on his cell he didn't answer he'll be fine let me think for a moment Noel was furious with me the last time we were together."

"I'm sure that's the furthest thought in his mind Mindy insist that he misses you deeply.' Leah said

"And so will Peter." Jill said

 India gave Jill an evil look seems like she was on a roll,

"Ok you can't drive me Leah, I'll catch a plane Jill how many little bottle do you have in that purse."

"I have the name of the hospital right here." Leah said

"Tell Shay where I am you have her number and here is Noel's address and home phone number and his cell number just in case."

"Good thing schools out India you don't have to rush back stay by his side as long as he needs you don't mess this up." Leah said

"Right, thanks Leah I needed that.'

Mindy and Sean forgot all about their secret they walked hand and hand into the hospital room they didn't notice for a minute that everyone was looking at them Mindy called to check on her grandfather as soon as they got off the plane. Noel was not suppose to be back yet but somehow he was sitting next to her grandfather they were talking quietly Mindy looked around the hospital room her stomach had fallen to the floor and then she took a deep breath when she didn't see Olivia Noel stood to his feet.

"Mindy who is this?"

"Uncle, this is the guy India told you about my, this is Sean he wanted to be here for us."

Noel gave Sean a firm look his mother reaching and grabbing Noel by the hand,

"Son while you all were gone your father and I have been talking and it's time honey."

334

"Time, time for what mom?"

"Time to let this beautiful young lady grow up she is not her mother she's a young women now she shouldn't have to hide things from us we have to trust her son.' Mrs. Olean said

Noel quickly remembered the conversation with India he was upset at first that Mindy didn't come to him India reminded him that even though she is surrounded by a loving family she needed   a friend she chose her words carefully not to say {mother figure}. Noel looked back at his mother and father then at Mindy the same look she had as a little girl but his parents were right she wasn't a little girl any more she deserve their trust and to be happy. He did not quite understand this feeling he had right then and this was not the place to call in his investigator another time he walked over to Sean and shook his trembling hand. Mindy burst into tears she hugged her Uncle for dear life they all turned as his father started gasping for air they called for the nurse as his father reminded everyone that he couldn't hold on much longer.   Even for his baby girl the nurse quickly gave Ned a check up he still was not feeling any pain Mrs. Olean called her pastor to come pray with them the nurse said after his prayer that everyone should clear the room Ned needed some rest.

India stomach was tossing and turning   45 more minutes and she would be face to face with Noel she got even more nervous when she thought about all of his family being there this would be the second time India's entrance would be while Noel had been angry with her. But like Leah said, she is sure that was the farthest thing from Noel mind right now India had to blend in give her support. She took a cab to the hospital she decided to call Mindy's phone from the hospital lobby she didn't answer she didn't know where to put her luggage so she dragged it along with her. She arrived on the 12th floor intensive care she looked down at the paper she wrote the room number on she walked around the corner then looked up to search for the room in a distance she saw Mindy, with a guy an then Noel her vision didn't go past Noel there were several other people. India's heart started beating faster and faster it felt like it was beating out of her chest she dropped her suitcase it suddenly felt like it weighted a thousand pounds. Noel was rubbing his head back and forth then he shook the pastors hand then waved goodbye to him when he looked beyond the pastor.   There she was this had to be a dream he had not had any rest but this woman staring he continued to focus on her when he notice it was his love India he put his hands to his face. As though he was praying   he was he hadn't realize she was standing before him he almost knocked over a doctor reaching for her they were now a few feet of one another India opened   her arms he held her like it was the first time he had seen her in life.

Every bone in her body still hurt but the little bottles of liquor that Jill gave her had her so numb and Noel's touch took away the rest of her pain. They continued to repeat each others name   one apologizing to the other telling the other it wasn't the each others fault . Noel had India dangling in the air when Mindy yelled out for them to come into the room Noel reached for India's hand his father reaching for everyone to move toward him. Mrs. Olean thanking God out loud and speaking to the doctor at the   same time Noel calling out to her never letting go of India's hand even though she was trying to stay back Noel walked over to his mother when he heard the doctor saying there was nothing else that can be done Mrs. Olean yelled out (God mercy and grace is sufficient enough). She looked at India and put her hands to her face Noel put his arms around his mother and India followed. Mindy walked over she could not get India from her uncles grip so she just hugged them from behind.

"Mom I have something to tell you and dad and Mindy.'

He walked over toward his father, Ned was smiling telling his family he was going home to see his parents asking everyone not to cry or be sad for him he has lived a good life and has a wonderful wife and children. He wanted his granddaughter to know she was one of the bravest woman and never forget that she could be anything that she wanted to be in life. She hugged him tight dropping tears on him he continued to smile he pointed toward Sean and shook his hand after asking who he was he demanded for him do right and only right by his baby girl,

"Yes sir I promise."

"Son, son."

"I'm here dad I have something to say Pops.'

Noel gave his father a kiss and a hug he let India get closer,

"Hi, Mr. Ned,"

"Baby call me dad you still a pretty little thing where have you been my son can't wait forever you know.'

"Dad I got this.' Noel said

He turned India toward him while his mother and father and Mindy and the rest of the family all held hands wondering what was about to happen Noel got down on one knee taking a box from his pocket he opened it you could hear a pin drop Ned eyes widened he shook his head yes in agreement.

"India Hype I love you will you be my wife forever?"

India thought she was going to throw up even though she had not eaten she put her hand to her mouth begging God to keep whatever tears down but they fell from her eyes she was overwhelmed. She could hardly stand Mindy was in the back ground whispering yes over and over India thinking to herself about what she said she wasn't going to mess this up she loved this man and she didn't want to be without him ever again she looked at Mrs. Olean. She whispered welcome to the family India's hands were shaking up and down but she could not speak.

"Is that a yes?' Noel said

"Wow that's a big ring if she don't want it I do." Noel aunt yelled out

"Yes Noel, yes I'll marry you.'

India's body and mouth was moving and she had no idea how the room filled with voices Ned told his son that he was the man now and should live on his legacy to always put God and then his wife first everything else will always fall into place India and Noel hugged him. When Mrs. Olean reached to kiss her husband he took every bit of strength he had and hugged his wife then he quietly whispered (Goodbye shining star) that's what he called her the first time they went out his grip loosened Mrs. Olean followed his eyes as they closed he was gone.

The funeral was three days later Noels parents had everything planned to the tee Ned and Olean will be buried together in the end. And their church cooked everything the pastor gave a good sermon he made people laugh instead of cry. Everyone's remembrance of him didn't make them sad Mindy cried like a baby and Noel cried the night before in India's arms she had never seen a man venerable before. But then said he had to be the man of family now he missed his father already and couldn't see his life without him but with India by his side he would make it through. A few days after the funeral Mindy said she would stay the rest of the summer but Noel wouldn't hear of her leaving school. He agreed to only the summer even if he would have to stay himself   Sean had to get back he had to work and take care of his son his parents wanted to also meet Mindy Noel still hadn't questioned him but told them that he would be up there the day Mindy went back to school.

"Mom can you come back and stay with me."

"Oh honey you going to have a wife I can't be inconveniencing you'll.'

"Mrs. Olean you can never be that."

Noel smiled at India that was the perfect thing to say he told his mom she should not be alone she has not been alone since she was 19 years old. She told Noel her sister Caren could come back down and she had her church family they would come over everyday they have lots of friends and good neighbors.

"I know mom but how long would that last."

"Look baby we don't have to worry about that now you and your partner Javier have to get back to work I know you you're a work alcoholic you cant be doing that with a new wife you know I'll be fine with Mindy we going to have a great time."

"Yes grandma we will, will shop everyday."

"Great just what I want to hear." Noel said he felt his wallet getting heavy

India didn't know what to say she still haven't been able to tell Noel anything not even the fact that she is homeless maybe she'll stay with his mother for the summer too. The church family was bringing food everyday they were gather in the dining room eating meatloaf mash potatoes and gravy homemade biscuit and fried chicken and corn, cabbage and a pound cake with glaze icing.

"Mindy baby get the door I hope it's not any more food I'm going to bust." Mrs. Olean said

"Yes ma am I hope it's a chocolate cake we haven't have one of those yet."

Mrs. Olean asked Ned brother and his wife will they be staying longer there was plenty of room. His brother could wear some of Ned clothes if he needed too Mindy rushed past everyone crying she did not stop she run into the kitchen and out the back door.

"Honey what wrong." Mrs. Olean asked as she tried to get up from the table

Noel and his partner Javier rushed to the living to see what was going on India told Mrs. Olean she would check on Mindy she grabbed a few napkins and walked through the kitchen out the back door Ned's brother helped Mrs. Olean up and then his wife and they walked toward the living room,

"What's going on?" Mrs. Olean asked

"Mama I'm here where's daddy I'm here."

She looked at the women in her doorway clothes torn and dirty a scarf on her head frail and shaking when she made it to the women's eyes she knew instantly it was her baby girl she hesitated for a moment. Then she tried to picture her a thousand times nothing could have prepared her she reached out to her and Olivia ran into her arms.

"Mama I told Mindy I am going to get myself together I need to tell daddy I'm ready."

Mrs. Olean was choked up she tried to tell her but the look in her eyes took her way back she could see the pigtails and missing teeth.

"Liv, daddy gone."

Noel was still standing in the doorway Olivia hugged him then walked straight passed him talking a mile a minute she thanked Noel for the plane tickets calling him little brother over and over. He finally walked over grabbing hold of his mother she was weak at the knees she could only focus on Olivia's eyes anywhere else would tear her down after trying to be so strong this week this was something she's prayed for but not prepared for Noel sat his mother down on the sofa.

"Mom, dad is he,"

Mrs. Olean slowly reached for Olivia whispering he's gone as Olivia slowly walked toward her mother she slowly sat next to her she took her mothers hands then looked into her eyes repeating she was sorry over and over and how she never meant to hurt her family or her child never she held her mothers hands tight and said,

"Mommy I didn't know how to forgive myself how can he be gone how could I not say goodbye."

"Liv, he knew you loved him and dad never stopped loving you he told me to tell you he loved you and that he wanted you to come home and stay home."

"How can I stay now, I worried my father to death mom how can you forgive me." Olivia said

"Baby your father lived a full life he is home with the Lord now no one is to blame."

"He had to live it without me I've been so selfish feeling sorry for myself you'll all didn't raise quitters or loser I'm so sorry." Olivia said

"I'll go make some coffee and make you a plate Liv let you and your mother talk." Ned sister and law said

Everyone was leaving the living room Noel was undecided his mother hadn't shed one tear she knew her husband would not have wanted her two but seeing her baby girl look this way seeing all the trials and tribulations in her daughter eyes wanting all along to take her pain away Noel was getting choke up too he held it in.

"I'm going to check on Mindy I'll be right back mom." Noel said

"I'm ok son go check on baby girl."

Mindy and India was sitting out back on   the picnic table Mindy was walking back and forth with her voice raised India watch her walk back and forth she knew exactly what Mindy was feeling but she didn't say. She knew Mindy was too young and emotional to understand she did not want her to think she was taking sides.

"Mindy honey I know we imagined seeing your mother in a different way but she's here baby she's finally here you can take this as slow as you'd like no one will rush you but we have to understand granddads leaving brought your mother here."

"I would rather have my grandfather any day." Mindy yelled out

"Sweet heart please try to understand this was the best she could do she could have sold the plane ticket but she didn't this is a gift from grandfather and from God grandmother wont be alone."

"You think I'm leaving that washed up crack head with my grandmother are you crazy." Mindy said

"Excuse me." Noel said

Mindy busted into tears again India held her she told Noel that Mindy would need more time that he should get Olivia washed up she has several tee shirts and sweats she could ran out and buy some undergarments she and Mindy were going to take a ride. Noel did not agree but India started walking off with out his approval Mindy did not stop crying he figured India's was right. Noel went back inside Olivia was eating like her life depended on it after eating he told her to follow him he'd give her clothes to put on after she showered she looked around like she'd never been in their childhood home before following behind Noel every step of the way. Noel gave his frail sister another big hug as she smiled going into the bathroom Noel sat in his old room while Olivia showered for an hour and a half she washed and brushed her hair back into a neat ponytail. India was a size 9 and her sweats were way to big even though Olivia was about 5 ft 10 inch she walked out the bathroom with her ragged clothes Noel rushed to her side with a plastic bag putting his arm around her,

"You wont need these anymore sis I'm glad you're here."

"Even though this is my fault little brother." Olivia said

"Hey, what did mom say dad's death brought us an angel."

"Do you mean that?"

"Look don't go trying to convince yourself to do that life of hell again Olivia this is your home you have a daughter and mother and brother that need you to do and get better."

"No more guilt trips live please." Noel said

They stood in the hallway talking until their mother called out for them they giggled going down the stairs Noel said that he would not leave going back home until Olivia was in a good treatment program they all agreed she needed in house treatment first. Mrs. Olean called over a church member that headed a drug program at their church she gave them a number to a head director of drug treatment center. It is suppose to be the best in the state of Illinois it was right outside of Chicago about an hour from where they lived they would call first thing Monday morning. The house became quiet once India and Mindy came into the house Mindy walked passed everyone going straight to the kitchen and back out back India stayed in the living room she asked Noel if she could speak to him alone she followed him up stairs to his old room that was still set as though he'd never left for college.

"Yes baby I was getting worried you know." Noel said

"Noel you have to learn to trust me.'

"India I do trust you but you need to learn that checking in is normal not a battle."

"Ok, I'll accept that for now we rode away for two hours before Mindy finally decided to stop at Kmart for the under garments for Olivia she seems she's so nice ." India said

India wiped her eyes she couldn't help but feel their pain and sorrow they have so many things in common that it began to seem scary to India she fumbled through her words.

"I, I just wanted to say that I'm not choosing sides I loved Mindy in a big way and I understand her pain more than you know, I also understand how hard it must be for your sister. To not only come home but come home and find out that her father has passed so I just want to say that I'm here for you and your family the best that I can be." India said

They hugged each other tightly he thanked India she had been more than a great presence especially for Mindy   he stated that things probably would be worse than they are if she wasn't there India felt better after hearing that Noel confirmed that giving Mindy all of her support was best. They discussed staying until Mindy felt comfortable with her mother even though she would be going into inpatient care. Noel had a big deal and the company only wanted to deal with him his partner Javier handle the smaller accounts since he also had his own real state company.

Mindy walked right by Olivia for the next few days she never knew she would react this way she thought things would be much different. Everyone continued to tell her losing her grandfather was difficult they even suggested she get some counseling Mindy wouldn't hear of it said she hasn't done anything wrong. She asked her uncle and India to stay longer India needed to check on Shay when she called Leah had Shay and their mother over for dinner Sharon had come for a few days after Shay contacted her and told her what happened she told her that she's been praying that their relationship gets better. Then showed up at the shelter the next day Leah has been checking on her and once she found out their mother was there she invited them over she'd never met India's mother India's mouth dropped opened she apologized for her family putting her out .   She wanted to know was anything broken was her godchildren all right. Leah laughed repeating that they all had a wonderful time and how India would be proud of them Shay had started working a part time job at IGA at local grocery and said she hasn't missed one day from her G.E.D class their mother even brought a bottle of champagne as a gift. India was at a lost for words her mother had been on her mind since the fire she was happy and nervous at the same time beside being newly engaged good news had been far and few. She had not told anyone about the engagement Noel wanted to have a small dinner party to tell everyone back home he said they both deserve a celebration India reluctantly agreed.

Noel had to get back to go to Atlanta for a seminar he been invited to months ago big wigs would be there Noel was trying to convince his business partner to become more invested. To do some of the traveling since he has met India but his business was also booming as CEO he needed to find someone to take off some of his load.

"Baby girl you can come with us for a few weeks but we have to get back I've been away for the office four weeks." Noel said
"I can't leave grandmother uncle you know that I'm just staying a few more days."
"Look were planning the engagement dinner first thing next month I'm planning for everyone to be there and well and I'll even fly in that young fellow if you take charge for me." Noel said

Both India and Mindy mouths dropped but Noel would do anything to make sure his niece would be ok with their leaving he wanted Mindy to ride with them to drop Olivia

off at the center Monday morning then they would be driving back home since Noel was

going all out Mindy agreed. Mrs. Olean put plenty of food for Olivia then made her a

picture album for her long stay at the center the car was quite at first until Olivia broke

the silence she was sitting up front with Noel they drive in their mothers mini caravan.

"Baby girl you'll see I'm going to finally be the one to make everyone proud you're a

beautiful smart and kind young lady and I'm sorry for everything, mommy will be back a

brand new person I promise." Olivia said

Mindy just shook her head holding back her tears she did not know what to say so she

said nothing just shook her head in agreement her grandmother and India consoling her

and patting Olivia on the back. Mrs. Olean starting singing {He didn't bring this far to

leave me} and the trust was restore Olivia was greeting by two counselors everyone had

to say their goodbye's at the front office Mindy took off the necklace her grandfather

gave to her on her birthday she put it around Olivia's neck then kissed her on the cheek.

"I'll need that back when you get better." Mindy said

Everyone laughed then said their goodbyes Olivia told India she looked forward to

getting to know her Mrs. Olean was happy she wept a little as Noel and India pulled off

but her sister, Mindy and some church friends where right by her side Noel promised to

call as soon as they got home.

They were on the rode for about an hour before India said a word she knew if she didn't

open up now she probably never would all of a sudden it hit her what she had survived

just a few weeks ago. She was no longer good at just sweeping things under the rug there

wouldn't be separate rooms like at Noel's parents India remembered she know longer had anywhere to go. Tears slowly started to run down India's face she felt guilty telling him this with what he was going through Noel India's problems has always been to put other people's feeling before her own today on this ride the buck stops. She just burst out crying Noel had to quickly pull onto the shoulder asking India over and over what was wrong what he needed to do he got out of the car and walked around to her side of the car. She did not open the door at first telling Noel she would be all right but he refused to get back into the car unless she unlocked her door he pulled India out of the car. She fell limb bent over crying trying to push Noel away he lifted her up and sat her down on the trunk of the car forcing her to face him,

"India, India your scaring me please what is it baby."

"I'm sorry Noel, I'll be fine."

"Let me help you were engaged now is that makeup on your eye wait what is that do you have a black eye."

"Who did this to you what's going on why didn't I notice this before?" Noel said

"I was wearing makeup Noel I tried to be strong I just can't do it anymore I'm so tired."

"Did Peter do this to you?"

"No Noel, He's done nothing but help."

"So what happening and why in the hell didn't you come to me India."

"It was EJ, Shay's boyfriend he got mad when Shay,"

India got choked up Noel hugged her so tight it made her yell out she pushed him back,

"What did he do to you India I'm so sorry I left you alone I didn't know?" Noel said

"It's not your fault Noel he was a bad person he got mad when Shay wouldn't rob the Federal Saving with him a few weeks ago." India said

"That was your sister's friend."

"Yes and when she would not go with him he beat her tight her up in his basement then came after me know one saw this coming.' India said

Noel walked away almost tripping from all the rocks car's were flying pass India didn't want them to get a ticket she jumped down off the car trying to hold her ribcage in place. Noel turned and starting walking back toward India,

"I'll kill that motherfucker I'll kill him dead that son of a bitch who is he India where is he."

Every vein in Noels body was showing some where popping out of his head he was rubbing his hands up and down his face India was calling out his name he didn't even hear her things were getting blurry Noel pound his fist into his hood over and over

"Noel I'm alright things are going to be alright as long as I have you in my life he's dead Noel the police shot and killed him."

"Baby I should have been there."

This time India held him close she knew at this moment she was in love and should have called him a long time ago maybe things would have been different but this happen for a reason. They are together now and she needed to do whatever it took to never convince herself other wise. They both continued to tell the other they were sorry for leaving each other as they continued to travel back down the interstate Noel told India she would be living with him from now on India immediately agreed.

"I don't want to hear it India your coming with me tonight-huh."

"That's fine Noel since were engaged that should be fine were kind of far from Shay though."

India knew she was making a big decision but right now at this moment it felt so good Noel could hardly keep his eyes on the wheel India just let him think she had surrendered she no longer wanted to be alone no need to tell him that for now he was in control and India stepped back. She continued to talk the more she did the easy it got telling Noel first about Ronald some of the things she felt had caused his death. Noel stayed in the slow lane stoking India's hand carefully paying close attention India was opening up and she had a mouth full asking Noel was he sure he wanted to risk it he told her he wouldn't have things any other way. India mumbled a bit when telling Noel about her nightmares and her relationship with her mother before she knew it they were in front of Noel place hugging all the way, until they got into the front door.

Their engagement party went off without a hitch everyone was so excited for India and Noel they flew Sharon in for the weekend. Shay decorated for the evening she and Mindy acted a little jealous of one another and Mrs. Olean   and Sharon connected right away sharing ideas on planning the wedding. There was no budget Mrs. Olean said she would pay for everything   mom I can't let you do that Noel and India gave up and set the date for June 27th school would be out they had less then a year and India would be Mrs. Hardman. India   stood and announced her bridal party she had everyone on pins and needles all month she would have two maid of honors   Leah then Shay bridesmaid Jill she called and asked Toshiba which she agreed. And of course baby girl Mindy they had Olivia call on Noel's cell phone at exactly 10 pm and   India asked her to be a bridesmaid she was overwhelmed she told her that her dress might had to be plus size India told her that didn't matter as long as she was doing well which she was.   Noel's choices were not as easy he had many friends he got as far as his partner Javier the honors for the best man his other best friend Jeff and of course Greg he included two other friends and one of his cousins and of course Mindy's bow.

No one wanted the night to end but by 2 am it did, everyone returned home safely two weeks later school started India ended her day with her new class some of the kids asked if she was married she told them not yet her children were getting more and more mature for their ages each year the day had ended. She was about to turn her classroom lights out when a soft hand touched hers which made her jump,

"Peter what are you doing here,"

"Well I didn't know what happened to you, you just left without a word."

"That not quite true I called your cell several time plus left you a note."

"Note you call that Dear John letter a note." Peter said

"Why are you yelling look I,"

"No India, you look I did not know where you were and I know you did not go back to that jerk that abandoned you in the first place." Peter said

India walked around Peter and started out the classroom he followed behind her asking repeatedly why she left and that he did not want to hear the excuse that his sister Leah gave.   He wanted to know what he had done wrong he has tried to be the man that India needed him to be not like the punk called Noel Peter jumped in front of India stopping her from putting her key in the car yelling out.

"Hell don't I deserve some kind of explanation?"

"I would talk to you but not like this not with you making a scene." India said

"Ok, I'm sorry I'll calm down please lets go somewhere and talk follow me."

He quickly rushed to his new Corvette then race around to India's car she was still standing there looking at Peter as if he was crazy she reminded him again that if his temper flares.

This time she would not wait around for him to calm down she got into her car and followed him to an elite bar and grill in the area where he lived the valet parked both there cars. Peter took India by the arm and escorted her threw the double doors the waitress knew Peter by name and seated them right away eyeballing India then rolling her eyes.   India gave her a look back holding her tongue not to say that she heard on the news that Hooters was missing one of their most ugliest waitress her nametag read (Tiff). She did not address India at all   Peter noticed he corrected her right away reminding India he would not let anything happen to her or anyone mistreat her India thanked him then let Peter know.   That she could protect herself he took her hands in his rubbing his thumb across her ring finger he immediately looked up then pulled India hand toward him,

"What in the fuck is this India'?" Peter yelled

India took a deep breath the couple from the next booth turned around to look, India tried to pull her hand back put Peter would not let go India didn't want to cause a scene,

"Peter, let go of my hand your hurting me.'

"Sir is everything alright   the manager asked?"

"Doesn't it look like everything is alright when I need your help I'll ask for it?" Peter said

The waitress sat down the expensive bottle of champagne Peter had ordered she popped open the bottle and began pouring Peter's glass first then she started to set the bottle down   Peter stopped her in her tracks and demanded she pour India a glass then reminded the girl that she would not be getting a tip.

 India didn't think keeping her promise would be a good idea right now she took a   big gulp   of her champagne then offered her explanation she apologized for leaving she thought   maybe this was partly her fault just like all the times with Noel maybe she should have done things different not stayed at his place at all.

"Peter I appreciate, everything that you have done for me offering your place everything but it's official I love Noel you were in a relationship with Jill when he and I met this has nothing to do with you he has asked me to marry him and I have accepted."

Peter laughed out loud drinking straight from the champagne bottle letting some of the champagne drip from his chin before he wiped it away he was convinced   India was out of her mind. He was convinced she could never love anyone and he felt that since she had confided in him that, that gave him just cause to make him be the only man in the world for her.

"India you and I both know what your capable of and being in love is not one of them you did not even want to have that one fellows baby, Now I'm not sure what kind of hold this guy has on you your probably still in shock that guy was killed right in front of you,"

"Peter, Peter I'm fine and I would not have told you private things had I known you were going to throw it back in my face I have to go and if things are going to continue to be this way then we can never ever see each other again.' India said

India got up from leather seated booth she grabbed her purse then   was about to say

goodbye when Peter slammed the champagne bottle on the table then stumble to get up

India grabbed the now empty champagne bottle she slightly lifted it,

"Peter I'm leaving and if you put your hands on me again I'm going to bust you upside

your head, again I'm sorry our friendship has to end but your making it impossible."

India back out of the restaurant still holding the bottle Peter did not move are say a word

he knew when India was serious he stood there with his mouth opened watching her back

out of the opening front doors. India turned around and her little   Celica was already

there she quickly got inside she didn't even tip the guy she started to cry as she fastened

her seat belt then burned rubber out of the parking lot all eye's were on her until Peter

made his exit yelling at the doorman.

"Where in the hell is my fucking car."

The guy carefully drove the shiny silver car toward Peter   he practically pulled the guy at

of the car then quickly drove off   he ran through two red lights before catching up to

India's car. He slowed down and tried to calm down so that she would not notice him

behind her India had her music blasting she was asking God over and over why her she

always tried to do the right thing. Treat people better than they treated her why she

promised God that she would make it work with Noel she would not lie to him or hide

things from him anymore she began to calm down the closer she got to the house. One

more exit to go she tried to check herself in the mirror at the red light when the car

behind her blew it's horn India jumped then drove off she started to fuss at the driver then

some how realized that would be stupid since she was not paying attention. She pulled

into the condominium complex and let out a sigh of relief she could not wait to be in

Noel's arm she rushed up the steps and opened then closed the door. Within seconds Peter pulled up behind Noel and India's car he sat there for a few seconds then quietly pulled off before India could put down her things Noel was behind her when she turned around he was wiping his hands on a napkin.

"Oh hi honey.' India said

"Baby where have you been I was worried I called Leah's Greg said Leah was in bed sick with the flu."

"Yes she did not come in today I need to check on her."

"So were where you I do not mean to sound like a broken record but I am not going to be driving myself crazy I'm going to get you a cell phone tomorrow and,"

"Ok, sure that would be great I'm sorry I just lost track of time I should have called." India remember what she talked to God about in the car so no news was good news and the news she always had never had a happy ending so she was going to keep quite as long as she could.

"India I'm not dealing with this, what did you say,

Ok." Noel said

"Sure just don't get one of those fancy one's a simple phone will do." India said Noel was at a lost for words a year of going through this and out of the blue India just agrees to a cell phone he didn't want to continue like he was arguing since India through him off but he still wanted an explanation.

"No problem I will stop and get you one on my lunch break so where have you been baby.'

"Noel I'm pretty tired should I start dinner." India replied

"No I've put some steaks on the grill and potatoes I just need to pour the wine." Noel said

India reached and kissed him on his cheek then said she was going to jump in the shower she would be right back down cutting Noel off when he demanded an answer from her India turned the shower as hot as it could go. She put her hair in a ponytail then took it back down to wash her hair she suddenly felt unclean she scrubbed until her skin was tender India had been doing this since she and Noel has been back together. Dr. Torres told India it is not her body that she feels is dirty she blaming herself for things that have been out her control.   India agrees but for some reason tonight triggered the feelings again.

Noel called out India's name she answered as she rinsed off then wrapped a towel around her body before she opened the shower curtain.

"Hey sweetie I am on my way down."

"That's good but I still would like to know where you where tonight I feel like your keeping something from me." Noel said

"And I feel like you have been talking to my father again." India said

"Wow, I have not talked to your dad since you gave me your consent to ask him for your hand in marriage."

India could not take another fight today she knew that she had made a promise with Noel to be more considerate but she could not fit that promise in today so instead of making the love of her life more upset she did the next best thing. She dropped her towel then pushed up on Noel so hard that it made him stumble backward she reached up and grabbed hold of his strong neck then lowered him down to her and began rolling her tongue as though her life depended on it.

"Hey one second baby, I thought you weren't ready for this yet are you sure."

Obviously it has been to long if he has to ask this question India did not want Noel to ask his demanding question again she did not. If he wanted to kill a dead person Lord only knew what he would do to Peter he's already said he has no more cheeks to turn he had demanded that India never see him again. So India forced herself to feel like this was the right time and the right place to redefine she and Noel's relationship she kissed him around his neck then slowly directed him backwards to the bed.   Pulling off his tee shirt she did not realize they would made it to the bed they fall in India jumped on top on him. Sucking his nipples soft and slowly she knew he wouldn't resist her after this he reached for her wet hair and India took his strong hands into hers then raised them above his head and tied both his hands tightly with his tee shirt India was now sitting on a mountain. If she allowed herself to turn into her erotic sexually being that loved to take control when ever India could not she held on to Noels arms. She whispered into his ear while licking on his earlobe saying (I love you today, tomorrow and forever) it made him go crazy he yelled out I love you too

" India you will be my wife forever."

He took his hands trying to loosen them India slapped his face telling him to keep them tied. He complied as India turned   him on from head to toe   she started to unbuckle his pants as he started to sweat when India lifted his penis with her tongue then with her hands behind her back. She looked up at Noel who was looking down at her as she slowly moved her head back and forth India gagged once it made it passed her throat over and over that was enough for her alter ego she moved down to his enter thighs licking and gently biting him. Causing Noel to loose his mind   she finally heard Noel calling her name. Pleading to touch her India before climbing on board again India gave Noel one last pleasure motioning her tongue around the tip on his penis she turned him around. Hoping he could take a little of her massage she reached into the night stand drawer and let a little oil drip on his back   then India   blew on it as her hands took every tense spot Noel had out within minutes. She turned him back around as the moon light shined through the window they both looked at each other Noel whisper,

"Baby I want you."

"Not yet"

Noel love India small soft hands massaging him her breast stroking against his back with her every move Noel turned around as she lifted her bottom up   to take a ride without using her hands. She infused his manhood with her wet vagina moving down until their bodies touch the sound of her soft moan made Noel break free there was nothing else for India to do. The ride became automatic her wet hair slide threw Noel's hand which made him grip it harder India leaned   back a bit but Noel wanted her close. Sucking her breast as with his entire passion he held on to her thighs for dear life causing his penis to feel like it was making a break through he once again needed to hold her. Sucking her lips until there was a burning sensation he forced her body down on the bed lifting her up by her legs only India's elbows and head were touching the bed Noel had her legs wrapped around his neck. And his face and tongue were covered with India bitter taste Noel arms were wrapped around India body as he drove her crazy she was no longer in control. Her body started to shake then Noel turned her around to the beat of the drum India spread her shaking legs then arched her back Noel eagerly grabs India   from behind. She called out his name looking back at him reaching for his wrist moaning "harder, harder" Noel could not take it any more his titanic was about to sink and India was not taking any prisoner. Noel thought his heart was going to beat out of his chest the silk sheets were so wet that he slipped back onto the floor he didn't have enough breath to laugh but India did she look over peaking at Noel on the floor reaching for her while he was still trying to caught his breath,

"Baby come to me please.'

India grabbed a pillow and sheet and slide down onto her man he cried as he said he loved her she laid her head on his fast beating chest looking at the moon she whispered "I love you too Noel."

While wiping his tears with her hand India   then without a doubt knew that she could no longer allow her brother's memories to affect her in a negative way she thought about visiting Ronald's grave thinking maybe letting off some balloons in his honor to say goodbye but let him know his memory would live on and Noel would be the perfect person to share her brothers honor with. India again realized that this is where she needed and should be she looked at her and Noel's reflections glaring on the wall from the moon light she was happy and nothing and no one would change things ever again.

Made in the USA
Charleston, SC
28 October 2013